Ancestors in Post-Contact Religion

Center for the Study of World Religions
Harvard Divinity School

Religions of the World
General Editor: Lawrence E. Sullivan

Cambridge, Massachusetts

Ancestors in Post-Contact Religion
Roots, Ruptures, and Modernity's Memory

edited by Steven J. Friesen

distributed by
Harvard University Press
for the
Center for the Study of World Religions
Harvard Divinity School

Book design by Eric Edstam

Library of Congress Cataloging-in-Publication Data

Ancestors in post-contact religion : roots, ruptures, and modernity's memory / edited by Steven J. Friesen.

     p. cm. – (Religions of the world)

   Includes bibliographical references and index.

   ISBN 0-945454-31-7 (alk. paper)

   ISBN 0-945454-32-5 (pbk. : alk. paper)

    1. Ancestor worship – Congresses. I. Friesen, Steven J. II. Religions of the world (Cambridge, Mass.)

BL467 .A54 2001

291.21'13 – dc21

2001037290

Wilfred Cantwell Smith
1916–2000

Contents

Ancestral Land

Preface

Tu Weiming

In the summer of 1990, at the invitation of President Victor Hao Li of the East-West Center in Honolulu, I took a leave of absence from Harvard University to assume the directorship of the Center's Institute of Culture and Communication. My purpose was to develop two projects: "A Dialogue of Civilizations" and "Cultural China." Since Cultural China was already underway,[1] I focused my attention on the Dialogue of Civilizations.

With generous support from Laurance and Mary Rockefeller, we were able to launch a series of workshops, seminars, and international conferences on axial-age civilizations. First proposed by Karl Jaspers, the idea of axial-age civilizations is predicated on religious pluralism and on the desirability and necessity of mutual, cross-cultural referencing. He observed that the civilizations that emerged as early as the first millennium B.C.E. in South Asia, the Middle East, and East Asia still define the main contours of the spiritual landscape of the human community in the contemporary world. For more than two thousand years, our worldviews and life orientations have been shaped by Greek, Judaic, Hindu, Chinese, and other historical religions.

Jaspers specifically identified Socrates, Buddha, Confucius, and Jesus as the four great thinkers of human flourishing for the global community. Jaspers's attempt to single out these four is suggestive but controversial from our multiculturalist, ecumenical perspective. Moreover, his notion of religious pluralism was restricted—if not exclusivistic—in its notion of human spirituality. We should also include at least Moses, Mohammed, and Laozi (Lao Tzu) in this list of ancestors who are, by implication, fundamental spiritual resources for the history of humankind.

As the project developed, other amendments to the axial-age theory were proposed. While the Dialogue of Civilizations project was initiated at the East-West Center, it was the continuation and expansion of an ongoing conversation under the leadership of Ewert Cousins of Fordham University. Indeed, as the editor-in-chief of *World Spirituality: An Encyclopedic History of the Religious Quest*, Professor Cousins painstakingly organized a comprehensive team of scholars to present an overview of the spiritual landscape of the human community.[2] At the international conference on world spirituality in 1990, senior scholars in the comparative study of world religions, including Balasubramanian, Seyyed Hossein Nasr, Raimundo Pannikar, Huston Smith, and Wilfred Cantwell Smith, urged us to expand the axial-age paradigm and to make a concerted effort to explore indigenous forms of spirituality.

Two reasons were crucial in the discussions. First, it is essential for our joint venture that we understand the primordial presence of indigenous traditions in each of the historical religions, not as an earlier sedimentation, but as an integral part of modern human religiosity in a comparative perspective. Second, for the sake of enhancing our own communal critical awareness of the human condition in the world today, it is imperative that we appreciate the cumulative wisdom found in the indigenous traditions. Understood in this way, claims of "primordiality" are not modernist cultural constructions dictated by the politics of recognition, but rather a recognition of dynamic modes of existence in the contemporary world that challenge us to develop a new anthropocosmic vision of human survival and human flourishing.

In response to this wise counsel, we organized a workshop on indigenous spirituality. Even a brief exposure to the rich symbolic resources generated in the workshop convinced us of the desirability of an interreligious dialogue among indigenous traditions. The synergy of Hawaiian, Māori, Native American, Melanesian, African, and Shinto scholars in a dialogical environment imbued with the aloha spirit of Hawai'i was exceptional. While the scholarly effort to capture the dynamism and resourcefulness of the encounter was difficult, Professor Steven Friesen—whom I invited to coordinate the project—asked the participants themselves to identify a common theme for further study. The veneration of ancestors was on the top of everyone's list. The result is an impressive pioneering exploration of primal spirituality in an academic context.

Huston Smith, in the completely revised and updated edition of his celebrated *The Religions of Man*, added a new chapter on "Primal Religions."[3] Thus, in addition to the seven so-called axial-age civilizations (Hinduism, Buddhism, Confucianism, Taoism, Islam, Judaism, and Christianity), a new dimension has been incorporated into the conceptualization of human religiousness in *The World's Religions*. Because this newest contribution in the worldwide academic study of religion is also the oldest heritage in human history, what Professor Friesen and his colleagues offer here is a way of seeing, a mode of experiencing, and a form of living that is fresh in its overall outlook precisely because it is deeply rooted in our communal memory. These essays and discussions are, therefore, profoundly significant for our self-reflexivity as students of religion. They enrich the breadth and depth of our understanding of human spirituality.

Since this book is dedicated to the memory of Wilfred Cantwell Smith, who passed away on 7 February 2000, of natural causes in his native Toronto at the age of eighty-three, it is fitting that I conclude with a tribute originally prepared for his memorial service on 5 May 2000, held in Memorial Church in Harvard Yard.

By thinking historically and comparatively about religion, Wilfred Cantwell Smith significantly transformed the study of religion from speculation on abstract universalism into a sustained and rigorous inquiry on lived concreteness. To Wilfred, the study of religion is not merely confined to orthodox ideas and truth claims. It is an exploration of human, indeed, personal ways of living that are informed by a cumulative tradition and inspired by a perennial quest for the ultimate meaning of life. This dynamic, transformative, and constantly self-reflective and continuously renewing sense of being religious envisions tradition as a flowing stream, theology as embodied thinking, faith as a defining characteristic of being human, and knowledge as praxis.

Wilfred Cantwell Smith was a brilliant scholar and an exemplary teacher, but, above all, he was a student exerting continuous effort to realize his calling as a comparative historian of world religions. What he exemplified is the mode of learning recommended by the *Doctrine of the Mean*:

> *Study it extensively, inquire into it accurately, think over it carefully, sift it clearly, and practice it earnestly. When there is anything not yet studied, or studied but not yet understood, do not give up. When there is any question not yet asked, or asked but its answer not yet known, do not give up. When there is anything not yet thought over, or thought over but not yet apprehended, do not give up. When there is anything not yet sifted, or sifted but not yet clear, do not give up. When there is anything not yet practiced, or practiced but not yet earnestly, do not give up. If another man succeed by one effort, I will use a hundred efforts. If another man succeed by ten efforts, I will use a thousand efforts. If one really follows this course, though stupid, he will surely become intelligent, and though weak, will surely become strong.*
> (20:19–21)

Indeed. What Wilfred aspired to do is the way of the profound person who honors the moral nature and follows the path of inquiry and study. He achieves breadth and greatness and pursues the refined and subtle to the limit. He seeks to reach the greatest height and brilliancy and follows the path of Centrality and Commonality. He goes over the old so as to find out what is new. He is earnest and deep and highly respects all propriety (*Doctrine of the Mean* 27:6).

Notes

1. The Cultural China project resulted in the publication of a special issue of *Daedalus*, the journal of the American Academy of Arts and Sciences (volume 12, spring 1991), which was in turn published as a book: Tu Weiming, ed., *The Living Tree: The Changing Meaning of Being Chinese Today* (Stanford, Calif.: Stanford University Press, 1994).

2. For a more extensive discussion of the work of Ewert Cousins and its implications, see Steven L. Chase, ed., *Doors of Understanding: Conversations on Global Spirituality in Honor of Ewert Cousins* (Quincy, Ill.: Franciscan Press, 1997).

3. See Huston Smith, *The World's Religions* (San Francisco: HarperSanFrancisco, 1991), 365–83.

Introduction
Modern Ancestors

Steven J. Friesen

It is difficult to discuss the significance of ancestors without talking about location—the land where they lived and the places where they were buried. So this introduction begins with an ancestral shrine located on the campus where I worked on the final editing of the manuscript. This obscure monument raises the central issue of the volume, which is the meaning of ancestors in modernity. The monument also suggests the crucial themes of the papers and discussions that follow: life, death, family, community, colonialism, religion, emotion, rationality, science, nature, materiality, politics, conquest, and territory.

The shrine in question is located on the campus of the University of Missouri at Columbia. The monument is a tombstone, a six-foot granite obelisk resting on a three-foot cube base. The original epitaph reads:

Here was buried
Thomas Jefferson
Author of the Declaration of American Independence
of the Statute of Virginia for religious freedom
and Father of the University of Virginia[1]

The monument is perplexing for at least two reasons. First, Thomas Jefferson was not buried here; he was buried at Monticello in Virginia. Jefferson designed this obelisk for his own grave and composed the epitaph sometime prior to his death on the Fourth of July, 1826. Congress later decided that this Founding Father deserved a better memorial stone. So a new, larger obelisk was dedicated over his grave at Monticello on the Fourth of July, 1883, to honor the national ancestor.[2] The original tombstone was then awarded to the University of Missouri—the first state university built in the Louisiana Purchase—in order to honor Jefferson's role in expanding the nation and in promoting higher education.[3]

The tombstone is no longer a grave marker. It has, instead, become a relic—a portable, tangible symbol that asserts the authority of an ancestor over colonized land where he never set foot.[4] The fact that the veneration of this mythic ancestor involves issues of authority, social relationships, and territory is not particularly surprising. The important point is that the roles of ancestors in societies have changed dramatically since the rise of the modern west, for modernity tends to denigrate local ancestors and to replace them with others. Continuity is supplanted through rupture. Memories are suppressed. And thus, this tombstone marks not a grave but a new style of knowledge and life on the land.

The monument is also perplexing because of what the epitaph does and does not say. Jefferson wanted to be remembered as an author and as the father of a university. He could have selected many other topics for this inscription, but he chose to identify himself with his work for political independence, religious freedom, and academic inquiry. These comprise a grand legacy, and in this sense all the contributors to this volume are his heirs. But Jefferson is an ambivalent forefather. One need only remember that political independence, religious freedom, and academic inquiry did not serve some of Jefferson's biological descendants so well, especially those whom he fathered by his African American slave Sally Hemings. Like any good epitaph, this one simultaneously hides and reveals, lest anyone speak ill of the dead.

One premise of this volume, then, is that western academic inquiry provides powerful methods for interpreting the world. But Jefferson's tombstone also reminds us that the western academy provides a limited interpretation of the meaning of ancestors in the world after contact. The tension generated by these contending styles of interpretation is responsible for the character of this volume. The study of ancestors—and by extension the study of religion—should not be left solely in the hands of the western scholar. The academy has developed dynamic tools for exploring religion, but these tools do not exhaust the topic. The complexity of such a fundamental phenomenon as ancestors requires a wider range of insight. Otherwise, we end up with the familiar academic genealogies: the heirs of Marx declare the veneration of ancestors to be a false consciousness that prevents us from addressing the real economic basis of our oppression; the offspring of Freud diagnose it as a neurosis based on the conflict of unconscious desires; the lineage of Durkheim defines it as an instrument of social control and cohesion; and so on.

This volume is not confined to one such perspective. It is comprised instead of a range of viewpoints that intersected in a conference setting. The conference took place 7–11 January 1992, at the East-West Center in Honolulu, Hawaiʻi. Some of the participants were specialists from the fields of religious studies, anthropology, linguistics, area studies, and theology. Experts in religion from outside the academy also took part, including clergy, chanters, woodcarvers, and poets. The conference did not attempt to provide exhaustive coverage of the religions of the world. Rather, a sufficient number of religious and secular traditions were included in order to provide a comparative perspective, and special attention was given to Hawaiian traditions that are related integrally to the place where the conference was actually held.

In this unusual setting of academic and personal diversity, the conference participants developed a dialogical method, which is reflected especially in the discussions that follow each paper in this volume. Since no particular theoretical perspective was granted a privileged status in this dialogical setting, the participants had to make their interpretive locations clear and they had to be able to make them understandable to others around the table. This had the effect of raising questions about all the theories that were employed and, if truth be told, it made all the participants uncomfortable at one time or another. Furthermore, the fact that the western academy was allowed to claim only limited control of interpretation raised questions about the relationships of scholars and practitioners. Thus, the focus was placed on the varieties of ways that one could approach the topic of ancestors. All participants had to declare their perspectives, and all were held accountable for how they dealt with their topics.

In this way the participants moved beyond the all-too-familiar dichotomy of the autobiographical self who represents the silenced "other." The participants chose instead to engage in a complex conversation with multiple partners that defied the facile labels of "insider" and "outsider," or "subject" and "object." Such labels often hide the exchanges that go on in the process of inquiry and conceal the transformations—both good and bad—that occur in the process of learning to know. It is the contention of this collection of papers and discussions that a dialogical method is required in order to understand the significance of ancestors in the midst of modernity. There are roots, ruptures, and repressed memories that need to be revealed, and the best way to approach the problem is collectively.

This dialogical method should not be mistaken for some sort of utopian egalitarianism. The conference did not transcend the barriers of domination built into our institutional and personal histories: it took place in Polynesia, it was conducted in the English language in an air-conditioned research center, and it resulted in a book distributed by a venerable university press. Within these limitations, arguments sometimes boiled over and at other times simmered on the back burner. Different styles of presentation were employed, and various authorities were invoked.[5] A concerted effort was made, however, to describe and to analyze religious traditions in ways that are recognizable to those from within the traditions as well as to those from without.

In this sense, the dialogical method is an experiment in the critical corporate self-consciousness and personalism advocated by Wilfred Cantwell Smith,[6] who passed away shortly after this volume was accepted for publication. For this reason the book is dedicated to his memory and to his honor. Smith influenced the thinking and practice of many of the contributors; his presence in these pages should not be underestimated.

Given the diversity of participants and perspectives, the reader should look for the unity of the contributions in two facets of our common experience. One is obvious: we are all descendants. We all have many ancestors who make powerful claims on our lives. Ancestry is a fundamental fact of life and should be a fundamental category in religious studies.

The other facet of our common experience is this. We all live in the aftermath of contact between Euroamerican powers and other civilizations. If there is a defining feature of the world today, it is a structure of life set in motion by these unequal and unjust meetings of cultures. This structure of life is not uniform, nor is it static, but it is our common inheritance.

Thus, "post-contact religion" should not be mistakenly applied only to the so-called indigenous religions. All religions today are in their post-contact phases. We have all been changed by contact—for better and for worse—and by taking this into account we will have a better understanding of ourselves and our world. This means that the emphasis on indigenous traditions in this book does not represent a fascination with the exotic. The focus on indigenous traditions was a choice based on the conviction that these are the ones that have suffered most overtly from the current state of affairs, and so they have the most to say about certain issues in the world today. One goal of the book, then, is to articulate from these perspectives some crucial issues in the study of post-contact religion.

This implies a critical stance toward Euroamerican traditions—not an ideological polarization but, rather, a range of nuanced appraisals of religious imperialism in colonial contact, with varying measures of appreciation and regret for the influences on our lives. Such a critique was not the primary focus of the conference, nor is it the primary focus of this book. Several critical stances emerged, however, as various people analyzed what they had experienced, and did so in a setting where they were held accountable by people with other experiences.

The exchanges that occurred in the conference cannot be replicated in print, so this volume is more like a translation than a transcription. As such, it is an effort to convey in a written artifact the conversations that took place in a mixed oral and written setting. Written papers have been revised; recorded discussions have been transcribed and edited. If errors resulted from this process, they occurred in spite of consultations among the participants and in spite of good faith efforts on all sides.

The structure of the volume is designed to match the content. Three related themes are evident throughout the chapters and discussions—the ancestral ordering of the world, intense personal attachments to forebears, and the catastrophes of colonization that are manifested in particular places. These themes have become the organizing principles for the three main sections of the volume, but the reader should be warned that all of these themes circulate through all of the chapters; the authority of ancestors is often invoked, passions are frequently enflamed, and references to Christianization abound.

No linear organization would do justice to these topics, and so I have adopted a cyclical structure for the volume. Each of the three main sections is composed of five chapters. In each section the final chapter returns to the geographical area discussed in the first chapter of the section. For the first section this is Melanesia, for the other two it is Hawai'i. The central chapter in each section tends to have a more theoretical orientation. There are also thematic bridges shared by the final essay in one section with the first chapter of the next section ("relationships with ancestors" between the first and second sections; "ancestral burials and land" between the second and third). Finally, there are parallels between the first and last chapters of the book, and between the second and second-to-last chapters: the first two chapters take us into a host of difficult issues and the last two chapters (in reverse order) seek a way out.

The thematic development through the volume can be summarized as follows. The first section of the volume is entitled "Ancestral Cosmologies" because it contains papers that focus on the ways in which ancestors shape the worlds we inhabit. The papers deal with various aspects of this issue, and through the diversity of interests we see a common thread. In most cultures, the dead play a vital role by integrating the experiences of life. They bring together family, society, land, even the spiritual and physical realms. Having been transformed themselves, the ancestors affect many of the crucial transformations that define our lives.

The chapter by William Ferea, "The Living Living and the Living Dead: A Source of Harmony in the Melanesian Worldview," begins with an examination of the dual self that moves between the physical and spiritual realms in Melanesian cosmologies. In this movement, ancestors provide communication and continuity between the realms and are crucial in the process of establishing harmony in the cosmos. Cargo cults developed after contact because the arrival of Europeans resembled the anticipated return of the ancestors, yet the greed and the violence of the colonizers violated the mythic pattern. In post-contact Melanesia, cargo cults have returned to a more normal lifeway and show that the ancestors can still be a source of harmony in a society that has changed radically in recent years.

The importance of ancestors is not foreign to Euroamerican Catholicism, but one has to seek out its manifestations. Ewert Cousins helps us do that in his discussion "The Cult of Saints and Souls in New Orleans." The Christian terminology of "saint" obscures the fact that there is a developed Catholic tradition of seeing ancestors (the "Church Triumphant") as helpers of both the living (the "Church Militant") and the souls in purgatory (the "Church Suffering"). Cousins alerts us to diversity within Christianity regarding ancestors: we need to distinguish not only Orthodox, Catholic, and Protestant attitudes toward ancestors, but also elite and popular views. A discussion of saints and ancestors in Dante's *Divine Comedy* shows that the popular piety of Roman Catholic New Orleans resonates with the high literary traditions of the church. Yet the expressions of popular piety suggest that many Christians sense a need for more active relationships with their ancestors.

The chapter by Rubellite Johnson returns to subjects introduced by William Ferea and works on them within the traditions of Hawaiian religious thought and practice. Johnson begins with a taxonomy of the spiritual and physical world and then shows how these various kinds of beings are related to each other. Hawaiian religion integrates the whole world—divine and mortal, animal and human, animate and inanimate, living and deceased—through a system of reciprocity, communication, and transformation. The 'aumakua (ancestors) play a crucial role in this process. The parent/child relationship expands across spiritual and physical realms, across generations, even across the divine and the mortal, embracing all experience.

Jacob Olupona draws on the religious traditions of sub-Saharan Africa to emphasize the importance of African ancestors. He examines expectations about who can become an efficacious ancestor and looks at how this process takes place. A description of the social functions of ancestors leads to the conclusion that the veneration of ancestors in Africa is particularly related to the maintenance of lineages and hierarchies. Thus, the ancestors have an important ethical responsibility to safeguard the moral order. They are called upon to assess the living, "To Praise and to Reprimand." This topic has not been given proper attention in the history of western scholarship on African religion because western definitions of religion tend to place ancestors in the human category rather than in the divine. A full appraisal of African views on ancestors and the sacred could change the course of religious studies.

The final paper in this section returns to Melanesia for a comparative discussion of ancestral piety among three highlands groups in Papua New Guinea. Mary MacDonald argues that institutions related to ancestors are primarily a way of overcoming death and affirming life. She does this by discussing the differences between sky beings, ghosts, founding ancestors, and ancestors; then by turning to well-known stories about ancestors; and finally by describing ritual actions that communicate with and feed the ancestors. Western theorists may dispute the "real" meaning of these institutions (are the institutions deception? social control? psychological therapy? ecological adjustment?), but ancestral piety somehow extends human relationships to include the departed as a way of promoting the value of life and the conquest of death.

The first section of the volume presents four proposals from various cultures about the functions of ancestors: providing social harmony (Ferea); transcendent mediators (Johnson); the establishment of lineage and moral order (Olupona); and the affirmation of life (MacDonald). Along the way, we are also reminded (by Cousins and others) that the ancestors are not absent from the Christian traditions. The dead are a lively issue in all religions.

The second section of this volume, "Intimate Ancestors," takes us into the area of epistemology and the ways in which we know the world around us. Throughout the five papers there is an antiphonal treatment of the tension generated by wide-ranging, existential commitments and the more limited rational commitments of western logic. The tension is not resolved; in some chapters the tension approaches dissonance, and in others a kind of contrapuntal arrangement prevails.

The first chapter works out of a particularly strong Hawaiian family context. Ulunui Garmon discusses the importance of narratives, names, and ceremony in this familial setting. By addressing the status of ancestors in this way, Garmon articulates an experiential epistemology (my term) that affirms the role of emotions and that is closely linked to land, to climate, to a specific topography, and to a particular time.

The second paper focuses on Māori literary texts that were published in the nineteenth century about the ancestors of one tribe. The Māori narratives and the ways these stories were used bring up several themes from the first section of the volume, such as the importance of ancestors for cosmogony, cosmology, and lineage. However, Margaret Orbell's paper and the ensuing discussions take us deeper into the personal significance of ancestors. We get a glimpse of the enduring persuasive power of ancestral narratives—especially when they are combined with ritual. We sense the flexibility of ancestors as they become part of the definition of post-contact religion and politics, and we confront the difficulty of defining "history" and "mythology" in a complicated, Christianized, colonial setting.

Charles Long's paper occupies the central position in the central section because it is the most concise statement of the problematic of this volume: we are all heirs of the Enlightenment, but that is not our only inheritance. Modernity is admittedly anti-ancestral, and questions about the viability of such a contrary orientation were raised as early as de Tocqueville's encounter with the Jeffersonians in America. Long argues that ancestors are an indispensible part of a functioning human community and that western rationalistic ways of knowing the world are insufficient in this regard. In the midst of modernity, however, there is no simple road back to an authentic relationship with the departed. Ideological constructions are inadequate, for ancestors must be intimately related to the existential structures of life. To this end, Long makes two suggestions. First, we should recognize that, in spite of hostilities toward the authority of ancestors, modernity also has its own ancestors. One step toward a recovery of memory would be a critical evaluation of the intellectual ancestors of western thought in order to produce a genealogy of modernity that could provide a new kind of memory. Second, there needs to be a recognition of the many ancestral influences that impinge upon us. There are no pure traditions, only complex histories of mixed exchanges. An honest attempt to build a connection with ancestors in modernity—and with the ancestors of modernity—involves a systematic examination of all aspects of our inheritance.

In the fourth chapter of the section, Laurel Kendall draws on her years of contact with Korean shamans to raise questions about the ways ancestors are known through trance and dream. Her chapter explores the twilight zone between insider and outsider interpretations in order to develop the idea that ancestors are not simply constructed by the actors in a seance according to the whims of the shaman. The ancestors are part of an ongoing process that is born in the family setting and that contributes to an evolving relationship between the living and the dead. It is too simple to say that the ancestors are "used" to make a performance convincing. Ancestors are not simply consoling, but are also intrusive; they do not simply provide solutions to life's problems, but also create new problems of their own.

The final paper in the section returns to the same Hawaiian family mentioned in the section's first paper. In this final paper, Pualani Kanahele develops further the notion of an experiential epistemology in which the na'au (gut, mind, heart) is given a role that is at least equal to, and perhaps more important than, the role of the rationalistic intellect. The mother of Garmon and Kanahele was one of the most accomplished hula masters of the twentieth century, and Kanahele draws on the family's dance traditions to show how her ancestors are influencing the larger community. Once again, we see that this is not without controversy. A commitment to the rhythms of bones, burial, land, and family quickly leads to severe conflicts in the practice of post-contact religion.

In a world after contact, conflicts between communities usually find expression in arguments over control of specific pieces of land. While this is clearly a question of domination, it is not *only* a question of brute force. Colonial conflicts over land also involve fundamentally different understandings of the significance of land. The meaning of territory—and the connection of territory to ancestors—is a crucial controversy in post-contact religion that raises serious questions about the long-term viability of expanding, western-style economies.

The last chapter of the second section of this volume highlighted the sacralization of the land in Hawai'i through the presence of the ancestral bones. The third section, "Ancestral Land," picks up this theme in several ways. David Ka'upu begins the third section by describing the way that Hawaiian 'aumakua integrate people with the land and the sea, thereby making the family the matrix for the formation of an ecological spirituality. Even the arrival of Christianity can be absorbed into this system that is mediated by the ancestors. The 'aumakua system provides the Reverend Ka'upu with crucial resources for understanding family, land, nature, and Christian theology.

The chapter by Diane Bell discusses Aboriginal Australia, where ancestral land claims have been argued in the courts of the colonizers. Anglo legal systems have denied the viability—and even the existence—of the ancestral connections to territory. Legal fictions, abductions, and massacres have all played a part in the attempt to alienate Aboriginal groups from their ancestral homelands. Bell quotes legal testimony from Aboriginal women and men involved in land disputes and helps us see that the stories and ceremonies of the ancestors do not simply perpetuate knowledge of the land. The ancestral rituals and narratives of the Dreamtime are flexible and relational, providing the resources by which the ethics of territory are negotiated.

Such negotiations are not unique to Oceania. John Grim's archival investigation into the Algonquian Feast of the Dead illuminates the way in which the bones of the ancestors played important roles in the establishment of alliances between native groups in the Great Lakes region of North America when various foreign powers were encroaching on their territories. As relations with European and American cultures became more urgent, the ancestral bones became the focus of different negotiations. Museums and universities claimed the right to possess and to examine the bones of native peoples, setting up a confrontation between indigenous knowledge and scientific knowledge (a theme that permeates section two of this volume). The Algonquian Feast of the Dead and the "bones controversy" with museums both point to a fundamental disagreement among post-contact religions regarding the status of the material world. Put bluntly, is the physical world a natural resource or a natural relationship? Are the ancestors with us or are they gone? The Native American Grave Protection and Repatriation Act of 1990 might set a new precedent in the United States for institutional cooperation in the treatment of the ancestors. It might even be a sign that the dominant culture is beginning to recognize the rights of ancestors to speak.

Jill Raitt's paper begins a process that is long overdue. Instead of imposing western categories on indigenous religions, she questions western religion in light of the religions of indigenous peoples. She asks specifically: "If ancestors are so prevalent and so important in the human religious experience, where are the ancestors in European Catholic Christianity? Why is there so little research on ancestors in the Christian tradition?" There are functional similarities to the importance of ancestors for indigenous peoples in three Catholic topics: the genealogy of Jesus, the veneration of saints, and the cult of martyrs. Yet, these three topics point to a distinction that surfaced in earlier chapters and discussions. Christianity forsakes the material, bodily relationships of family, preferring instead a spiritual kinship with heroes. These Christian "ancestors" have no bodily connection with their "descendants." Is this broken connection desirable or dangerous? Should European-based Christianity try to learn from other religions, or is there a need for Christians to dig back into the indigenous roots of their own traditions?

The third section and the volume conclude with a paper by Puanani Burgess entitled "Disconnection and Reconnection." Burgess picks up the theme of contact between religions and cultures from one Hawaiian perspective. Communities that have been subjected to a long history of domination and discrimination tend to be ambivalent (at best) toward dialogue. Burgess's paper reminds us of the corporate and personal suffering that is a constituent part of post-contact religion. It is a suffering born of disruption and alienation; it is distance, departure. She recounts some of the efforts that have been made in one community on the west coast of Oʻahu and, in this way, reflects on one model for action.

A great debt of gratitude has accumulated during the development of this volume. The conference in which these discussions took place could not have been held without the help of the East-West Center and its Institute of Culture and Communication in Honolulu. Thanks go especially to Helen Griffin, Sandi Osaki, Helen Palmore, Anna Tanaka, Geoff White, and Meg White for their assistance at many levels. The funding for the conference was provided by Laurance and Mary Rockefeller. Intellectual leadership came from Ewert Cousins and Tu Weiming.

The final stages of manuscript preparation were made possible by a research grant from the American Academy of Religion. Special appreciation also goes: to Mary MacDonald; to Kathryn Dodgson; to the anonymous readers whose comments strengthened the volume; and to my colleagues in the Department of Religious Studies at the University of Missouri-Columbia for their continuing efforts to put indigenous religions at the center of the discipline.

Thanks is due to each of these, and to others too numerous to mention here.

As you consider the papers and discussions in this book, you will notice that the topic of ancestors evoked numerous stories, both personal and corporate. So I close the introduction with an excerpt from another narrative. It comes from the first chapter of V. S. Naipaul's *A Way in the World*, and it suggests a reason why a discussion of the religious significance of ancestors quickly draws people into some fairly deep waters. The chapter introduces a character from St. James, Trinidad, by the name of Leonard Side. Leonard Side worked part-time teaching courses in baking for the Women's Auxiliary Association and also worked across the street at the funeral parlor, dressing bodies for burial. Whether decorating cakes, arranging flowers, or preparing a corpse, he displayed an uncanny and inexplicable aesthetic understanding. Where did this strange sense of beauty come from? Like many people in the post-contact world, Leonard Side knew little of his own history. In his case, it went back through India and beyond.

He knew he was a Mohammedan, in spite of the picture of Christ in his bedroom. But he would have had almost no idea of where he or his ancestors had come from. . . . All Leonard Side would have known of himself and his ancestors would have been what he had awakened to in his mother's house in St. James. In that he was like the rest of us.

With learning now I can tell you more or less how we all came to be where we were. I can tell you that the Amerindian name for the land of St. James would have been Cumucurapo, which the early travellers from Europe turned to Conquerabia. I can look at the vegetation and tell you what was there when Columbus came and what was imported later. I can reconstruct the plantations that were laid out on that area of St. James. The recorded history of the place is short, three centuries of depopulation followed by two centuries of resettlement. The documents of the resettlement are available in the city, in the Registrar-General's Office. While the documents last we can hunt up the story of every strip of occupied land.

I can give you that historical bird's eye view. But I cannot really explain the mystery of Leonard Side's inheritance. Most of us know the parents or grandparents we come from. But we go back and back forever; we go back all of us to the very beginning; in our blood and bone and brain we carry the memories of thousands of beings. I might say that an ancestor of Leonard Side's came from the dancing groups of Lucknow, the lewd men who painted their faces and tried to live like women. But that would only be a fragment of his inheritance, a fragment of the truth. We cannot understand all the traits we have inherited. Sometimes we can be strangers to ourselves.[7]

Fourth of July, 2000
Columbia, Missouri

Notes

1. Andrew Burstein, *The Inner Jefferson: Portrait of a Grieving Optimist* (Charlottesville: University of Virginia Press, 1995), 265; William Peden, "The Jefferson Monument at the University of Missouri," Ellis Library, University of Missouri-Columbia, 1–3.

2. Peden, "The Jefferson Monument," 7–9. For photos of the old and new tombstones, see William Howard Adams, *Jefferson's Monticello* (New York: Abbeville Press, 1983), 248–49.

3. Frank F. Stephens, *A History of the University of Missouri* (Columbia: University of Missouri Press, 1962), 295–96.

4. The stone was even lent to the World's Fair in St. Louis in 1904; Stephens, *History of the University of Missouri*, 381.

5. Styles of documentation varied widely. Some contributors sensed no need to use footnotes to buttress their claims, while others of us felt compelled to supply such information. This phenomenon seems to confirm Bruce Lincoln's conclusion that footnoting is a ritual used by western scholars for the invocation of their ancestors; "Two Notes on Modern Rituals," *Journal of the American Academy of Religion* 45, no. 2 (1977): 152–56.

6. W. C. Smith, "Objectivity and the Humane Sciences: A New Proposal," in Willard G. Oxtoby, ed., *Religious Diversity* (New York: Crossroad, 1982), 158–80.

7. V. S. Naipaul, *A Way in the World* (New York: Alfred A. Knopf, 1994), 10–11.

I. Ancestral Cosmologies

The Living Living and the Living Dead

A Source of Harmony in Melanesia

William B. Ferea

The topic of ancestors in Melanesia is discussed in this paper in terms of the problem of the "self." There are other ways to approach the problem; I have chosen this method because I am convinced that the dual conception of the self that characterizes Melanesian cultures provides the basis for harmony in society between the "living living" and the "living dead" (i.e., the ancestors). I prefer to avoid an approach that focuses on linguistic analysis. This paper adopts instead a descriptive approach that depicts the general conception of self that is found throughout Melanesian groups. This allows us to study the meaning—or at least the possible meanings—of a particular conception of self in Melanesia, and then to speculate on its value in a wider cultural context. That is to say, the descriptive approach involves explaining the problem of "identity" in Melanesia as seen by Melanesians, with some evaluative commentary on my part.

After preliminary remarks on early, foreign Christian interpretations of self and culture in Melanesia, my paper makes a general statement on the distinctive and common cultural features of identity in Melanesia. The second section of the paper then takes a particular tribal perspective on selfhood, drawing especially on cultural historian and physician Wulf Schiefenhoevel's study of the body and soul among the Eipo Melanesians of Irian Jaya.[1] The final section deals with the way this view of the self is cultivated in ritual and myth and illustrates how this view played itself out in the changing relationships with ancestors after contact in the cargo cults.

A Short History of the Melanesian Self

Before the introduction of writing by Europeans in the 1800s, cultural information in Melanesia was passed down from generation to generation exclusively
by word of mouth and through oral tradition. With the advent of writing, we
now have both oral and written media for the transmission of cultural definitions of topics like selfhood. The forms of oral tradition include songs, poems,
legends, and myths, and we will return to these later in the paper. At this point
we should consider the role that has been played by the written sources.

The early documentation of Melanesian cultures comes from European explorers, miners, plantation owners, government officers, and Christian missionaries. Most of this documentation, especially that by Christian missionaries, was meant to degrade and to destroy Melanesian cultures. For example, Karl
Panzer was a German Lutheran missionary who worked among the Wampar
tribe of Papua New Guinea. Panzer wrote that the Wampar people should forget
their oral traditions and pay attention only to God's gospel in the Bible.[2] Similar
Christian attitudes toward Melanesian values are found in the writings of other
missionaries, for example, in John Nicholson's work on the Vella Lavella
Melanesians of the Solomon Islands and John Paton's work on the Tanna
Melanesians of Vanuatu.

During the late 1800s the emergence of the discipline of anthropology paved
the way for Europeans to study Melanesian cultures in a more sympathetic and
more objective way. John Beattie highlighted two factors that led to this sort of
study about non-western cultures in their own right in the nineteenth century.
First, the improvement in quantity and quality of ethnographic information led
scholars to demand serious comparative analysis instead of the earlier efforts to
degrade other cultures. Second, the colonial governments and missionaries finally realized that for the purposes of actually understanding the peoples of the
new worlds, the anthropological studies of other cultures were much more
helpful than the old declamations.[3]

One thing we learn from the more disciplined studies of the last one hundred years is that it is impossible to discuss all the notions of self from all the
groups in Melanesia. There are about three thousand different Melanesian
tribes. About one thousand of these tribes speak various forms of Austronesian
languages, while the other two thousand speak non-Austronesian languages.
The great variety of languages in Melanesia is due to the huge gaps of time
between the various migrations into the area, ranging from sixty thousand to
three thousand years ago. In spite of this linguistic diversity, however, there are
still some common cultural features, such as general social organization, leadership style, and religion. The structural similarities of Melanesian religion are

important for our purposes since one common element is a cosmology that harmonizes or unifies the material and spiritual world. Though the various tribes may have different linguistic references to the soul/body relationship, they are based on this same cosmology.

The Eipo conception of physical body and spirit-soul provides an exemplary case in this regard that allows us to discuss a specific cultural configuration within the general category. The Eipo conception of body and soul presupposes the Melanesian cosmology of the unification of the material and the spiritual world. Within this process of unification, there seems to be a temporary or final movement of "beings" (or self) from one realm to another. This movement suggests the dual nature of selfhood in Melanesia. This temporary movement from the material/empirical to the spiritual/non-empirical world is possible through the process of unconsciousness, while the temporary movement from the non-empirical to the empirical world is possible through the process of metamorphosis. Of course, the final movement of "beings" from the empirical to the non-empirical world is death, and the final movement from the non-empirical to the empirical is birth.

According to Schiefenhoevel, the Eipo Melanesians conceive of the person's appearance in the empirical realm as the body, or physical body. At the opposite end, in the non-empirical realm, they conceive of the person's appearance as spirit-soul, the *isa dib*.[4] What happens, so it seems, is that when an Eipo person is alive, the person's identity, or self, is referred to as *na*, "I." After death, however, that person's isa dib will still use the term na, but this time referring to the spiritual being. In Melanesia, the spirit-soul's identity or self-reference as na is proven by the event of a physical person's body being occupied by a spirit and, thus, making the self-referential statements.

We could say, then, that in the Eipo cosmology, a person in physical form is the self in actual bodily form (the *pasre*), but he or she is potentially a self in the spirit-soul form (the *yanon*). Conversely, a person in the spirit-soul form is an actual self in that form, but potentially a self in the physical body form.

We should note that the final movement from spirit-soul to the physical body during birth does not mean the return of the same person in the form of a new baby. Rather, that person's spirit-soul, or isa dib, remains in a mythic village where the ancestors reside. Throughout Melanesia it is common for people to speak of a village to which people travel after death. This place, or ancestral village, may be found in a remote part of the forest, on or inside a mountain, along a river, or within a cave. It is often located in a place associated with the origins of a particular clan. Such places will, then, be sacred to the clan and when activities, such as hunting or gardening, are carried out there, they must be accompanied by rituals to placate ancestral spirits who are believed to be living in a community similar to the community of the living.[5] This "return" to the place of origin by spirit-souls helps create a sense of completion of the diaspora for clans that have moved to other locations (due to wars, migration, and the like) and a sense of reaffirmation of communal living by clans that have remained in one location. As a "final" and "blissful" place for spirits, the ancestral village is similar in some ways to the Christian notion of heaven.

While ancestors do not return to the material world, they do send their essence (*kenye*) to a newborn baby in their families. Kenye for the Eipo is the human essence or intelligence that a person possesses. This transfer of kenye, as opposed to a direct return, helps the Eipo avoid the cycle of birth and rebirth evident in the Hindu tradition. Thus, between the realms of the physical body and the spirit-soul there are temporary movements in both directions. From the physical body, this temporary movement of self happens during unconsciousness. During this time, the Eipo would say that the person's body-soul, or *furume*, leaves the physical body and may return. If it does not return, that furume becomes the isa dib, or the actual self in the spirit-soul form.

In regard to the spirit-soul form, the temporary movement of self to the physical body form occurs during metamorphosis. This is when a spirit-soul enters the physical body of another living person, or when the spirit-soul changes (or transforms) into a physical being or into another animal form. This spirit-soul returns, however, to the non-empirical world, and must necessarily do so. The spirit-soul must always return and remain in the ancestral village; the non-empirical world is the final end of the Melanesian cosmos. As stated above, a spirit-soul's final return to the physical body during birth can only be marked by the transfer of this kenye to a newborn baby, most often a relative residing in the empirical world. In that way, the cosmology of connecting the empirical and non-empirical world is complete.

There is also frequent communication between the living living and the living dead. This occurs in various ways: through dreaming, through near-death experiences, through trances, and so on. Sometimes the yanon, the spirit-soul self, goes to the ancestors, and at other times ancestors might come to the living with a message of some sort. These sorts of communications help establish harmony between the spiritual and material realms.

In light of the movements of the self through the material and spiritual aspects of reality, and the ongoing relationship with the ancestors, we can say that Melanesian selfhood is a totality of being, for it encompasses both the material and the spiritual worlds. Although the various Melanesian tribes will have different linguistic references to the soul-body and the self, the two realms of exist-ence are always present in their cosmology. The Melanesian's aim is to connect these two realms, and in this way to promote universal harmony.

I would say that, for the living living in Melanesia, this general aim of har-mony is composed of six purposes in life. The first purpose is *gom*, to cultivate food and to eat; without this the Melanesian cosmology would come to an end. Second, humans have a responsibility to cultivate the species, to propagate hu-manity (*sagaseg*). A third purpose is *usitdaorab*, the cultivation of trade. Since life is lived communally and not individualistically, reciprocal exchanges must be promoted that allow society to continue. Fourth, the cultivation of peace between people (*umunerom*) allows the community to survive politically. The fifth purpose is *umu-unumurin*, the cultivation of education. Without a lively intellectual life (which includes the maintenance of medical knowledge) there would be no unity of the material and spiritual worlds. Finally, there is also *utigfaum*, which is the duty to cultivate the religious life that allows the commu-nity to survive spiritually.

All six of these purposes are very pragmatic; they are put into practice in daily life rather than enshrined as abstract ideas. They are the natural result of the general Melanesian cosmology that locates the human within the material and spiritual realms and that allows the ancestors to play a crucial role in the production of harmony. This process of unification is not simply a matter of everyday life, however. It is also evident in stories and ceremonies. Once contact with Europeans began, the process took on some unusual characteristics in the so-called cargo cults. To these topics we now turn.

Ritual, Myth, Ancestors, and Cargo

One reason for the specific role of ancestors in Melanesian cosmology and in the goals of human life is that Melanesians pay more attention to the ancestral spirits than to the gods and goddesses. This is not the case in Micronesia and Polynesia where the deities are more prominent. For Melanesians, the gods did exist at the beginning of time, creating humanity and the universe. According to Melanesians, however, those gods and goddesses have now withdrawn into par-tial or total oblivion. So Melanesians pay more attention to the ancestral spirits, the isa dib, in order to ensure their future safe entry into the spirit world. The ancestral spirits also support the physical beings in their daily life, while the gods do not. This cosmology is summed up by the Melanesian scholar Esau Tuza as that which unifies the empirical and the non-empirical realms of the universe.[6]

The practical reenactment of unification is done through the various rituals and ceremonies that Melanesians perform in their daily activities, especially during the funeral ceremonies.[7] Karl Hesse made a careful account of such ceremonies.[8] He lived among the Baining of East New Britain in Papua New Guinea as a Catholic missionary and is now archbishop of Rabaul. According to Hesse, the death of an important man (a *barka a nijipki*), a man who has many gardens and pigs and a knowledge of magic and sorcery, is marked by destroying gardens and killing his pigs.[9] All his spears, axes, knives, and fighting sticks are also destroyed by being broken. Broken, they can then be taken by the dead man's spirit to the spirit world. For the Baining, the physical destruction of objects ensures the entry of a dead person into the spirit world, the *a rimbab*.

The Baining belief that it is necessary to break or destroy the possessions of a dead person so that they and he, all in their changed or broken state, can enter the spirit world is opposite to our understanding of the ancient Egyptian practice in which safe passage to the afterlife of an important person and his implements is dependent upon the preservation of his body and his implements. Hesse also mentions that at the night vigil prior to burial, a man's wife and children must touch his corpse. Their failure to do so can result in calamity for the individuals concerned.[10] The touching, I think, symbolizes the final bonding of the living with the dead person's spirit. Like most Melanesians, the Baining hold big mortuary feasts. But, according to Hesse, the taro to be cooked and eaten are placed beside the dead person's body. It is hoped that the taro will capture the knowledge and energy that emanates from the important person's body. Again, this is a ritual bonding of the living and the dead.[11] Many of the Baining dances and the associated body paintings and paraphernalia also symbolize the "intimate connection between the living (*chachet*) and the dead (*a jos*)."[12]

The unification of the empirical and non-empirical realms is also effected through myths about cosmology and the dual nature of the self. Myths, according to Wendy Flannery, "reveal the inner meaning" of the Melanesian universe or cosmology, the cosmology that presupposes the connecting of the empirical and the non-empirical worlds. This is especially the case with eschatological myths.[13] The eschatological myths are of special importance in this study because 1) they not only encompass the Melanesian cosmology (as do the other three types of myths), but 2) they also portray the movement of self (in the form of a mythical being) from the physical body to the spirit-soul, with an expectation for the return of that same self. The eschatological myths in Melanesia explain the "going-away" of a mythical being or a culture hero and then presuppose his "return," bringing some form of material and spiritual enlightenment. This "going-away and returning" seems to suggest the completion of the connection of the empirical and non-empirical worlds.

According to the Biak Islanders of Irian Jaya, for instance, one of their mythical ancestors, by the name of Manarmakeri (Mansren Manggundi, "Lord Himself"), had left in a canoe for the west a long time ago. Manarmakeri was said to have had so much magical power he could do almost anything. One day, however, when his people realized that he could not raise a child from death, they staged a revolt, and so he left to go west. Manarmakeri's going-away could be seen as a state of unconsciousness. According to the Biak Islanders, however, Manarmakeri will someday return to the Biak physical world, thus bringing the *koreri*, or enlightenment. This koreri, for the Biak, will be marked by the abundance of food, material goods, and spiritual happiness.[14] We could say that Manarmakeri's return assumes a state of the body-soul, or furume, coming back to the physical world.

Likewise, among the Rai-Coast of Madang in Papua New Guinea, a mythical ancestor by the name of Kilibob had paddled away in a canoe to the west. He left in anger and shame after discovering that his twin brother, Maup, had printed a tatoo on the genitals of Kilibob's wife Rorpain. Kilibob will return, according to the story, to reunite with his brother and thus will bring about a new cosmos, a new universe.[15] Like Manarmakeri, Kilibob's going-away was through unconsciousness; but his return is in fact his furume coming back to the empirical world.

The events described by these myths are symbolic of the fundamental meaning of the Melanesian cosmology, the dual movement of self from the physical body to the spirit-soul, and back. We not only see Manarmakeri's self and Kilibob's self moving from the physical world to the spiritual world (through unconsciousness), but we also see their return—or rather, their expected return—from the spiritual world to the physical world. The going-away and return of both Manarmakeri and Kilibob are in the form of furume. They have not really died yet, so their self cannot be isa dib (spirit-soul). Their self, however, is potentially spirit-soul. Nevertheless, the event of going into the spiritual world and back to the physical world still serves the Melanesian attempt to unite the empirical and non-empirical world.

The dual notion of self in Melanesia manifests a communal relationship between the living living and the living dead. The effect of this duality became evident in the early 1800s when the Europeans arrived in Melanesia. The initial response of the Melanesians to contact was exemplified by the attitudes of the Biak and the Rai-Coast Melanesians at that time. They concluded that the Dutch and the Germans were the descendants of Manarmakeri and Kilibob, respectively. When the Europeans did not distribute the goods that came with them on the ships to the Melanesians, the latter thought that the Europeans had cheated them; they had not brought back gifts from the spiritual realm. The Melanesians resorted to traditional ritual and to Christian practices in order to obtain the cargo from the Europeans, and, thus, the so-called cargo cults of Melanesia were born.

For this reason, the cargo cults are a uniquely Melanesian kind of millenarian movement. Millenarian movements have existed throughout the world in various times and places. The cargo cults, however, stem from the Melanesian worldview, which portrays the communal and obligatory relationships between humans and ancestors. But the cargo cults also arose out of the grave miscalculation of the meaning of contact that resulted in an aberration in regard to the ancestors—some Melanesians no longer pursued the six purposes of life but waited for the alleged descendants of their ancestors (that is, the colonizers) to provide material goods for them.

Post-contact history has brought significant changes in Melanesia, but among Melanesians there has also been a return to the ancestral spirituality that was once the norm. In the face of modern developments, Melanesian gods, culture heroes, and ancestral spirits can still be worshiped, especially as a source of inspiration for the mundane activities of daily life. This was the case before the coming of Europeans. Melanesians did their carving, fishing, hunting, gardening, building, and dancing with the inspiration of the ancestral spirits. They never sat and waited for the ancestors to do these mundane tasks for them. In line with this traditional lifeway, many of the cargo cult movements in Melanesia have become indigenous political movements that have fought for independence from the colonial powers. Such were the Taukei Movement of Fiji, the John Frum Movement of Vanuatu, and the Tanget cult of Papua New Guinea. Others, like the Pomio-Kivung Group of East New Britain and the Pitenamu of Morobe Province in Papua New Guinea, became successful modern business cooperatives. Members of these movements maintained their faith in the guidance of their ancestors but worked hard to achieve success in their political and business activities.

This consideration of the dual self in Melanesian cosmology leads to three conclusions that point us toward a future for our ancestors. First, the spirituality of contemporary Melanesians can be strengthened by continued communion between the spiritual and physical worlds. It makes little difference whether the spiritual realm is thought to be populated by the Christian God, the Muslim Allah, or the ancestors. All of these can operate within a Melanesian cosmology. Second, the Melanesian conception of the ancestral village is similar in some ways to the Christian heaven. The symbol of the ancestral village can help contemporary Melanesians cultivate the pragmatic purposes of life that establish cosmic harmony. Finally, the communal relationship between the living living and the living dead can continue to flow from the spiritual realm to the social policies that regulate our mundane existence. To put it in other words, the relationship of the ancestors with those of us who are still living can become a source of harmony within human communities.

Notes

1. Wulf Schiefenhoevel, "Of Body and Soul among the Eipo of Irian Jaya," *Bikmaus* 4 (1983).

2. *Usingis num ngaeng amogamog ages azob, ban edaom? Ofos ages azob anin dojanon Anutu dongkang ari garamut, en Jesu efai mur agea onowaro fuzun. Usingis Anutu gea zob, gea ban edaom en agea zob nizin.* "If you read your ancestor's words, will it be of any good to you? If you continue to like their words, you run away from God, and it is Jesus who stepped on the Serpent's head [i.e., Jesus saved you from evil]. Read God's word and it will do you good because it is the only truth." From Karl Panzer, *Garagab Egerenon Anutu Imuam en Anzob Egereneran* (Logaweng-Neuguinea: Neuendettelsauer Missionsdruckerei, 1917), 64.

3. John Beattie, *Other Cultures* (New York: Free Press, 1964), 9.

4. Schiefenhoevel, "Body and Soul."

5. G. W. Trompf, *Melanesian Religion* (Cambridge: Cambridge University Press, 1991), 44–45.

6. Esau Tuza, "A Melanesian Cosmological Process," in H. Olela, ed., *Total Cosmic Vision of Life: An Introduction to Melanesian Philosophy* (Port Moresby: University of Papua New Guinea, 1981), 56.

7. Ibid., 90.

8. Karl Hesse, *Baining Life and Lore* (Port Moresby: Institute of Papua New Guinea Studies, 1982), 22–26.

9. Ibid., 23.

10. Ibid., 25.

11. Ibid.

12. Ibid., 33.

13. Wendy Flannery, "Appreciating Melanesian Myths," in Norman C. Habel, ed., *Powers, Plumes, and Piglets: Phenomena of Melanesian Religions* (Bedford Park, South Australia: Australian Association for the Study of Religions, 1979), 161–72.

14. Friedrich Steinbauer, *Melanesian Cargo Cults: New Salvation Movements in the South Pacific* (St. Lucia: University of Queensland Press, 1979), 5–9.

15. Ibid., 39–41.

Discussion

Diane Bell

How are the six purposes you mentioned articulated in your culture? Are they articulated in ritual, in mundane conversation? How does someone acquire this knowledge?

William Ferea

The six purposes that allow someone to survive spiritually are communicated through rituals. One becomes religious when one observes the tribal rules: performing rituals before canoe-making or planting bananas, dancing, and so on. All these activities involve the ancestral spirits. So, one cultivates the religious life by abiding with the performance of rituals during one's mundane life. Failing to do the rituals or failing to attend the performances before going out on a canoe, before dancing, and so on, is irreligious and may have serious consequences because you are failing to recognize the other side of humanity, the ancestors. You may not progress in society, you may not progress spiritually. People will see you as someone who is not upholding the religious, cosmic order.

Jacob Olupona

Diane asked where these purposes of life are manifested, which raises the problem of method in research. It is quite hard to study these traditions, even for people who are in some sense insiders to the culture. My experience studying in Africa suggests that it works well to approach the elders through rituals, to observe them in the context of rituals, and then to ask them to explain what these beliefs are. I'd be interested in knowing how you go about your own research, in collecting these materials. The second question is that I am also interested in knowing how people become ancestors in your tribe. My understanding from your paper is that once you fulfill these six purposes of life and you do not commit suicide, you are qualified to become an ancestor. Now, what about people who commit evil deeds in your culture? Is there an equivalent of hell in this culture? How do you punish people who do evil? Are they qualified to become ancestors?

William Ferea

Regarding the six purposes and the methodology of research, 60 to 80 percent of the people in Papua New Guinea live in villages in a tribal context, performing their rituals as a part of daily life. I grew up in a village and took part myself in the garden ceremonies and in all the activities in the six purposes that I mentioned here. In a sense, I am talking about what I have been doing. But besides that, regarding the songs that were brought back by the ancestors, there is a list of elders with whom I sat through the night, chewed betel nut, and listened to them singing. I didn't go out with a set of questionaires and ask the elders, "What is this and what are the six purposes of life?" I come from that culture. I took part in all the rituals, and I have expressed the goal of these experiences as six or so purposes.

Jacob Olupona

What sort of rituals are you talking about here?

William Ferea

Rituals involved in the preparation of food, rituals for the cultivation of bananas, rituals of dancing, rituals of canoe-making, and so on. Peacemaking involves various rituals like shaking hands, exchanging pigs, exchanging betel nuts. To cultivate the species, you have to go through the rituals of a lot of magic, such as magic to attract the right woman for you to marry.

There was another question about hell, conceptions of good and evil, and ancestral places of bliss and punishment. No one is going to die and go to a place of non-bliss. We simply do not have any concept of non-bliss. There will be problems, and those who have done evil, like not following tribal norms or not doing the right rituals, will be punished by the ancestors one way or another; at one time or another they will face some sort of calamity. There is also punishment meted out by the social institutions of the material society, but the culprit would be brought back into society. Or, there are many other practices that now seem like cruelties and excesses, such as the old practice of killing a woman who committed adultery. There were punishments meted out for evil acts, but negation of rituals results in not being respected in society as a religious person. So one did not become a Big Man. Please remember that we don't have chiefs in Melanesia; we don't have inherited leadership, with the exception of a few tribes. We compete for leadership. If you have more pigs and a big garden, and if you give more feasts, then you are a leader. If not, then you are just somebody, a villager.

Charles Long

I have some questions about translation. I ask because words in our vocabulary like "physical," "spiritual," and "soul" are confusing even in western languages. There is no standard understanding of what these words really mean in English. What does "yanon" mean? What does "the purposes of life" mean to your people? The word "religion" is a strange word in the western vocabulary, too. I guess I'm trying to get around the idea that the world can be squeezed into western categories. I'm trying to get a new kind of meaning out of what your tribe was about. If we don't do this, we run the risk of just saying, "Well, that's nothing but what we already know. They just happen to do it that way."

Ulunui Garmon

Maybe we need more definition here, especially for the terms "spirituality" and "religion." I can listen to you, William, and understand that you are coming from a very deep cultural and spiritual tradition. So when you say the word "religion," I am not too concerned about the particular word. But since the question has been raised, what do you mean by "religion?"

William Ferea

I use the word "religion" to refer to activities that are already present in those various tribes. But the tribes themselves don't have a word for "religion." The problem is that one tribe is trying to convey to another tribe—the western tribe—certain aspects of their worldview. You have to use accepted terms in order to help that other tribe understand approximately what you mean. Translation is never perfect; and we may never find a way of resolving the differences, but we do have to be aware of the problem. There is no word for religion in my tribe nor in the various languages in Melanesia.

Puanani Burgess

William, in listening to what you were saying and especially in the discussion, I was reminded of a meeting where our *kupuna*, our elders, were speaking English in deference to the fact that a lot of us who attended the meeting could not speak Hawaiian. And they began to argue. They argued and argued, and it was getting louder and louder. Then they turned back to speak to each other in Hawaiian, and they found that they could agree quite easily. The language that they were able to communicate to us in, in this case English, could not carry the meaning. So my question to you is, how is western training and western education interfering in the process of understanding your own culture and your own spirituality, and in being able to transmit that to your own people first and then to outsiders?

William Ferea

There certainly is a tension between tradition and education, for me and for others in Papua New Guinea. Here's an example of the expectations people now have regarding the influence of foreign cultures. There is a part of a river that my parents have put aside and it is taboo for anyone to go fishing there. They let the fish grow big and multiply and on special occasions, like when I come home from the university on holidays, we can go there and catch the big fish. Once when I went home for the Christmas holidays, I swam across this huge river with my brothers and sisters and went into the forest where my great-grandfather used to live. The protocol is that the oldest male member of the family will cry out incantations for the ancestral spirits to help us by coming out of the river so that we can catch the fish. My elder brothers didn't come along on this trip and it fell to me to perform the rituals. So I was chanting, "Oh, ancestors, please come out of the water and let us catch the fish!" and so on, and my sisters and younger brothers were laughing and laughing. Then I realized what the problem was. They thought I was an atheist now that I went to the university. You see, if my elder brother had done the chanting, or if I hadn't gone and my younger brother who lives in the village had done the chanting, nobody would have laughed. Maybe if I had prayed to the Christian god it would have been different.

Rubellite Johnson

Was the problem related to the influence of Christianity, or to the attempt to practice a spirituality that is both Melanesian and Christian?

William Ferea

Christianity wasn't so much the issue. It was staying away for years in an urban place, spending two years in America and then going back. My brothers and sisters probably were thinking, "You don't fit anymore. Maybe the ancestors don't know you very well. Your chanting will not have any effect. We're going to go home without any fish."

Steven Friesen

Did you catch anything on that trip?

William Ferea

We did, but not my favorite kind of fish.

The Cult of Saints and Souls in New Orleans

Ewert Cousins

Before plunging into my topic, I would like to situate it within the context of our conference. I must confess that at first I had some difficulty choosing a topic for a conference on primal spirituality. I do not belong to an indigenous group. I am not a cultural anthropologist, nor am I a historian of religion who has done in-depth research on such cultures, although I have had prolonged first-hand contact with Native American people and have participated in interreligious dialogue with members of many different indigenous cultures.

My academic specialization is in Christianity, particularly the Franciscan movement in the Middle Ages. My role in the ongoing project of the Dialogue of Civilizations[1] has been chiefly to explore the interface between primal spiritualities and axial religions. So, I thought I might compare the spirituality of ancestors in primal traditions with the Christian doctrine of the communion of saints as expressed in Dante's *Divine Comedy*. In so doing I will be presenting the Roman Catholic tradition. By the communion of saints I mean the interrelation between those living on earth and those who have died and gone to heaven or who are in the state of purification called purgatory. The term "saints" here is taken in a broad sense and not restricted to the officially canonized saints. It includes the entire Church community, living and dead: one's immediate and distant ancestors, the canonized saints, and the larger community of the faithful. This interrelationship is expressed in the terms: the Church Militant on earth, the Church Suffering in purgatory, and the Church Triumphant in heaven. The military metaphor contained in the term the Church Militant should not be taken literally. It suggests rather the struggle against temptation and the forces of evil that one encounters in one's spiritual life on earth and for which one needs aid. An essential element of this doctrine is the belief that these different groups of souls can communicate. Those on earth can help those in purgatory through prayers and good works, which can reduce the period of purgation. The saints in heaven can assist those on earth either spontaneously or in response to prayers.

This is the general topic I will explore. To make it concrete, I will take my point of departure from the experience of the communion of saints as I encountered it growing up in New Orleans. Since the culture of New Orleans is pervasively Roman Catholic, I will be speaking out of that tradition. It is important to note that there are significant differences between the Catholic, Protestant, and Orthodox positions in this area, especially on the doctrine of purgatory. The choice of New Orleans is especially relevant to our conference since popular religion there contains a remarkable blend of primal and axial elements—primal elements that the French and Spanish colonists brought with them from their own archaic Mediterranean European roots, which blended with primal elements imported from Africa and the islands of the Caribbean.[2]

It is difficult to describe the culture of New Orleans. It is located in the southern United States, but it is unlike any other part of the American South. In many respects it is much more European than American. It has rich ethnic diversity—not only French and Spanish, but Italian, German, Irish, and others as well. There are even two French cultures: the one centered in the city and nurtured from Paris in the nineteenth century, the other in the bayous south and west of the city, the Cajun country, which has increasingly influenced life in the city.

New Orleans is a city that celebrates life—in the superb cuisine that it cultivates as a fine art, in the sound of jazz that flows through its streets, and in its fantasy world of Mardi Gras. But it is also a city that celebrates death—in its elaborate wakes and funerals, in its monumental cemeteries, and perhaps most strikingly in its observance of the religious feasts of All Saints and All Souls. It is here in the cemeteries on the feasts of All Saints and All Souls, November 1 and 2, that we encounter one of the rich expressions of the Christian doctrine of the communion of saints and one of the most vital contacts with the primal spirituality of ancestors.

All Saints and All Souls

The liturgical feast of All Saints commemorates all those who have died and reached heaven, whether they are officially canonized or not. The liturgical feast of All Souls commemorates those who have died and are presently in the state of purgatory, where they are being purified through suffering for the remains of sin in their souls before they can be admitted to heaven. In the popular observance of these feasts this distinction is blurred, since the focus of the observance is the family grave in the cemetery. It is here that we connect most concretely with the spirituality of ancestors. It is customary for families to spend days and even weeks before the feasts preparing the graves—cleaning and painting the tombs, trimming the grass and plants on the graves, and filling the vases with flowers, usually white and yellow chrysanthemums. All Saints' Day is an official holiday in New Orleans, with banks and post offices closed. Many families spend hours in the cemetery on All Saints' Day and also on All Souls' Day, praying privately, attending Mass in the cemetery, and joining in prayers led by priests. Their primary purpose is to be present to the deceased members of their families and to honor their memory. It is the public feast for establishing concrete relationships with their ancestors.

As a young boy I remember taking part in this cemetery ritual on these feasts. Yet, the close contact with the deceased was not limited to All Saints' Day and All Souls' Day. It was customary for our family—as for many in the city—to visit the family grave each Sunday, placing flowers on the grave and saying silent prayers. Many people would spend hours at the family graves each Sunday and on religious feast days. These practices continue to the present.

The mystique of death in New Orleans is manifested by the observance of the feasts of All Saints and All Souls described above, but also by the cemeteries themselves. The cemeteries are very visible in the city, gracing the urban landscape in prominent locations, adorned with stately monuments. Because the city is built on marshland, burials cannot take place deep in the soil. As a consequence, even ordinary graves are raised above ground by marble or stone borders. A high percentage of the burials take place in tombs and large monuments that are often decorated with statuary. Cemeteries in New Orleans are among the leading tourist sites and are visited regularly by touring busses.

This mystique of death has connections with the origin of jazz. The beginnings of jazz have been traced to the music played by blacks in the nineteenth century in Congo Square on the edge of the French Quarter, but it was developed by the black musicians who played for funeral processions. On the way to the cemetery they solemnly played the Funeral March, but on the way back they let out their emotions in the rhythms of jazz. These processions have become a crucial aspect of the city's culture. Some years ago when visiting my family in New Orleans, I heard a jazz band playing in the street one Sunday afternoon. Thinking it was a funeral procession, I ran outside, saw the procession but no hearse with a body. A bystander told me that it was a funeral organization whose members pay dues so that each will have a procession for his funeral. In this case, however, the man died and was buried in the middle of the week when the members of the organization were working. So they gathered for the funeral procession on Sunday.

The Cult of Saints

Prominent in New Orleans is the cult of saints who have been formally canonized by the Church. This means that they can be the object of a public cult, of veneration, of a place in the liturgy. Since the early centuries of Christianity, such saints have been honored, their relics venerated, and their shrines visited. They have been the models of virtue and the source of benefits for those who petition them.[3] They are the spiritual heroes of the past—admirable and powerful ancestors—who will guide and protect their devotees in the present and future.

Popular devotion to saints also flourishes in New Orleans. Among the favorite saints is Mary the Mother of Jesus, who is venerated under many titles, chief of which are Our Lady of Prompt Succor and Our Lady of Perpetual Help. For example, when in 1969 the devastating hurricane Camille was heading across the Gulf of Mexico on a straight course toward New Orleans, the archbishop went to the shrine of Our Lady of Prompt Succor, the patroness of the city. There, he said a Mass for the deliverance of the city. At that moment the hurricane dramatically turned to the east and bypassed the city completely.

Another popular saint is St. Joseph, the husband of Mary and foster father of Jesus. When I was a boy, I took part in a special devotion to St. Joseph that flourished among the Italians in the French Quarter. Each year on the eve of the feast of St. Joseph, which was celebrated on March 19, my aunt and I visited nine St. Joseph altars, as they were called. We would walk through the French Quarter looking for the sign of an altar—a torch surrounded by flowers, at the entrance to an alley. The altars were often beyond a patio and up several flights of stairs, set up in the homes of families who had made a vow to St. Joseph in return for a favor. The shrines consisted of a picture or statue of St. Joseph displayed at the center of decorations of elaborately prepared Italian bread and food of all kinds. In some of the rooms which housed these shrines, the walls and tables seemed completely covered with food. The aromas were delicious.

We were told that on the next day twelve poor children, symbolizing the twelve apostles, would be invited to the home for a meal, and then the rest of the food would be distributed to the poor. In later years, after moving away from New Orleans, I often thought of these St. Joseph altars and surmised that the custom had probably waned. To my surprise, I learned recently that it is still flourishing and, in fact, the custom has extended from the French Quarter throughout the city.

St. Ann, the mother of Mary, is another popular saint, whose shrine on the edge of the French Quarter attracts many pilgrims. St. Jude, the patron of impossible cases, draws large crowds to novenas in his honor. St. Patrick, of course, is a favorite among the Irish community in the district called the Irish Channel. Many also pray to St. Francis of Assisi and especially to the Franciscan St. Anthony, who is famous for helping to find lost objects.

Last year while watching a video made for public television about devotion to saints in New Orleans, I learned of a saint I had never hear of—St. Expedite. The story of his cult was told in the video. A parish in New Orleans had ordered from France the statue of a young male saint of the patristic era. When the statue arrived, the recipients noticed that on the shipping crate was written: Expedite. They concluded that inside was the statue of St. Expedite, which they proceeded to remove and place on a pedestal in the church for veneration. A cult soon grew up around him, especially because he had the reputation of obtaining favors quickly.[4]

Dante and Saints

We will now turn to Dante and his treatment of the communion of saints in the *Divine Comedy*. In doing this, we move from popular to learned religion. Within Christianity Dante has provided the classical presentation of this doctrine. It is true that he has done this in poetry, but it is a poetic expression that faithfully mirrors the most sophisticated scholastic theology of the Middle Ages. It represents the position of western Christianity in that era, and although the Protestant Reformation rejected Dante's view of purgatory, his position remains that of Roman Catholicism to this day. It provides the learned explanation behind the popular religion of Roman Catholic New Orleans.

The narrative of the *Divine Comedy* is woven within the fabric of the doctrine of the communion of saints. In the opening lines of the poem, we find Dante lost in a dark wood after he has turned away from the straight path of his spiritual journey. He gets his bearings through the assistance of the poet Vergil, whom we soon learn has been sent by Beatrice, Dante's beloved. She had died some years before and was given a high place in heaven, making her a saint in the sense of one who is in heaven, although she has not been canonized. We learn that the original impetus to help Dante came spontaneously from Mary, who called St. Lucy to send Beatrice. So, in the communion of saints, help for those on earth can arise spontaneously from the saints in heaven.

Vergil tells Dante that he must go on a journey into hell, purgatory, and heaven. The damned in hell do not share in the communion of saints, but Dante has much to learn from their plight. It is when he enters purgatory that the interrelatedness of the three branches of the communion of saints becomes clear. As a member of the Church Militant on earth, Dante can assist the souls in purgatory, who are members of the Church Suffering, by praying for them and requesting their relatives and friends to pray for them so that their sufferings in purgatory can be reduced. When he enters heaven, the realm of the Church Triumphant, he is constantly enlightened by the wisdom and enflamed by the love that is mediated by the saints who come to meet him. Finally, in Dante's beautiful image of the mystical rose formed by the souls of the blessed in heaven, we see the ultimate fulfillment of the communion of saints. Here, the members of the Church Militant and the Church Suffering take their place with the Church Triumphant in their communion among themselves in the eternal union of the beatific vision of God. Here, in the eternal presence of the mystical rose—where all of the saints are present to each other and are present to God— the spirituality of the ancestors reaches it culmination. This state will be enhanced and the intensity of joy increased when, after the resurrection and final judgment, the bodies of the saints will be joined to their souls for all eternity.

Dante's Examples

As Dante tells the story of his journey through purgatory and heaven, he gives concrete examples of how he interacts with the souls of the deceased in the communion of saints. Throughout purgatory, when the souls realize that he has not yet died and that he will return to earth, they implore him to urge their families and friends to pray for them so that their time in purgatory may be shortened. This is especially the case of the penitents of the last hour, those who had led sinful lives and at the hour of their death repented and were saved, but whose repentance was private and not known to their family and friends. For example, Jacopo del Cassero, a soldier who died alone of wounds received in battle, urges Dante: "I beg of thee, if ever thou see the land that lies between Romagna and that of Charles, that thou do me the courtesy to beg those in Fano that good prayers be made for me, only that I may purge away my grievous sins."[5]

The role of the saints in heaven is highlighted by Beatrice when she meets Dante at the end of his journey through purgatory. He, too, must repent and be absolved from his deepest fault: his failing to follow his spiritual journey to which Beatrice had awakened him while she was still on earth. Now she confronts him with his failure even in the face of all that she did for him after her death from her position in heaven. In this passage she speaks of Dante in the third person:

> . . . *he bent his steps in a way not true, following after false images of good which fulfill no promise; nor did it avail me to gain inspirations for him with which both in dream and in other ways I call him back, so little did he heed them. He fell so low that all the means for his salvation now came short except to show him the lost people; for this I visited the threshold of the dead and to him who brought him up here my prayers were offered with tears.*[6]

When Dante enters the celestial spheres that lead to heaven, he is constantly met by the saints, who instruct him in knowledge and virtue in order to enable him to enter into the vision of God. He is instructed in the four cardinal virtues—justice, wisdom, courage, and temperance—and in the three theological virtues of faith, hope, and charity. His instruction in the latter is carried out respectively by the apostles Peter, James, and John.

The most specific treatment of Dante's own ancestor is in Cacciaguida, his great-great-grandfather, who lived almost two centuries before him. Dante meets Cacciaguida as he climbs the celestial spheres toward heaven. This noble ancestor, a warrior and a knight, speaks of Dante as "my blood," "my seed," "my son," "my branch." Dante, in turn, speaks to him reciprocally: "You are my father, you give me all boldness to speak, you uplift me so that I am more than myself. . . . Tell me then, dear stock from which I spring, what were your ancestors and what years were chronicled in your boyhood."[7] He tells of the great Florentines of his era and the virtue of the city that has in Dante's time fallen into such turmoil, and he urges Dante to face his future with courage.

As Dante proceeds on his journey, he reaches heaven itself and there beholds the assembly of the saints, whose souls form a white shining rose (*candida rosa*): "I saw, rising above the light all round in more than a thousand tiers, as many of us as have returned there above. And if the lowest rank encloses within it so great a light, what is the expanse of this rose in its farthest petals?" Beatrice speaks to Dante: "Behold how great is the assembly of the white robes! See our city, how great is the circuit!"[8] This is the ultimate fulfillment of the communion of saints. It is the mystical community of this heavenly rose to which the Church Militant on earth and the Church Suffering in purgatory are destined for their completion.

Having reached this heavenly community of saints, Dante is drawn to its ultimate source and ground: communion with God. Once again it is through the communion of saints that Dante is led in this final stage of his journey. Beatrice leaves him and takes her place in the celestial rose. Then Bernard of Clairvaux appears, the great love mystic and spiritual teacher of the twelfth century. He leads Dante to Mary, who in turn directs his eyes to the divine light. Gazing there in wonderment, he is drawn into the community of divine love—the Trinity—where at the heart of the divinity is found the basis of the human community and the communion of saints that transcends space and time. It is here that Dante, in gazing on this circling love of the Trinity, is drawn into the communion of saints in its full cosmic dimension by the divine love that "moves the sun and the other stars."[9]

Popular and Elite Religiosity

Within the Roman Catholic tradition of Christianity, ancestors have played and continue to play a prominent role on both the popular and elite levels of religious archetype. It is especially the case if we consider that this archetype is central to Dante's *Divine Comedy*, which many critics consider the most sophisticated poem written in the history of western culture and which is studied extensively to this day in the universities of Europe and North America. In contemporary Roman Catholicism, the doctrine of saints, especially Mary, continues to be a matter of theological investigation.

As is clear from the case of New Orleans, the religious archetype of ancestors continues to be alive in Roman Catholic popular culture. New Orleans is not exceptional in this respect; one can find this popular cult of saints in many ethnic neighborhoods of New York and other cities in America and Europe. It is especially strong in Central and South American Catholicism. In medieval Europe, however, the energies of popular religion flowed more directly into the literary and theological levels of culture, producing the *Divine Comedy* and great cathedrals.

As in the case of ancestors, and in other areas as well, the axial religions have tended to lose contact with fundamental religious archetypes. This is especially true where the forces of secularization have taken their toll. Yet these archetypes often remain alive in these religions on the level of popular culture. It is here—on the level of popular culture—that a fruitful dialogue, and mutual enrichment, can take place between the axial religions and the primal traditions. But the primal traditions as well as the axial religions have their elite levels of culture—their poets and sacred teachers. Thus, the dialogue can be extended to all levels of religious culture.

Notes

1. See the preface for a description of the Dialogue of Civilizations program.

2. See Peter Brown, *The Cult of the Saints: Its Rise and Function in Latin Christianity* (Chicago: University of Chicago Press, 1981); Philippe Ariès, *The Hour of Our Death* (New York: Alfred A. Knopf, 1981); Robert E. Hood, *Must God Remain Greek? Afro Cultures and God-Talk* (Minneapolis: Fortress Press, 1990).

3. See Brown, *The Cult of the Saints.*

4. I have been unable to determine whether this incident actually happened in New Orleans, although many there claim they have heard the story. I have discovered an account of a similar incident that is described as having occurred in Paris in the nineteenth century; see Donald Attwater, *The Penguin Dictionary of Saints* (New York: Penguin, 1983), 125.

5. Dante, *Divine Comedy* Purgatorio, v. 68–73, from Charles Sinclair, trans., *The Divine Comedy of Dante Alighieri: II Purgatorio; III Paradiso* (New York: Oxford University Press, 1961).

6. Ibid., xxx, 130–41.

7. Ibid., Paradiso, xvi, 16–24.

8. Ibid., xxx, 113–17; 128–30.

9. Ibid., xxxiv, 145.

Discussion

Jill Raitt

In a hierarchical church organization like that of the Roman Catholic Church there will always be a good deal of social control that is exercised. One thing that occurred to me in your presentation, though, is that the spectrum of saints also provides a good deal of flexibility. Any good Catholic can say, "I'm going to choose the saint I want. I'm going to make somebody else my spiritual ancestor."

Theodore de Bary

When you choose your own saints, do you choose them as fictive ancestors alone or also as models for living?

Jill Raitt

Baptismal names are saints' names and you don't have a choice in that. When you're older you can relate more to a saint that you feel is a challenge or a model. But Christians in general don't seek saints particularly as ancestors; they're more interested in the help of a certain saint. Devotion to a saint is almost always in some sense modeling oneself on that saint. It can become a commercialized transaction, though, where someone says, "I'm going to worship you for ninety days and at the end I get a Cadillac." But if an ancestor is active in one's life, there must be some living relationship to that person.

Theodore de Bary

The issue I find interesting is the degree of freedom one has in choosing a saint as an ancestor. Do you choose someone with whom you wish to identify, or do you try to express a kind of rootedness that explains where you are from and where you are going?

Ewert Cousins

A place where that modeling takes place in the Roman Catholic tradition is in religious orders, and it is related to the virtues or charism of the founder. For example, Franciscans are drawn to the spirit of St. Francis and within the orders those virtues are held up as models. The person chooses the whole lifestyle within the charism of the founder, and that charism is a source of spiritual nourishment to which you can always return.

Theodore de Bary

It relates to the question about the great mobility of the Christian religion, which probably tends to leave in its wake a feeling of being unrooted. The contrast is very sharp with Confucian ancestor worship, for example, which is very closely identified with a particular place and with remaining in that place, with fixity of residence. That rootedness is very weak in Christianity, but that transience does not necessarily mean that the need to be rooted is not there.

Ewert Cousins

One way of dealing with this problem is the Roman martyrology. In monastic houses, the Roman martyrology is read daily at dinnertime for all the saints whose feasts are celebrated on that day. The martyrology usually begins with the martyrs or a confessor or the major feast of the day. A long paragraph is devoted to each one, and the cumulative effect is that you feel yourself to be a part of the communion of saints. The emphasis isn't on individual saints. You begin to sense that you belong to an army, the Church Militant along with the Church Triumphant.

Lawrence Sullivan

In this sense, martyrologies seem to be a way of transforming a localized, particular event into a portable phenomenon. They take martyrs who are connected to one landscape and recast them in terms of the calendar. Place becomes time and can be enacted easily in another location. A similar process is at work in the relationship of the liturgical calendars to the Holy Land. The calendar tracks the movements of Jesus during his life in Palestine in a one-year cycle that can be repeated indefinitely. The church year thus embodies a pilgrimage through the Holy Land. Physical and spatial relations become temporal realities.

Theodore de Bary

I think the idea of the Church Militant and the Church Triumphant suggests the same problem. The Church Militant is a church on the march; it's on the move. The Church Triumphant has heaven as its home, but that tends to remove you from any rootedness in space.

Ewert Cousins

That's right. The image of the *homo viator*, the pilgrim, is exactly the framework in which it occurs.

Laurel Kendall

Isn't pilgrimage in the Christian world one way of bridging the contradictions of mobility and identity? Christians move, Christianity is a global phenomenon, and yet it seeks identification with places tied to the ancestors. And through the pilgrimage process itself, more of these portable relics are acquired and diffused.

The Hawaiian 'Aumakua
Ancestors as Gods

Rubellite Kawena Johnson

There are several words in the Hawaiian language referring to "god" and "spirit," indicating a level of contact commensurate with the importance of community, occupational, or family guardianship roles:

1) *Akua*, "God," as of a major god of the pantheon, such as Ku, god of war; Lono, god of peace; Kane, god of fertility; Kanaloa, god of the ocean; therefore, a "departmental" deity, one having charge over a part of the natural world and thus personified, i.e.: Ku, god of all upright, firm, erect things; Lono, god of all vining plants; Kane, god of jointed-stemmed plants; Kanaloa, god of all cordage fiber plants; or Ku, god of the east (sunrise); Kane, god in the "eyeball" of the sun disk; Hina, goddess of the west (sunset, moonrise); Kane, god of the northern solstice; Kanaloa, god of the southern solstice; Lono, personified in the star Sirius, etc. These are the "community" or "national gods," society's major temple gods, requiring community ritual and performed rituals conducted by a titled, hereditary priesthood order.

2) *akua*, "god," major or minor god, classified as a "patron deity," or occupational god; same as the major Akua, including lesser deities, but kept in daily contact on shrines used for daily offerings (*ko'a* coastal/upland shrines); patronized by farmers, fishermen, tapa-makers, warriors, etc.

3) *'aumakua*, "god," as an ancestral god, guardian spirit, family god, ancestral spirit, including those in categories 1 and 2 above in family guardianship roles, in both formal and informal worship/ritual.

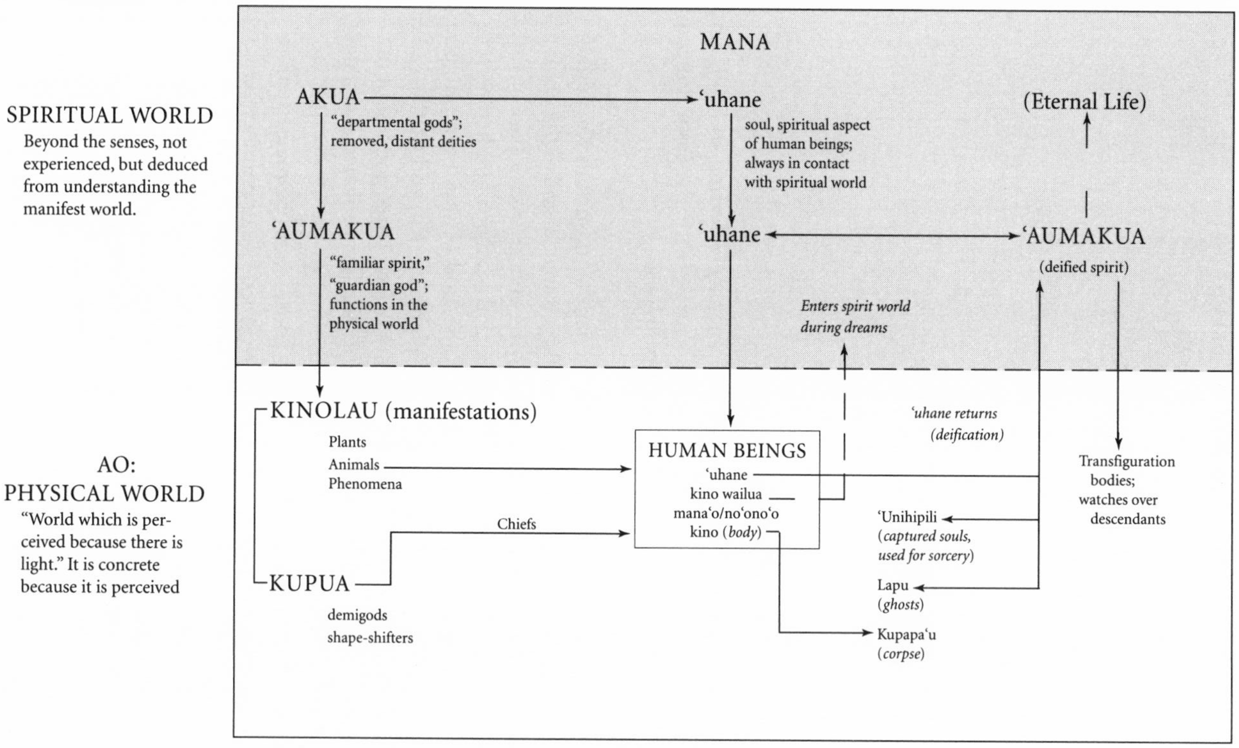

Figure 1. Relationship of Material to Spiritual World in Hawaiian Tradition. (Designed by Rubellite K. Johnson)

Stories about Life, Death, and the Divine

The best understanding of this relationship between the "God(s)" and "god(s)," the Akua/akua, to the 'aumakua ancestral spirits common among all of them is to be found in this folktale, the "Kneecap Fishhook Legend," told by Robert Kailianu of Kohala in 1955.

Fishing contests were this chief's sport. He was from Kona. I don't even know his name. He and his group of fishing comrades made bonito fishing their speciality, and their fame for this was great. One day they saw a man from Makalawena heading out on canoe with his son, in the breaking waves at that! Here's what the chief said to his men: "What is that canoe going toward and then returning from the breakers?"

"Perhaps the fish is po'opa'a?"[1]

Again and again the man went out looking for fish. The chief saw a chance to challenge him at a bonito fishing contest. If the chief won, the man would become his servant, and if the man won, the chief would be his servant.

One day the chief saw the same man going into the breakers again. He said to one of his men, "I'm sending you where those men are. Tomorrow you will ask them what kind of fish they have been going to catch there. Go."

The man sent by the chief asked the fishermen, "What are you both coming here to fish for outside the breakers? Is it for the po'opa'a fish?"

The father said, "Aku [i.e., bonito]."

"How can that be? How is it the aku are in the breakers when aku are to be found in the deep ocean?"

When he finished his questioning he returned to tell the chief. "Say, aku is the fish these men are fishing for here every day."

"Oh? Where can aku be in breaking waves?" asked the chief. "I am commanding you to tell those men to come and challenge me at aku fishing."

The father knew what this meant. He was a wise man, a seer. He knew about things which were going to happen in the future. Here's what he said to his son: "Kill me, put my kneecap into a sea pool, and let the sea moss grow on it. Make yourself a hook for catching bonito."

"Why should I kill you when you are my father?"

"I can't escape death, son, because I am old. My days have been many. The chief would kill us both, if he could. Death is good for me, but you should live, so do as I ask." The son obeyed, killing his father and depositing the kneecap in a seapool. When the seaweed had grown, he started to shape this into a hook for catching bonito.

His father had said, "Take the first fish to my grave, and such should you do everyday you go to fish for bonito, remember me with one fish for the day. And when the chief arrives and asks you where your companion is, say that I've gone to Waipi'o. But you stay right here."

The chief's messenger came. "A contest is announced, and where is your companion?"

"He has gone to Waipi'o."

"Just you?"

"Yes."

"Cha! The chief wants to challenge the both of you at aku fishing."

"Ka, perhaps I may want to. My father has gone to Waipi'o."

So the messenger returned to the chief saying, "Tomorrow your opponent will arrive, but only one, the son. The father is at Waipi'o."

The chief then selected the canoe paddlers, the strong people for himself; the weaker ones, for his opponent. When the boy arrived at dawn, the chief had already gone out. But the hook which this boy had made was full of power. This hook was merely shown, without pole, without line. It was held in the hand and placed outside the calabash for the fish, which leaped into it from the sea, that's the story of this hook.

The native people looked at this handsome malihini *and said, "We feel sorry for you. The chief has already gone with people strong at the oars, and those who are left can't help you at all. But the gods go with you."*

The boy said, "The fish isn't way out there; it's close to shore." The chief was way out there. The boy sighted him, seeking the chief's face on the canoe heading out. Over there the chief would start fishing for bonito. The boy started his canoe and disappeared into the breakers.

The chief then said, "Say, let's go back. Let's go home." And he started back. On returning he left his canoe, which was filled with aku.

The boy said to the first paddler, "Don't turn back yet. Look here! If you turn around, I'll kill you all. Forge your canoe ahead until I tell you to turn back to land!" The men obeyed. When the chief came back, and the boy's canoe was close he saw that the canoe was filled with tuna, and his were only half-filled.

The chief grabbed a fish from the boy's canoe, the first of which was his, with the mouth stopped on a hook. What of this big mistake of daring, so swift to the breakers and back to land?

"How did you get this fish?"

"Cha! The fish is out here in the breakers."

The bet was won. The chief became the boy's servant. The chief said, "You

will be chief, and I will be your servant. Yours to say, mine to do; my prop-
erty, my daughters are yours. And my daughters shall be your wives. Here is
the time to agree," said the chief.

The boy neither agreed nor disagreed. He just grabbed a fish and fled.

Then the chief told his daughters that the boy was now their husband.

The boy said, "Give the fish to the common people."

Then he returned with the hook in a calabash. This was his pillow for
sleeping.

The girls waited. "Say, to whom shall this man go, to you, perhaps, or to
me? Tsk! This fellow doesn't like women. Wait! This thing here, the hook is
his bird feather for sleeping!" They wondered, whatever was this sort of hook.

The boy said, "Well, I go to sleep with it, not with women!"

"Goodness," said one woman to the other. "If he falls asleep and snores,
we ought to take a look at this hook that's inside this calabash."

The boy went to sleep and snored. When the girls took a good look at the
hook, they saw it was a mere nothing. They got a knife and cut the hook
from the ʻolona *fibre, every day a little bit until only a little string was left.*
One day when he went fishing, a fish grabbed it, and the hook was lost. This
hook, lost! When it disappeared, the boy saw the flying of the body of his
father in the air. A bird body came, a black bird. He didn't see his father,
just this bird over the surface of the ocean. And it was following the fish
with the lost hook *[emphasis mine].*

The boy went home, taking a tuna fish for his father, *and the next day*
he went out again with a fish pole. When he got there the fish was uneaten
because the father had gone to seek the lost hook *[emphasis mine].*

After a week passed, the boy went to Waipiʻo. He asked a fisherman there
if a hook had been found in the sea, and the people wondered about this.
When he wanted to go fishing with them, they grumbled. "Here comes that
runny-nosed brat who doesn't know how to fish. He wants to go." The chief
of Waipiʻo told them, "Take this fellow, and if he can't do the work, kill
him!"

When he went, his luck was incomparable. The people went back to the
chief, but the boy stayed out fishing. "No! I haven't found what I want."

He left and swam to Maui; no boat. Nothing with which to swim but just
his strength. He arrived at Maui. Then he saw the bird which he had seen
in the sea, sitting upon the hut of the chief.

"Say, this is my bird which I saw at sea, the one over here on Maui"
[emphasis mine]. Then he thought, *"Cha! I'll meet with these folks and ask*
who the fishermen are."

As he went along, he met people coming with canoes. They wanted to go out. He stopped the fleet, and said, "Say, wait. I'm a stranger in this place. I'm looking for work. If you agree to let me go with you, we'll go fishing. How about it?"

Perhaps he should ask the chief. He went to see the chief.

One day they had a contest. The chief took the strong people and left the weaklings for him. The boy said, "I can't go fishing. Wait till I find my hook."

The chief said, "What hook?"

"I want to find a hook."

The chief asked his girls if they would fetch the hook basket and pour it (out) in the presence of the boy. He looked. "No, this is not my hook."

The father said to the daughter, "Get one from my hooks which are behind the door."

The boy looked. "Yes! This is my choice hook. So let's go!"

Then they wagered that if the boy won, the chief would be his servant, and his daughters, wives for him. As at Kona, he won the bet. He loved the hook more than anything else including the chief's wealth, which he didn't prize. He prized the hook.

Well, this is a story about fishing.[2]

In this legend, among others in recent times, the 'aumakua ancestral spirit, as an akua of the family, is only a generation away from the hero. In life, he was *makua*, a parent. He contributes a choice part of his body, the kneecap, or patella, which, because of its flat surface, makes an ideal source for a bonito fishhook.

The father gives to the son the twofold method of securing the power (*mana*), or of increasing the power of the bone:

1) *ho'omana* ritual process of:
   a) placing the kneecap into a *kaheka kai* sea pool
   b) waiting for *limu* (seaweed) to grow on the bone
2) *hanai akua* ritual offerings to the deceased at the gravesite: *hanai* a "feeding," or food offering, from the first fish of the daily catch.

The 'aumakua presence of the father's spirit as the ancestral guardian god of the son is realized when the kneecap fishhook, or father's bone tool, is lost. The body in which the spirit manifests itself is a bird, a black bird, and its appearance is classified in Hawaiian as a "sign" (*ho'ailona*) of the 'aumakua by which the son recognizes that the black bird would show him where to recover the lost hook. This suggests that in the family's 'aumakua background, certain birds are the *kinolau*, or "many-bodies," through which their ʻaumakua ancestral guardian spirits/gods make themselves manifest.

How many black sea birds in the kinolau sets of the major akua gods of the general Hawaiian pantheon are identifiable? Ku is manifest in the red-tailed, white, tropic bird *koaʻa* and in the hawk *ʻio* (a symbol of a high-ranking chief). Kaneʻs bird kinolau is the *pueo*, owl. Kanaloa is symbolized in the *peʻa* shape of the insect-eating bat and the stingray. Lono is in bird form a *kaʻupu*, albatross, ranging from brown and gray to black, and the *kolea*, golden plover. Since none of these birds are identified within the narrative, the lineage of the family from which both father and son descend is not of the high chiefs who are *kupua*, or "god(s)-incarnate," that is, "demigod" descendants of the major akua. But, the fact that it is a bird (*manu*) through which the ʻaumakua manifest themselves (*kinolau*) to their human relations in the physical world means that the family is more closely connected to the priestly groups than to ruling chiefs, as birds are messengers of the akua in the priesthood (*kahuna*).

The ritual process through which the fatherʻs role as ʻaumakua is maintained is called hoʻomana, "to-cause-power," a word which in broad terms means "religion" or "religious worship"; and the basis of belief in mana, supernatural power, that is, the universal presence of the cosmic agency through which matter manifests bodily the form in which power asserts presence, activity, intelligence, and creativity in body and spirit (*ʻuhane*). This ʻuhane is the spiritual actuality transcending corporeal physicality of form in which it is, in concrete life, visualized, felt, and understood. Ultimately, it is assumed that the spiritual entity of the ʻuhane is light, or perceived as light small enough to enter and exit the body during the lifetime of a person. Physical death does not extinguish this light, which exits through the tear duct of the eye; in the afterlife it may be extinguished if it enters the everlasting night forever. The Hawaiian "hell" is a place without light, and the spiritual afterlife of the ʻuhane takes abode in a place where light continues, as may be seen in the example of the next two family stories.

In the family background of my mother are two examples of travels of the "soul," or "second-body" (*kino wailua*, from *wailua*, "second-stream"), that illuminate the issue of spirit, death, and afterlife.

Great-grandmother ʻEkekela (Esther) Kaʻaikaula Kaʻulili, a descendant of Molokaʻi chiefs and priests in the line of Kaiakea, was one of the first converts to the Mormon faith. She resisted Christianity until she experienced the flight of her spirit from her body. All she remembered when she awoke after four days' spirit travel was that her body suddenly felt light, that she began to lift from the ground where she had been tending her garden, and that her spirit traveled into the sky toward a great light in the east. When she reached the place from which the light shone, she found an open door. Inside were angels, praying to the light, and it was so beautiful that she started to enter through the open doorway. At that instant, a hand slapped her on the chest, and there was a voice, saying, "You are not ready yet. You must go back from where you came," and she started back to her body. When she found it, it was like a mountain, but she started to enter through the big toe. It was dark inside, and darker still in the knee, and even darker when she awoke. It was after this experience that she became a Christian. This happened a year before she died, and because of this experience, the family all converted to Christianity.

An uncle by the name of Lono suffered periodically from what appeared to be catatonic fits. To him, these states of physical suspension were times when his kino wailua left his body and went on many travels through the universe. He married late in life, and one day he took one of his "trips." Not knowing that this was one of those times, his wife called the undertaker, and the ka'a kupapa'u (hearse) came to pick up the body. On the way to the morgue, through a window, the driver saw the body of the corpse sit up, and thinking that it was a reflex, stopped the car to go back and straighten it out again. Instead, he found a live person sitting up and talking, so he drove Uncle Lono home, to his wife's great surprise. Alone together again, the puzzled wife asked, "Where do you go on these journeys?"

"All over the place."

"Where?"

"I go everywhere. I fly around. The sun, the moon, planets, here and there."

"Oh, my. Tell me, have you seen that place, hell? What is it like there?"

"I've never been there. I've never seen it, but I can hear the people there moaning and groaning. That's all. Crying and crying. Awful."

"Oh."

"Have you been to heaven? Did you see that place?"

"No. But everywhere I go, I see these little, tiny blue lights. Everywhere. Millions of them. Millions of tiny blue lights. And so I thought, I must be one of those blue lights."

In each of these family stories, passed down orally since the time of 'Ekekela and Lono two generations ago, the experience of the kino wailua spirit travel is the basis for belief in the afterlife of a person—the belief that death of the body does not extinguish personality or consciousness or memory. These experiences that parallel the same kinds of spirit travel related in the classic tales of Pele's spirit travel to Haʻena, where she met Lohiau, while her real body lay inert at Puʻu Pahoehoe, Hawaiʻi; or Hiʻiaka's descent to the underworld to recover the spirit of Lohiau after Pele's eruption engulfed his body; or when Hiku traveled into the underworld to bring Kawelu's spirit back to the real world by attracting it with a swinging morning-glory vine. Hawaiians once believed—if now they seem not to believe actively—that the kino wailua would return after the death of the body if the life of a person was not yet over, so Hawaiian burial practices allowed four days after death when the body was left intact. The postponement of interment was requisite treatment of the dead, allowing time for the kino wailua to return.

There is, however, another aspect to the belief in the indestructibility of the ʻuhane and the longevity of the ʻaumakua ancestry through which family life insures the regeneration of the akua through posterity. In the context of the dream (*moe ʻuhane*, "dream", i.e., "spirit-sleep") and vision (*akaku*, from *aka*, "shadow/embryo," + *ku*, "stand"), the ʻaumakua relates an expectation, so as to continue his or her name/tradition to a yet unborn child. The next family story concerning my brother's given Hawaiian name is an example.

When my mother was expecting her first child, she was loathe to go to the family doctor because he was also a member of her church, and wishing not to expose herself to him and desiring greater privacy, she traveled eight miles away from her home in Lawai to Makaweli to see another doctor. My father, who worked several miles away also in another direction, did not know this, and as my mother's condition became more and more obvious to the church members, the doctor queried my father as to when his wife was going to go to the clinic for an examination. Rather late, and against her own wishes, she went back to the family doctor, and as the birth of her child was imminent, she went to the hospital to be delivered. After examining her, noting that the child was not in proper position, the doctor sent her home a distance of three to five miles. It was not viewed by the family as a good sign, and through the day and the night they prayed.

By the bed where she lay, awake and drifting through pain, she saw a little man come into her room. She had seen this man in her dreams before, three times before she told her mother that he had come for her in a canoe, taking her to his house on another island where he took her through empty rooms until reaching the last room in the house, where he opened a large trunk, and, after taking out all kinds of fishing gear, nets, hooks, bait baskets, he lifted out a ball of many colors and handed it to her, saying, "This is all that I have which is my very own, and I am giving it to you. I want you to have this." This dream was interpreted as the gift of a child, a son, and the ʻaumakua was Kanaka-o-Kai, the shark-god of Molokaʻi, to the effect that a son born to my mother should be given his name. Now, the same ʻaumakua, in the red malo *loincloth he wore in the canoe and with the same webbed feet to indicate that he belonged to the sea, was by her bedside as a real person, not as a dream.*

As in the dream, he was silent, saying nothing, but he bent close to her ear and blew into it, and having satisfied himself that she was all right, he left. It was then that the child began to move again, and all that she remembered later was that she was in the hospital, that it was raining outside, and as the child cried its first cry, the doctor said, "It's a boy, and he came feet first."

This breech birth came to identify my older brother, Kanaka-o-Kai, "Man-of-the-sea," as belonging to the shark ʻaumakua side of the family, and when he was finished with high school, as prophesied and directed, he was sent to sea to live a life as a fisherman. He was told that, wherever he would go on the ocean, this ʻaumakua, Kanaka-o-Kai, would fill his boat with fish, that he would never have to work hard, that the supply from the sea would be inexhaustible. I used to ask him if he believed that story, and all he would say was that on several boats on which he was crew, he would watch the sea for birds, the presence of which means there is a school of fish, and would see none, but a shark would surface and turn over on its belly, and where this happened there would be a school of fish. This area is between Kauaʻi and Niʻihau, and not by Molokaʻi where Kanaka-o-Kai is the ʻaumakua. Rather, it is a place where my father's family has ancient connections.

My father is part Portuguese, at least half, and considers himself above superstition and brooks no nonsense at sea, being a nuts-and-bolts kind of person. But he has his own ʻaumakua stories, all of which are personal experiences. One of these represents how the ʻaumakua of a particular place protect their own descendants.

During World War II my father's fishing boat, the Taihei Maru, was taken by the United States Navy to be a reconnaisance vessel after the loss of several ships in the 7 December 1941 attack on Pearl Harbor. On that particular day he was at Niʻihau, saw the Japanese planes fly overhead, and, knowing nothing about Pearl Harbor, continued fishing. The sampan was just out of dry dock and recently reoutfitted, but it had its old crew of alien Japanese. After a few days he decided to go back to Port Allen, and reaching port, found it unlighted, which was odd, and the Japanese fish captain protested going into the harbor under these conditions, but my father insisted on going in, that it was Port Allen, rest assured. No sooner, however, had the sampan cleared the breakwater through the wide pass than guns started firing, bullets flying through the cabin, and in the excitement the Japanese, screaming in their own language, signalled that the boat was a foreign, enemy vessel. An alert portmaster, however, realized that there was no return fire from the sampan and ordered the National Guard to stop firing. All they heard after that were four-letter words from my father until explanations on both sides were exchanged and it became clear that the alien Japanese were now to be sent to relocation camps because of martial law. Devoid of crew, there was no fishing for the sampan, no business, no income, and my parents had to leave the island to find other employment on O'ahu. After a while, longing to go to sea again, and with proper licenses, boat, and fishing permits allowing him to fish for bait in Pearl Harbor, my father got another boat and outfitted it with a Portuguese-Filipino crew.

On one trip far out and beyond Kaua'i they had fished enough and were on their way back, nearing the north coast of Napali at night. Asleep in his bunk, my father knew something was wrong by the feel of the boat and, going topside, found the helmsman asleep. There was no time to lose because the sampan was already in the breakers, ready to strike ground. His eyes had not yet adjusted to the darkness, and he couldn't see where he was, where the land was, in which direction. At that moment, flares started falling from the cliffs, lighting up the coastline. He could see where the land was, and where the open sea was, and turned his ship around in time to save himself, the boat, and the crew. But from where came the flares? There's no one living there. The cliffs are empty of people. The place is off-limits to everyone. There is no military personnel. There are no trails there, except ancient ones traveled by people along that coast a long time ago who used to go up into the mountains to throw flares in the traditional art of firebrand throwing (papala, a Kaua'i sport on the northwest and western side of Napali cliffs). Who was there at that particular place when my father's boat was in trouble? Who was there, and who threw the flares to light the way? A long time ago, my father's people lived there, ancient Hawaiians. Who else but the 'aumakua would know he was there and was in trouble and would show him where to go, as the black bird showed the father's son where the lost hook had gone after the fish ate it? In this instance, however, my father had

*not done any ritual promotion to deserve the help, and still, even then, the
'aumakua do not forget who among the descendants still live and need protection.*

Transformations According to Hawaiian Religion

As the generations lengthen and the identities of ancestors dim into obscurity
(except as names in genealogies), the 'aumakua fade into the past, except that
Hawaiians today will identify the kinolau. "Our 'aumakua is the shark," or "Ours
is the owl," or "We have the *mo'o*" (lizard). One student made a rare announce-
ment in a class one day when she said her family had the spider for an 'aumakua.
People may have no family connection consanguineally, but if they identify a
certain group of kinolau associated with a particular akua, such as Ku, they have
common ground assumed to exist in the lineal past. For example, if someone
uses the *palai* fern for medicine, I know their principal akua/'aumakua ancestor
god is Kane. If they use salt water for healing, they are also Kane people. If they
place an aborted fetus in a pool of fresh water, they belong to the mo'o (lizard,
reptile) family and probably venerate the turtle as mother. The *lehua 'ohi'a* is a
form of Ku—Ku-ka-'ohi'a-laka, the principal god in the form of a carved image
on the luakini po'okanaka war heiau temple, where human sacrifice was practiced in ancient times. The lehua flower is, therefore, symbolic of a warrior's
courage, one who invokes Ku.

These multiple 'aumakua forms are present all around Hawaiian families for
whom plants, animals, the earth itself, the ocean, the atmosphere invoke
'aumakua associations everyday of their lives, in their names and in the patterns
of their religious practices and beliefs. The validity of any herbalist who prog-
nosticates remedies for diseases or any practicing kahuna who prophesies on
the basis of dream interpretation usually rests on knowing what the 'aumakua
associations are from the kind of disease, from the presence of key ho'ailona in
a person's dreams, or even from his name, before he prescribes any kind of
treatment or course of action. This is done by asking what kinds of medicine
were used by the family for certain kinds of illnesses, and from the list the
'aumakua connections are identified, if they were not previously known.

There is a point, however, in these associations where 'aumakua identities—
until now rooted in Hawaiian tradition—merge with other traditions on levels
of religious reflection that are not racially or nationally prescriptive, or at a
juncture where "spirit" ('uhane) and "god" (akua) or ancestral guardian spirit/
god ('aumakua), or "divinity-incarnate" (kupua), or "deity-manifest" (kinolau)
merge the primal spirituality into the axial tradition. This is accomplished on a

level of metaphysical thought about human spiritual nature as a reflection of "cosmic spirit," that is, if the cosmos itself is "father" creator.

How or where is that level reached, in the abstraction of "spirit" (ʻuhane) and in "spirit" as "matter" in "form/body" (kino)? Hawaiian thought on that level, like Greek thought, looks at matter as a reflection of "power" (mana) of the "spirit" (ʻuhane) that resides with the akua—that is, in and at that plane of existence where power is not confined to nature in the living bodies of things, but exists where regeneration of life is possible from nonliving things, power (mana) of the spirit (ʻuhane) being incorruptible or unlimited.

In Polynesian thought, or in several cosmogonic traditions, a set of ideas about creation will cite inanimate natural objects, such as rocks (Tahitian) as generating sources of organic being.[3] How does "rock" (which carries connotations of earth and moon, and of female ʻaumakua/akua) become animate life? Inside the human body is a hard structure of bone, the ʻiwi, the character of which is a quality akin to rock, which does not decompose or dematerialize easily. ʻIwi, "bone," extends to shell, to the hard midribs of leaves, to hard casings. A nutshell is an ʻiwi encasing its seed (hua), just as a coconut shell encases its seed (hua), or an eggshell, another hard casing, its own egg (hua), or the placenta (honua), a soft casing, its own egg (hua), or the earth (honua), the placenta encasing other seeds (hua) and fruits (hua). In all of this vegetable and animal growth and fertility, which is organic life, a process has taken place in which bony, hard, rock-like substance has been transferred from the outside of bodies into the inner structure of the skeletons of bodies, or what was the ʻiwi of a nutshell is the ʻiwi of a crabshell and the ʻiwi of a human skeleton. Something of the earth entered into the life of all creatures and remained of earth's bone.

What about earth's soil? In Hawaiian religious practice of ancient times, two rituals featured the use of salt water (poʻokea rite, using an empty human skull to hold salt water) and red earth (ʻalaea, iron oxide, red earth, used to color salt). Why these two rituals and why the elements concerned? The salt water is a thing of atmosphere, of water and air, a sphere of Kane kinolau, and its saltiness is an element, also, of human blood (koko), one of the many wai (waters) of the human body. Over the wai of the human body Kane is in control, as he is manifest in all reproductive water (wai ola, "living/healing" water; semen), in all watery fluids, such as saliva, mucus, reproductive fluids, tears, and blood. Water is the principal element of the blood, and what of its salt and red color? Consider menstrual blood, connected to birth, reproduction, life-giving ʻinaʻina blood show at the time of parturition, and how it dries; what residue is left will be the substance of soil, as well as the soil's redness.

When the gods Ku, Kane, and Lono made man, they went to the shores of

Ki'i in Mokapu Peninsula, O'ahu. Three kinds of soil were brought to put into the body of man. One was *kele*, a dark, muddy earth; another *palolo*, a whitish clay; and the third, *honua'ula* (*'alaea*), a reddish soil. The whitish earth went to form those parts of the body that are white, such as brain, lungs, tendons; the dark earth, skin; and the red earth, muscle.

To bring life into the body, to activate the inert mass of earth, Kane spat saliva into the soil, and man came to life. Both water and earth are fundamentally present in his body, but into his lungs the "breath" of the gods (*'ea*) must be ingested before the living person is considered a personality. Kane's province of control is over water, sunlight, and air, and this part of the akua—excluding the fundamental element of "mother" (Papa, "female earth") in blood, bone, tissue—is the masculine component within the living body of man. Air and water are masculine; flesh and bone are feminine. It is understood that the body, which is of the earth and female, must have air and water to live, other food or nourishment being of secondary importance to the body's needs.

Life in Hawaiian thought is thus not restricted to human life in the concrete world, felt and seen by the senses of the human body. The Hawaiian idea of the reality of life in the world supersedes the world that is seen and experienced by the material body and enters into the life of the spirit that is beyond the physical senses of the body. The total life of humanity involves the ability of the spirit to move back and forth between the world of the live physical senses and the world of the "extra" spiritual senses. Thus, the Hawaiian mind places greater reality on the life of the human individual in the spiritual realm, the present material life being regarded as ground for the discipline of the spirit in preparation for the afterlife. Therefore, a human being, either male or female, has spiritual origin, material birth, and spiritual eternity of complete unceasing existence.

Persons, such as Uncle Lono, who have experienced soul journeys are often described by relatives as living a daily life of prayer and having an expectation of dying with no fear of passage from human life to death. Stories told by persons having had these experiences usually fortify strong Hawaiian faith in the reality of an afterlife and tend to assist in the conversion to western and eastern forms of religion *without* any loss of faith in the older religious beliefs. Where there has been no experience of this kind, there is conversion, accompanied usually by rejection of the older religious beliefs and total absorption of the family into the adopted norms.

Modern political movements trying to restore pre-contact Hawaiian society and religion at pre-contact sacred sites blame this condition of conversion and absorption on the influx of Christian missionaries since 1820. It seems to me, however, that the rejection comes from an incomplete experience of Hawaiian traditions. The archetypal truths of Hawaiian religion allow Hawaiians to acclimate themselves in any historical situation that arises, even contact with the so-called axial civilizations. The acclimated Hawaiian Christian is primarily affiliated with his or her church rather than with ancient religious practice and belief, except for those practices that continue within the family, such as naming for ancestors, dream interpretation, and prophecy related to dreams and visions. These Hawaiians simply keep native Hawaiian beliefs separate as it suits them, or they will work beliefs into home rituals combining Christian and Hawaiian forms of worship, with no fear that they may be violating either tradition.

The concept that one's spiritual destiny is 'aumakua status, that one's parental role is stretched between spiritual and physical worlds, may be an attempt to keep the spiritual life that is familiar to the deceased and to comfort those left behind, who otherwise would be out of contact with the deceased person. But how many living people in the society have considered what expectations may encumber the deceased, whose spiritual destiny has been to support the living throughout generations? How faithful can 'aumakua be to supplications uttered by generations of descendants? The story of the flares along the coast of Napali illustrates precisely that kind of 'aumakua tenacity, the unfailing source of ancestral care for the unwary son hundreds of years later. Along with the responsibility of 'aumakua, there is also the story of the blue lights that course from universe to universe, unbound by obligation to descendants or spouses, free to roam, to explore, to experience another realm of promise. We have the choice to be in both situations, as Hawaiian 'aumakua, being close to earth yet venturing afar.

To illustrate this power of the spirit to be in and out of the body and in two worlds—the spiritual and the material—at once, I tell this story from my own experience.

> I work late at night at school, and one night I went home and found my daughter in the kitchen, doing her chores, and I asked her a question that had been on my mind all day.
>
> "Did anything happen today?"
>
> "No, nothing."
>
> "Did you fall asleep at the wheel of your van?"
>
> She worked for a tour company with small mini-buses that hold about seven people, and in the early morning I had said goodbye to her. She had driven to the hotel and picked up passengers who needed to be taken to the airport.
>
> "Yes, I did. I fell asleep at the wheel."

"Was there a woman talking loudly at the back of the van?"

"Yes, there was."

"Was anybody in the front seat, next to the driver?"

"No, there was nobody there. No one is allowed to sit in that seat. That's company policy."

"Well, there was somebody there this morning, and whoever it was saved your life."

I was aware of this situation because after she had walked out the door and I had gone back to sleep, I dreamt that I was in the front seat of the van next to the driver. I saw that she was losing control of the van. *"Get up, Hana,"* I said. *"You're falling asleep at the wheel."* But her head finally fell across the wheel, and at that moment the van was skidding out of control down a concrete ramp. It spun around a corner, and up another concrete ramp, as I tried to get one foot on the brake by reaching across the gear shift controls on the floor before waking up.

"Where were you, Hana, when you awoke?"

"I was going up a concrete ramp at the airport."

"And where did you fall asleep? What is the last thing you remember before you lost consciousness?"

"I was passing the Bishop Museum on the freeway."

When cars go past this part of the freeway in Honolulu on the way to the airport, the traffic divides awkwardly onto three ramps. The lowest ramp goes to Nimitz Highway and of the other two, which briefly merge, the uppermost goes to Middle Street and the one that goes to the airport is between both of those. As the ramp to the airport continues, it makes a wide turn left for a while, then it winds to the right onto a larger ramp. The distance between the Bishop Museum and the airport is three to four miles, and the last part winds down into the airport, with its macadamia tree–lined cross streets, before another wide left swing requires that the driver choose to stay the course or accelerate up a broad concrete ramp to the departing gates of a number of airlines. The full distance may be more than four or five miles, during which she was asleep at the wheel. Nothing happened. There was no accident. No one was injured. No one died. She drove another long circle-island tour the same day.

How could a person who was dreaming in a bed at home be sitting in the seat of a tourist van trying to stop a runaway vehicle?

"Well, you're lucky," I told her.

"Who do you think was in the seat this morning?"

"God was sitting there, and he told me all about it."

Notes

1. The bonito is a deep-sea fish, and the poʻopaʻa is an ugly but tasty rock cod caught near shore.

2. Tape recording H42, Bishop Museum Archive, Honolulu.

3. Another set of ideas about creation indicates that life came from thought, from conception as idea before conception became the birth of life.

Discussion

From the audience

There is one consistent theme that has struck me in all of the Hawaiian presentations. Even though we recognize that Hawaiian culture has changed since contact, although it has been hit and devastated by a stronger force from outside, there is a tremendous amount of tolerance of the people who have nearly destroyed their culture. This is in stark contrast to the ways in which the invading forces look upon themselves. When their own culture is invaded or threatened, they themselves are so intolerant. Perhaps this comes from a difference in religious disposition—Christianity with its crusades, belief in the one and only true god, not accepting other gods. These things perhaps make them intolerant of others, of outsiders, while the Hawaiians seem to be able to take differences, accept them, and try to live with them.

Jacob Olupona

The same processes are evident on the African continent. Both Christianity and Islam are strong in Africa, and both are monotheistic traditions that are intolerant of other deities. In my country and elsewhere, African hospitality and tolerance has often been mistaken for stupidity by those coming in from the outside. The foreigners don't see it as a sign of strength. The ability to incorporate new experiences is almost threatening to the outsiders.

Rubellite Johnson

Even though we're tolerant, it's taken a long time for this tolerance to develop into its current form, and there have been plenty of altercations all along the way. It hasn't gone quickly, even with so much intermarriage. For instance, I have this *haole* [Caucasian] name, Kinney, with twelve ancestors from the Mayflower. But I can't go to my relatives and say, "Hey, I'm your cousin!" They'd show me the door. I'm proud of them, though. I'd never give up my Portuguese grandmother, either; she came all the way around the Horn as a little girl and ended up marrying a Hawaiian man. I'd never give up my Scottish grandfather from Nova Scotia who had a haole wife on Kaua'i and a couple of Hawaiian wives on every other island. I would never give up my American and English ancestors. I treasure that side of my heritage.

Now, as a Hawaiian, I grew up as the dark-skinned kid in schools full of Asian children. There weren't any other Hawaiians there, so I had to be nice just to survive. That doesn't mean we didn't fight; we fought all the way. When I made it to college, I thought, "Okay, I'm not going to make Phi Beta Kappa, but you are not going to kick me out." In 1954 when I graduated from the University of Hawai'i, there were 350 international scholarships. Of the twenty-five American scholarships, there were three from Hawai'i, but I was the only Native Hawaiian. After that, I worked for a while for a dollar an hour. I tried to get a job teaching Hawaiian language at a Hawaiian school but ended up going to work for the Bishop Museum. Along the way I noticed that there were always some individuals who opened some doors for me. And that's when I decided I couldn't harbor any more grudges against people who tried to keep me under their thumbs—not against haole, not against Asians, not against other Native Hawaiians. We all suffer in making these accommodations. But the worst thing we could do now is to let tensions flare. We can't afford to have a war between the different ethnic groups.

To Praise and to Reprimand

Ancestors and Spirituality in African Society and Culture

Jacob K. Olupona

Introduction

A conference like this one on ancestors and spirituality in an international, comparative perspective provides a unique opportunity for us to reexamine some of the unresolved issues in the study of indigenous religions. One such problem among Africanists is the nature of ancestral veneration in African religions. By implication, this also relates to the central question of what constitutes the quest for the transcendent and the sacred in African society and culture. The need for such a discussion will become clearer as we also examine the unforeseen consequences of some of the anthropological works on African religions, especially works that tend to overemphasize the centrality of social systems and cultural symbolic expressions in the interpretations of African cosmology and thought patterns, almost to the exclusion of the indigenous meanings and interpretations of these phenomena. Such one-sided interpretation has blurred the African understandings of the sacred and the African answers to their human quest.

Africa's religious system, like other indigenous belief systems the world over, is a pragmatic faith; it espouses a proximate, this-worldly salvation rather than just an otherworldly salvation. It is community-oriented rather than individualistic. African religion is also embedded in, and expressed through, the culture and society in which it is found. Unfortunately, these features have led some scholars to jump quickly to the conclusion that African religions, at best, are merely a projection of African social systems and of mundane activities. No better place is this expressed than in discussions about ancestral spirituality in Africa.[1]

The discussion about the definition of ancestors has been between those anthropologists who argue that ancestors are more "transformed elders" than spiritual beings,[2] and those who are inclined to classify the ancestors more as supernatural entities than as mere social constructions of reality.[3] A central issue for those who argue for the humanity rather than the divinity of ancestors (to borrow from the metaphor used in similar debates about the nature of Jesus) is that Africans approach the ancestors in ways that tend to be casual and conversational, even taking the form of satire and reprimand. Such behavior seems to contradict ideas like those of Rudolf Otto concerning the human response to the transcendent. Can ancestral spirituality be analyzed in terms of western definitions of spirituality and religion?

The truth is that in several African communities, references to the ancestors apparently portray them as mere human entities. For example, among the Yoruba people of Nigeria, Egungun, the ancestral masquerades, move around the village during the annual town's festival, saluting and greeting friends and important chiefs. The Yoruba jokingly say in proverb, "If the underworld [the land of the ancestors] were that prosperous, would the ancestor spirits be returning back to this world to beg for dimes and cents?"[4] In another context, they would say to someone who is being pursued by a stronger person, "The one pursued by the ancestor masquerade should have patience; just as the people on earth get tired running, so will the ancestors from heaven."[5] These two proverbs point to a significant meaning in the conception of the power of ancestors, their spirit lives, and their relationship with the living. Ancestor spirits are not exclusively otherworldly. Like humans, they drink, eat, and excrete, yet they are regarded as supernatural beings. As Evan Zuesse rightly pointed out for the Bantu, which undoubtedly applies to other African groups: "The society . . . is not the core of African religions, even though it is one of the chief media through which [religion] is expressed. Everyday life and society as well as the ancestors reflect trancendental structures pervading the cosmos."[6]

The first section of this paper provides some description of ancestors in African contexts. After that, I explore the roles played by ancestors in African societies. The paper then concludes with some observations about ancestral spirituality and the forces of secularization. Normally, I would rather explore these issues within a specific religious system, such as that of the Yoruba, the Bambara, the Nuer, or the Akan. No single group could bring out the depth and complexity of ancestral spirituality in Africa, however. So in this chapter I provide an overview of the ideas, beliefs, and practices regarding ancestors across sub-Saharan Africa and illustrate these general observations with examples from specific groups.

Distinguishing Ancestors

The first task is to locate the ancestors among the supernatural beings in African religious systems. It is possible to distinguish conceptually between four hierarchies of deities: the Supreme Being, lesser gods, culture heroes, and ancestral spirits. In general, the Supreme Being is the head of the pantheon and the creator of the universe and the inhabited world. The lesser gods are the messengers of the Supreme Being and, unlike the latter, are direct objects of worship and sacrifices. It is more difficult to make distinctions between culture heroes and ancestors. Culture heroes have not been given prominence in the study of African religions, and the question is complicated by the fact that the roles of the two groups sometimes overlap. In general, however, ancestors are often regarded as the deceased members of the lineage inhabiting the underworld, while culture heroes are mythic founders of communities and villages who go through an apotheosis after their heroic sojourn on earth. They are regarded as greater in importance and authority than the ancestors, whose sphere of influence is more or less limited to their lineage and their descendants. In several places in West Africa, there is a tradition that indicates that culture heroes/founders in their old age disappeared into the earth's crust, having promised the descendants that in time of war or epidemic they could be approached for help. Two frivolous village people, quarreling between themselves, called in the heroes only to unleash havoc on their innocent descendants. Realizing their mistake, the heroes vowed not to answer any call again, and once more they disappeared into the earth. While scholars may never succeed in sorting out this complex issue, it seems to me that the tradition may serve as a distinguishing mark between deified culture heroes and ancestors.

A major issue in ancestral spirituality is who can become an ancestor: male, female, or even children? Available ethnographic data present diverse but logically related views across the continent. While it is difficult to suggest a standard common characteristic for becoming an ancestor, the criteria used across the continent are similar. In most African communities, such as among the Manyinka of Zimbabwe, ancestor status is bestowed only on male members of the lineage. It is connected with a male's "sexual potency" and not necessarily with fatherhood.[7] To prove this point, Anita Jacobson-Widding observed that a grown Manyinka male who dies before procreating may become an ancestor if one of his nephews acts as a classifactory son and includes him in his own ancestor cult (*Vadzimu*) assemblage.[8] There is also abundant evidence that female ancestors exist in African societies. For the matrilineal, agricultural Ila people in central Zambia, while the men make sacrifices to ancestresses on the right side of the threshold, their wives offer similar sacrifices to the ancestresses on the left side of the threshold.[9]

Certain sacred children can also become ancestors. Among the Sukuna-Nyamwezi people, the largest ethnic group in Tanzania, twins are regarded as ancestors by virtue of their multiple birth.[10] Here, multiple birth signifies "excess of human fertility."[11] Women are exclusively in charge of the rituals relating to twin ancestors.

The process of becoming an ancestor begins at death. Death, as we have observed, does not end or annihilate human life, but rather is regarded as an inevitable passage to the next stage of life. This peaceful passage is ensured through proper burial rites and ceremonies. For the Bambara of Mali, the occasion of death brings about great anxiety, confusion, and unpredictability. It is a liminal period when the community is in danger and the fortunes of the deceased and his descendants are equally unpredictable. One of the strongest prayerful wishes for the descendants of a deceased person among the Yoruba is "may God not make his/her death a successive one."[12] Coupled with the possibility of successive death, the Yoruba also face the disruption of the lineage-orderly life. It is believed that the death of the head of a lineage may bring about the total disintegration of the lineage line, because it presumes that once the elder who provides unity and strength has departed, the household becomes empty (*bale ile ku, ile di ahoro*) and devoid of any source of coherent unity.

To become an ancestor, the deceased must be properly buried by the kinsmen and women. Proper burial entails performing elaborate funeral ceremonies, participated in by all of the deceased's descendants. Also, the deceased must have died a good death. Africans regard death that occurs as a result of an accident or a shameful disease, such as smallpox or leprosy, as a bad death. Most significantly, the deceased must have lived to a very old age, signifying wisdom and experience. As Dominique Zahan observed, "the individual venerated by succeeding generations is considered by society to be a moral, social, and religious model whom the living must try to imitate, in order to prevent the deterioration of their conduct and the decay of their powers."[13] When an aged individual passes away, Africans generally avoid the use of the word "death." The transition is put in metaphoric language that connotes a traumatic event. The Yoruba would say that "the elephant has fallen" (*erin wo*), or that "the tiger is gone" (*ekun lo*). By avoiding the use of the word death, it is assumed that an individual is greater than death itself, and that death is simply the beginning of another life after this life.

African ancestors sometimes go through a process something like reincarnation. The ancestors are responsible for perpetuating their lineage, not only by making procreation by the living members of the lineage possible, but also through reincarnation. On face value, there is an apparent contradiction in a simultaneous belief in ancestral veneration and reincarnation. How can the ancestors live in the underworld and at the same time return to their lineages to relive a previous life? The case of the Lupupa people of Zaire would illustrate how this works in most African communities. The Lupupa believe that the body (*mbidi*) houses the spirit (*kikudi*) and when death occurs, the spirit leaves for a special land (*elungu*) that the ancestors inhabit. This special place is protected by wild pigs who guide it and run errands for the ancestors.[14] If the living maintain a cordial relationship with the ancestors, one of the spirits returns to be reborn into the lineage. In principle, it is held that an individual's spirit can live in a body on earth three times, after which the cycle is complete, and he may be reborn the fourth time as a strong animal, perhaps a leopard.[15] The rebirth of the deceased spirit occurs through a grandchild, not one's own the child, as the spirit must "skip a generation."[16] As such, newly born grandsons are often named after their deceased grandfathers.[17] Alan Merriam, who had worked among the Lupupa, remarked that "the idea of three reincarnations after an original existence delays the matter so substantially that ideas of a permanent afterlife do not emerge with clarity. . . . Indeed, the joy of afterlife lies precisely in reincarnation because everybody wants to come back to be with his children and family."[18] The western notion of afterlife came with the arrival of Christianity among the Lupupa. While other African societies may not possess such elaborate details of the reincarnation process, several of them hold the view that ancestors are born into their lineages. The Yoruba assume that children born after the death of a grandfather or a grandmother are reincarnations of the latter. These children are given special names, such as Babatunde (father has returned) and Yetunde (mother has returned). They are regarded as special and are pampered and adored.

The African idea of the ancestorhood would not be complete without a consideration of the place of royal ancestors in African communities. The institution of sacred kingship and, by extension, royal ancestors, is an important aspect of African belief systems. From the myths of origin of several communities, we learn that the first man to be created by God became the founder of a lineage, clan, and village that became the basis of the community. In societies with centralized state structures, such as the Buganda of Uganda, the Swazi of Swaziland, and the Yoruba of Nigeria, the first ruler or king also established the kingship system and, upon his death, became the first royal ancestor. The incumbent ruler must not only be able to trace his descent—real or ficticious—to this first ruler, but is regarded also as a reincarnation of the first royal ancestor. The kingship ideology and rituals in contemporary societies are most pervasive because they continue to relate the dominant ideology and the sociopolitical order to the royal ancestral beliefs. These beliefs in turn legitimize the status quo. Through this process the kingship system is perpetually maintained. For the Yoruba, a reigning king is immortal (*aiku*) and the kingship itself is a timeless and enduring institution. Hence, the physical demise of a king is denied and, upon death, a king is said to have ascended into the ceiling (*oba waja*), since a god personified in principle cannot suffer physical mortality.

Among the Shilluk of South Sudan, where there is an equally strong tradition of sacred kingship, the king-founder of the kingdom (*niwang*) cannot suffer physical death, but at the time of his demise is said to go like the wind.[19] The Kabaka in Uganda is regarded as the descendant of Kintu, the mythical founder of the Ganda people and the Buganda kingship system. The Kabaka maintains his rule and hegemony over the Ganda people through the power derived from the founding royal ancestors. The well-being of the Ganda people, and his authority over them, is sustained partly through the numerous "sacrifices" he offers at the shrine of his ancestors.[20] At these royal shrines, mediums are possessed by the royal spirits, and they give advice to the king on issues of state governance and assist in protecting him from his enemies.[21]

The Participation of Ancestors in African Societies

African cosmological stories locate the place of the ancestors in the earth. A fairly similar story found throughout Africa indicates that the cosmos was created by the instruction of the Supreme Being at a certain time in the distant past. The highest, and the first, layer of the cosmic universe is the location which the Supreme Being, the lesser gods, and other spirits inhabit. The Supreme Being is the inexhaustible source of life and vital power, and the unique agent of the vital breath of life.[22] The second, and lower, layer of the cosmos is the earth, the "dwelling of the ancestors and ancestresses."[23] The third layer is the center of the cosmos and the inhabited land of the living beings that "stretched endlessly to the ocean."[24] This is the vitalizing center, the point at which all forces and vital powers intersect.[25]

There is a regular movement between the inhabitants of the second and the third layers, that is, between the human world and the ancestors in the underworld. The African idea of death and afterlife is at the foundation of this relationship. Throughout Africa, there is the belief that death does not end the life of the living but is, instead, a mere passage from the second layer of the living to the third layer of the ancestral world, where life continues ad infinitum. A practical demonstration of the regularity of the interaction of the living living and the living dead, as the African dead are known,[26] is the involvement of the ancestor spirits in the rites of passage for the living: naming, puberty, marriage, and death. Without their assistance and support, this transition cannot be successfully accomplished, since evil forces personified as witchcraft, sorcery, and the "evil eye" are positioned to disrupt the passage as individuals endeavor to accomplish these rites. Such evil machinations, if allowed, could disrupt the continued existence of human life and the cosmic order. Blessings of the ancestors act as the proper means of warding off these disruptive forces, and thus ensure success.

The foregoing description represents an ideal construct of African religious systems. In several other places, the ancestor belief system constitutes the core of the religion and the focus of ritual action. Among the Kono people of Sierra Leone, ancestor beliefs play the most significant role in their religious life.[27] Robert T. Parsons, who worked in Kono society, observed various sets of supernatural elements in the Kono religious worldview: impersonal power, ancestral spirits, lesser gods, and the Supreme Being. Of all these powers, the ancestral spirits have the most significant leverage over the Kono universe because "they are the most real, nearer to him and of the same nature."[28]

In spite of the closeness of the ancestral spirits and the regular contact the Kono people have with them, they also consult other spiritual entities because of the limitations of the power of the ancestral spirits.[29] Thus, nature spirits, such as the mountain, river, and hill deities, complement the work of the ancestors, especially in spheres where the latter cannot adequately function. The Kono example presents a somewhat different religious set-up from the rest of African groups, where the lesser gods and nature deities occupy a higher status than the ancestral spirits.

A similar situation exists among the Jarawa of Bununu in Plateau State, Nigeria. Like that of the Kono people, the central element of the religious system of the Jarawa is based on the cult of the ancestors. Indeed, the idea of a Supreme Being in contemporary Bununu life only emerged with the coming of Islam.[30] Among the Katana, the ancestors (*dodo*) control all aspects of life—political, economic, and cultural—so much so that the people themselves describe their system of parliament as a "hierarchy of [ancestral] masquerades."[31] The ancestral masquerades controlled by different patrilineages took charge of various sectors of their civil and cultural life: warfare, ritual initiation ceremonies, and the "social control of women and children."[32]

In the previous section I suggested that there is a strong linkage between ancestors and the lineage, the clan, and the community. Indeed, it is probably correct to say that ancestor belief is a lineage religion, since it derives its continued values from the lineage or clan structure. This is one of the reasons, as we observed earlier, why there has been a problem in interpreting aspects of African religious worldviews that relate to this belief. A central focus in anthropological study of ancestor cult in Africa is the importance of lineage in ancestral spirituality. Unfortunately, this linkage between lineage and ancestor is often taken for the essence rather than the expression of ancestor sprituality. African understandings of this relationship will help us to understand this process.

The Yoruba people refer to the collective bond of unity existing in a lineage as *ajobi* (literally, the bond of co-birth). This is an abstract concept referring to the sacred bond arising from a common origin and descent. When invoked, ajobi commands power (*ase*) and energy (*agbara*) that cause whatever is said or invoked, be it for good or for evil, to come to pass. On the other hand, ajobi invokes a distinctive African characteristic of "collective self."[33] The idea of personhood and identity within the lineage is defined in terms of the common membership of the ancestral lineage. In the Yoruba town of Oke-Igbo, my maternal place, an ancestral masquerade (Egungun) bears the name and identity of my lineage. There are two well-known masquerades, named Eegun Ile-Kuole (the masquerade of the lineage of the Kuoles) and Eegun Olomo (the masquerade of the lineage of "the one with bountiful children"). Each of these masquerades portrays the lineage traits, mannerisms, and professional roles in the community. The wooden head masks even bear the facial marks that are distinctive features of the lineage. The first masquerade, Eegun Ile-Kuole, and the oldest in the town, is a warrior masquerade. He is highly respected and whenever he appears in public, all other masquerades must go into hiding because his extraordinary magical power can cause harm to the other masquerades. Being greeted as Omo ile Kuole, the son or daughter of Kuole lineages, is a unique praise name that makes one feel honored and elated. Among the Ila people, every hut must have a fireplace containing a continuously burning fire that signifies the continued presence of the ancestor in the lineage. It is taboo to take a fire stick from one hut to another hut, because "to mix fires is to confuse the ancestral essence and mingle with other families."[34]

These examples further support the view that ancestor belief is a form of lineage spirituality. The linkage between ancestor and lineage is even more pronounced in the African communities where a further distinction is made between those who have recently passed away and are still remembered and those whose identities have passed human memory. Teddy Aarni, who studied the Ovambo people of northern Namibia, made a distinction between "ancestors" and the "living dead." The former (*aathithi*) refer to the "forgotten deceased," those who had gone long ago, beyond the fourth generation, and whose activities and memory cannot be remembered by the living members of their lineages, and the latter, the recently deceased.[35] The Ovambo themselves make a further distinction between deceased relatives (*oohe nooyina*),[36] regarded as those constituting one's living dead, and the living dead of all others, say, for example, a man's spouse's relatives. While the deceased relatives command respect and attention, the ancestors of others are virtually unacknowledged, a tradition that further points to the significance of maintaining a direct genealogical link with the living members of the ancestral lineage.

For the Kono people of Sierra Leone, the ancestors' habitation (Faa) is designed just like the earthly abode, except that the ancestors' is more beautiful and prosperous than the earthly one. Ancestors have the same human characteristics, but they exercise a "superior power" and have the ability to help the living.[37] Just as on earth, the families and clans live separately in the ancestral world. The heads of Faa lineages and clans constitute the council of ancestral spirit elders, which decides on cases in the spirit world.[38] The Kono people believe that these uncompleted cases on earth are taken to the ancestral world for completion. The ancestors possess more power and strength and have the freedom and liberty to exercise their authority in ways that earthly elders cannot. This explains why they are able to maintain such social and moral control over the living. Through regular offerings and sacrifices, the living secure the ancestors' blessings of good health, good fortune, and plentiful harvest. From the general structure of Kono life, one sees that their ancestral worldview tallies very much with the notion of religion as pragmatic and with a result-oriented belief system. Such a cosmology that sees the underworld as a continuum of the earthly abode of the living has much influence on the idea of death and afterlife. Death as signifying life after life makes practical and more meaningful sense to the African mind.

We have established that there is a strong relationship between the ancestors and the members of their lineage and also that the ancestral spirits mirror much of the sociocultural systems of the living. Yet, the ancestors differ significantly from the living and have special responsibilities for establishing the moral order of society. In order to function in this way, the ancestors are freed of the human weaknesses and conditions of pettiness, particularly common among living lineage members. They are, therefore, eminently qualified to act as the guardians of social and moral order in the world.[39] Writing about the Zezuru society, Peter Fry remarked that "the society of the ancestors is a kind of ideal paradigm for Zezuru society as a whole, a society in which people behave without self-interest and enjoy their rights and obey their obligations defined by the ideals of descent and affinity."[40] In a society devoid of the direct intervention of God in the daily activities of humans—which Islamic and Christian worldviews later introduced to African communities—it makes perfect sense that the ancestral spirits would act as regulators of human activities and conduct. Whenever the living fail "to live up to their social and ritual obligations,"[41] the ancestors withdraw their support and protection against the evil forces of sorcery, witchcraft, and other malevolent spirits.

The question has also been raised that if the ancestors maintain the same human personalities that they have while on earth, they may not be able to fulfill the role of policing the social order. In theory, the ancestors are devoid of negative individual characteristics and traits noticeable in the living beings. As ideal men and women, who have shelved their individual traits and "personal peculiarities and petty jealousies," they are "able to act as moral and just guardians of pure morality."[42] After death, the dead assume a new moral personality that is right, just, and basically good. That is why it is taboo to speak evil of the dead. Through the process of death, ancestors undergo a change in their ontological status that makes them into supernatural entities. The Yoruba would say, "It is at death that we become an (ancestral) masquerade" (*Igba a ba ku la ndi ere*). Masquerades signify sacredness and god-like status. With the rituals of death, "the ancestors are on the side of group values and openness; free from purely personal interests, they stand opposed to the mechanisms of those who would go against collective ideals and ignore their social obligations for reasons of jealousy or personal advancement."[43] This is why in several African communities, the cult of the ancestors, signified in the ancestral masquerades, constitutes the traditional supreme court of the land, where appeals are brought for final arbitration. There, the power of the ancestors are juxtaposed with that of the evil forces of the society, personified in witches and sorcerers. The latter represent disruptive forces of the universe, whose powers are harnessed by selfish members of the community to disrupt the social and moral order.

The normative power of the ancestors is given concrete expression in ceremonies and rituals. This can be seen by the propitiation, rather than the worship, of ancestral spirits in the ritual observances of two African communities—the Bambara of Mali and the Yoruba of Nigeria. The focus of propitiation of the ancestors is generally the lineage shrine located at the threshold or the pillar supporting the house. The shrine may also be located outside the house at the center of the compound of the homestead. The ancestor's habitation, in principle, must be close to the living. The responsibility for the daily or weekly propitiation at the shrine lies with the oldest member of the lineage, who is in closer proximity to the ancestors than other members of the lineage. While propitiation takes different forms, as the occasion warrants, in general it commences with the invocation of the ancestors and the pouring of a libation at the designated shrine. For the Bambara people, fresh water, millet flour, and kola nut are the materials offered at this stage,[44] while for the Yoruba, palm wine, water, and kola nut are used. Libation is regarded as a prelude to proper rituals. It awakens the ancestral spirits to the prayers and request of the supplicants. In the Yoruba context, the dead are "awakened" to the presence of the living through an invocation of their names and their lineage praise words (*Oriki*).

More formal offerings follow this initial rite. The kola nut is now split into its lobes and shared among the participants. For the Yoruba, a brief kola nut divination is cast to ensure that the ancestral spirits have accepted the offerings. The Bambara serve boiled fermented millet drink to the guests, while the Yoruba serve white palm wine. Through the breaking of the kola nut, the lineage reasserts its bond with the ancestors. Kola nut, for the Yoruba people, symbolizes that which expels evil, including premature death, away from the habitation of the living. Both the boiled millet beer and white foaming palm wine produce effervescence which, Dominique Zahan observed, "awakened" the dead to the supplications of the living: boiling the fermented drink "sets the dead in effervescence; it awakens and excites them and makes them more disposed to intervene in human affairs."[45] Palm wine naturally foams; the more foam fresh palm wine produces, the purer and stronger it is and the sweeter it tastes.

The ancestors, like humans, get intoxicated with strong drinks, which energize and "boost their morale" and make them more prone to influence.[46] Libation is followed by the sacrifice of an animal, which could be chicken, goat, or ram. The throat of the animal is slashed and the blood let out on the shrine. The release of life's vital force and energy is regarded as a substitute for a human life. In the prayer that takes place, the ancestor spirit is informed of special needs of the members of the lineage and, in return, the spirit bestows blessings on the lineage members.

Occasions of special rituals are periods when the ancestors manifest themselves to the living. The ancestors, as guests, come in the form of masquerades. A masquerade consists of a cloth costume, usually with a carved wooden mask on top of it, worn by a member of the lineage, personifying the deceased ancestor. Since they are regulators of the life of the living members of their lineage, the masks are worn on occasions of the funerals of important people in the community, during harvest festivals, and in emergency and in troubled times, such as periods of epidemic, war, and drought.[47] These are liminal periods when the community needs assurances of the presence of ancestors, and when the ancestors can be relied upon for peaceful transition to normal, ordinary time.

Throughout Africa, ancestral images are widely dispersed and multifarious in style and design and, as Elizabeth Isichei has observed, they have "religious, political and aesthetic dimensions."[48] Undoubtedly, the place of art in the understanding of ancestral spirituality in Africa deserves separate treatment. Here, I will concern myself with some of the meanings implicit in the religious and social dimensions of ancestral spirit-masking traditions, as I observed them in my mother's town, Oke-Igbo, in the Yoruba-speaking area of Nigeria.

A revered ancient masquerade appears yearly in Oke-Igbo. As he parades through the town at night, human sight of him forbidden, he stops in front of houses of important lineages in the community to give his annual felicitations. As part of this annual ritual, the masquerade must praise and reprimand his host, wherever he stops. "I will praise you a little and abuse you a little,"[49] he says, recounting the good deeds and the misdemeanors of the lineage in the past year. As he recites all this, his voice is echoed by a large contingent of followers who must stand at a great distance in order not to catch a glimpse of him. The masquerade must give praise and abuse at every place. However, once in a while, he will only praise his host and never reprimand him. The people believe that when he does this, it signifies that an important member of the lineage, most probably the most senior member, will die before the next festival year. As a result, people look with apprehension toward this festival occasion.

My understanding of this tradition is that the surest sign of ancestral favor is to praise and to reprimand. This is what brings life. This ritual of praising and reprimanding in ancestral veneration is common in Africa. Henri Junod, for example, also observed in his classic, *Life of a South African Tribe*, that among the Thonga of South Africa, prayer to the ancestor spirits is conveyed in two forms: *khongota* (to plead) and *bulaabulele* (to reprimand).[50] For the Oke-Igbo Yoruba people cited above, the ancestor masquerades assume this role of the elders who, by societal requirements, are obliged to praise when praise is due and to abuse when things go wrong. But why does the combination of praise and reprimand represent life, while silence on the subject of misdemeanor signifies death? First, to praise and to reprimand means that there is equilibrium in the community life. In Yoruba thought, it is argued that "the child whom the father (elder) loves is the one that is reprimanded for a misdemeanor" (*Omo ti baba ba feran ni ma nbu*). By the same token, the elder's silence in the face of a child's misdemeanor is regarded as more serious than a lineage curse. It also signifies a reversal of the accepted custom and a reference to death. Unlike in the west, where silence means consent, here silence connotes something harmful, evil, and disastrous.

As I remarked earlier, scholars who have observed this apparently mundane attitude and behavior of the ancestors often have concluded that such practices cannot be an approach to the trancendent and the sacred—that, at best, ancestors are elders but not supernatural entities, and not of the same ontological status as deities and spirits. The Africans themselves are aware of the problem the mundane practices create in the context of belief and ritual practices. However, in their view, the line drawn between sacred and profane attitudes, as construed in the western traditions, is blurred in the African setting.

Conclusion: Secularization and Social Change

Changes have taken place in African conceptions of ancestorhood in light of social developments and the secularization process in contemporary Africa, and historians of religion must constantly examine the connection between developments in religious beliefs and practices and the historical and social changes taking place around them. A relevant question here is: "Why is it that, long after several ancient gods have disappeared from the African pantheon, ancestor beliefs are still as strong as they were in the distant past?" Ancestor beliefs continue to respond to modernity and social changes in contemporary Africa without losing too much of their raison d'être. As most of Africa's great empires collapsed under colonial rule and nation-states emerged in the independent era, ancestral rituals became one of the avenues that served as a link between the present and the past. Quite often, ancestral ideology is invoked to legitimize ethnic identity reinforced by a bond of unity. Ethnicity and communalism—which modern political theorists often condemn as anti-progress and at the root cause of underdevelopment—have served as rallying points for collective community development at the grassroots level. While most Africans have converted to Islam and Christianity and some have become secular, allegiance to the ancestor beliefs remains strong and is the main source of cultural revitalization.

Ancestral symbols and metaphors have also played a somewhat different role in Africa's quest for cultural authenticity. They have been invoked against threats to Africa's culture by literary writers such as Wole Soyinka, Chinua Achebe, and Ngugi. The chief proponent of negritude, Léopold Senghor, reflects on the tenacity of ancestor beliefs in his poem by referring to the ancestors as follows: "O you dead, who have always refused to die, who have always resisted death."[51]

Ancestor imagery has also become the instrument with which African literary figures have expressed anger against colonialism, political domination, and the subtle racism they come across in foreign lands. In this context, Senghor also wrote in one of his books of poetry:

> I must hide him down in my deepest veins
> The Ancestor whose stormy skin
> Streaks with lightning and thunder
> He is the guardian animal I must hide
> Lest I burst the dam of scandal.
> He is my loyal blood demanding loyalty,
> Protecting my naked pride against myself
> And the arrogance of fortunate races. . . .[52]

Beyond the African literary genres, in the battlefield against the remaining vestiges of colonial occupation of Afria's territory, the ancestors become the most formidable weapon for liberation struggles. At the height of the struggle for freedom in countries of southern Africa, such as Zimbabwe,[53] Angola, Mozambique, and Namibia, ancestral spirits allied with the so-called guerrilla fighters to wrench their land from foreign control.

How has ancestorhood responded to Christianity and Islam, the new agents of religious change? What impact has conversion to these two world religions had on ancestral spirituality? First, beliefs and concepts within Christianity and Islam similar to African ancestral traditions were reinterpreted to suit the African's model. For example, in European mission churches the feast of All Saints' Day has become a substitute for the indigenous ancestral festival and second burial ceremonies.[54] During this ceremony in the Anglican Church of Nigeria, the cemetery is cleaned and decorated with flowers, and a memorial service is held there while members stand by the graves of their deceased ones. Many Muslims, who by Islamic tradition should maintain a low profile around customs of death and funeral ceremonies, make yearly sacrifices in honor of their dead relatives.

In the Independent African Churches that have synthesized African and European spirituality, the response to ancestor veneration is more radically in tune with ancient African beliefs. A case in point, addressed by Benetta Jules-Rosette, is the Lulu Church of the Ancestors (Eglise des Ancêtres) in the West Dasai region of the Republic of Zaire: she recorded that "traditional forms of ancestor worship and animism are retained."[55] While some other Independent African Churches may not have adopted the word "ancestor church," some of their practices historically fall very squarely within the traditional African ancestral practices. As an example, the Celestial Church of Christ, the most widespread independent church in West Africa, entered a new stage in church ritual life when it enshrined the body of its deceased founder Oschaaffa in his hometown, Imeko, in Nigeria. The burial place quickly became a major pilgrimage center for the church's members. The annual pilgrimage has officially been incorporated into Celestial's ritual calendar. It is no wonder, then, that in the African Christian quest for an indigenous theology, ancestor spirituality has taken a central place in theological discourse.

Notes

1. I take ancestral spirituality to mean all the ideology, beliefs, and ritual practices related to ancestor veneration in Africa.

2. The works of the following anthropologists are representative of this view. Jack Goody, *Death, Property, and the Ancestors: A Study of the Mortuary Customs of the LoDagaa of West Africa* (Stanford: Stanford University Press, 1962); Meyer Fortes, "Pietas in Ancestor Worship," *Man* 91 (1961): 166–91; Igor Kopytoff, "Ancestors as Elders in Africa," *Africa* 41 (1971): 124–42; T. Cullen Young, "The Idea of God in Northern Nyasaland," in Edwin W. Smith, ed., *African Ideas of God: A Symposium* (London: Edinburgh House Press, 1966), 36–60; J. H. Driberg, "The Secular Aspect of Ancestor Worship in Africa," *Journal of the Royal African Society*, 36 (1936), supplement.

3. See the following works: Victor C. Uchendu, "Ancestorcide: Are African Ancestors Dead?" in William H. Newell, ed., *Ancestors* (The Hague: Mouton, 1976), 282–96; James Brian, "Ancestors as Elders in Africa," *Africa* 43 (1973): 122–33. Evan Zuesse's work also contains a summary of the key arguments of both sides: *Ritual Cosmos: The Sanctification of Life in African Religions* (Athens: Ohio University Press, 1979), 127–28.

4. *Orun san egun lo mu w'asaye wa toro kobo toro?*

5. *Eniti eegun ba nle ko ma roju, b'oti nre ara aiye lo nre, ara orun.*

6. Zuesse, *Ritual Cosmos*, 27.

7. Anita Jacobson-Widding, "The Fertility of Incest," in Anita Jacobson-Widding and Walter van Beek, eds. *The Creative Communion: African Folk Models of Fertility and the Regeneration of Life*, Uppsala Studies in Cultural Anthropology, 15 (Uppasala: Academiae Ubsaliensis; Stockholm: Almquist and Wiksell International, 1990), 51.

8. Ibid.

9. Zuesse, *Ritual Cosmos*, 82.

10. Per Brandstrom, in Zuesse, *Ritual Cosmos*, 182.

11. Ibid.

12. *Ki Olorun ma se ni oku akufa.*

13. Dominique Zahan, *The Bambara*, Iconography of Religions (Leiden: E. J. Brill, 1974), 10.

14. Alan P. Merriam, *An African World: The Basongye Village of Lupupa Ngye* (Bloomington: Indiana University Press, 1974), 120.

15. Ibid., 112.

16. Ibid., 113

17. Ibid.

18. Ibid., 116.

19. Burkhard Schnepel, "Continuity despite and through Death: Regicide and Royal Shrines among the Shilluck of Southern Sudan," *Africa* 61 (1991): 40.

20. Benjamin C. Ray, *Myth, Ritual, and Kingship in Buganda* (New York: Oxford University Press, 1991), 205.

21. Ibid.

22. Isiaka Prosper Laleye, *La conception de la personne dans la pensée traditionnelle Yoruba* (Berne: Herbert Lang, 1970), 72–73.

23. Noel Q. King, *African Cosmos: An Introduction to Religion in Africa* (Belmont, Calif.: Wadsworth, 1986), 46.

24. Ibid.

25. Laleye, *La Conception*, 72.

26. See also the chapter by William Ferea in this volume, above.

27. Robert T. Parsons, *Religion in an African Society: A Study of the Religion of the Kono People of Sierra Leone* (Leiden: E. J. Brill, 1964), 167.

28. Ibid., 169.

29. Ibid.

30. Elizabeth Isichei, introduction to Elizabeth Isichei, ed., *Studies in the History of Plateau State, Nigeria* (London: Macmillan, 1982), 24.

31. Ibid., 25.

32. Ibid.

33. Anita Jacobson-Widding and Walter van Beek, introduction to Jacobson-Widding and van Beek, eds., *The Creative Communion*, 34.

34. Zuesse, *Ritual Cosmos*, 82.

35. Teddy Aarni, *The Kalunga Concept in Ovambo Religion from 1870 Onwards*, Stockholm Studies in Comparative Religion, 22 (Stockholm: University of Stockholm, 1982), 15.

36. Ibid.

37. Parsons, *Religion in an African Society*, 167.

38. Ibid. The accounts of Parsons are summaries from Kenneth L. Little, *The Mende of Sierra Leone: A West African People in Transition*, rev.ed. (London: Routledge and K. Paul, 1967).

39 Peter Fry, *Spirits of Protest: Spirit-Mediums and the Articulation of Consensus among the Zezuru of Southern Rhodesia (Zimbabwe)* (Cambridge: University of Cambridge Press, 1976), 21.

40. Ibid.

41. Ibid.

42. Ibid.

43. Ibid.

44. The materials on Yoruba ancestral rituals come from my fieldnotes, while my references to the Bambara follow Zahan, *The Bambara*, 9–11.

45. Zahan, *The Bambara*, 11.

46. Ibid.

47. Ibid.

48. Isichei, *Studies in the History of Plateau State, Nigeria*, 24.

49. *Ma bu o di e, ma yin o di e.*

50. Henri A. Junod, *The Life of a South African Tribe*, 2 vols. (Neuchâtel: Attinger Frères, 1912–13); cited in Luc de Heusch, *Sacrifice in Africa: A Structuralist Approach*, trans. Linda O'Brien and Alice Morton (Bloomington; Indiana University Press, 1985), 71.

51. Léopold S. Senghor, "Totem," in Melvin Dixon, trans., *The Collected Poetry* (Charlottesville: University Press of Virginia, 1991), 14.

52. Ibid.

53. David Lan, *Guns and Rain: Guerrillas and Spirit Mediums in Zimbabwe* (Berkeley: University of California Press, 1985).

54. See also Ewert Cousins's chapter in this volume, above.

55. Benetta Jules-Rosette, "Symbols of Culture Transformation in Urban Africa: Indigenous Religion and Popular Art as Expressive Forms," in Pearl T. Robinson and Elliot P. Skinner, eds., *Transformation and Resiliency in Africa* (Washington, D.C.: Howard University Press, 1983), 236.

Discussion

Esau Tzau

Thank you, Jacob, for the presentation. It is very much like my country's situation, particularly in the western part of the Solomons. The issue of good and bad deaths is very prevalent, even now. Those who die in old age are said to be sleeping, not dead. When people die young, we become suspicious; something must have gone wrong. If someone dies who is in their thirties, people question whether that person might have been killed with European poisons or by some other means. Divination might be employed to find out who the culprit is so that we can deal with him. That's the kind of explanation you have. But it's the people who die young, the people who still have so much to accomplish whose deaths are so resented.

Laurel Kendall

In Chinese funeral custom and to some extent in Korea, to die before your parents is a breach of filial piety. There are stories of the father being expected to come out and pound on the coffin to blame the son for dying young. Renato Rosaldo wrote a very moving essay about the death of his wife and how he finally understood the concept of rage. He had asked the Philippine people among whom he was working what they felt when they took heads from their victims and they said that for them it was an expression of rage over the death of others. Rosaldo was trained in social anthropology—social, structural, ecological explanations—but when his own wife died suddenly, he said he finally understood rage and its relationship to death. It's a very moving essay that would contribute to these discussions. One question I had for Jacob, though, is what happens to the dead who are not ancestors? Do they become troubling and malevolent dead?

Jacob Olupona

Yes, that happens. I'll just give you an example from my own family. One of my sisters died at the age of eighteen, on the first of January one year when my father was getting ready for the New Year's Day church service. Some time later, a younger sister took ill. My mother went down to the vicarage, went into the room, stood at the open window and started calling out the name of the dead sister, warning her not to disturb the younger sister. So there is a strong belief that if you die before your time, you are still around and can cause all sorts of trouble. This applies to most African societies.

Laurel Kendall

In the literature on Korea, there is a good deal of discussion on the distinction between ancestors and ghosts. The ancestors are said to be the proper dead who died after a full life and have descendants, and the ghosts are those who didn't make it to a ripe old age, so they still rattle around and disturb the living. But in practical terms, there are crossovers. There are old people who meet every criterion of ancestor, but they didn't get to meet this particular grandchild in life, so they are drawn to it and touch it. Or the son is having trouble now, so they come back and they express their grief but, because they are dead, they come too close and that causes further trouble. Similarly, you can die young and you still get your offerings and you still can be called "ancestor." You even get summoned up in ancestor categories in ritual settings. Reality blurs it, but the basic distinction is clearly there.

I was also interested because there are East Asian parallels to the observation that ancestors remain active even when a society loses interest in their deities. There is a notion that Christianity comes in and certain deities fade out. But the ancestors have stayed. Why is it? Is it that ancestors are "good to think?" Is it that Christianity recognizes a moral role for ancestors as models in certain cultures? Or, is it something more profound than that?

Jacob Olupona

I'm not too sure that the missionaries cared about maintaining role models from African cultures. By and large, they just wanted to go to Africa, clear the people's minds, and turn them to Christianity. That was their mission. But they found that it was just impossible in most cases. The ancestors are real to the people, they are built into their daily lives through rituals and festivals. In some of these places, ancestral rituals and the kingship rituals happen at the same time. That is when you really celebrate the significance of your lineage.

I'll give you an example. We normally go to my mother's church in Oke-Igbo, Nigeria, once a year for the harvest ceremony. In that church they call us according to lineages to come and to give our offerings. I remember a particular occasion when we were called to come to the altar for prayer and they were singing a normal Christian song for harvest. The church was so dull and nothing was happening. Then the old organist simply changed the tune of the song and started singing a traditional war song about the oldest masquerade (*kuole*) in the town, which happened to be part of our ancestral heritage. And as soon as he sang that song, the whole church just stood up in response and in respect to the lineage. My mother and my aunts had been dragging their feet before, but then everyone went wild in the church. So how does an outsider deal with this kind of power? You can't just do away with it. It isn't possible.

Jill Raitt

Most of us here are speaking in terms of a body and a soul. But many cultures hold that there are several "souls" in an individual. It is something different from the western notion of the body and soul as the components of a person.

Jacob Olupona

Yes, that is true in many places in Africa. Take the Ibo or even the Yoruba of Nigeria. There is the reference to the *chi* among the Ibo people and *ori* among the Yoruba, which is the second self, and there is some reference to the soul which is different from the body. Their belief is that once you die, you die with the body and the soul. There is no separation between them. But your chi is something like what you call in the west your guardian angel. It also goes with you, but it is not seen as just the main soul, nor is it separate from the body. They realize, of course, that the body will perish and decay; and they do not keep the corpse at home for long. But, at the same time, they believe that the body is part of the individual that is making the journey to the other world. It's not as if the body remains there and the soul goes somewhere else. They don't separate body and soul. Even from the burial ritual we can say that.

William Ferea

Are there beliefs in reincarnation, as in the Hindu tradition?

Jacob Olupona

There is a kind of reincarnation but not like that in the Hindu tradition. Reincarnation in the African sense takes different forms. An example in Yoruba culture is *abiku,* which is also called reincarnation. When you die very young, you belong to the category we call "children of repeated birth," or *abiku* among the Yoruba, which refers to people who die and come back over and over again. Some people even test this empirically. There are cases when the African mother who is very angry that this young girl or boy has died will cut off one of the fingers. That child will then be reborn without one of its fingers. That is a clear test and very common. We cannot explain it, we don't really want to go into it, but it is real. Then you have to go to the diviner to find out what to do, and he or she tells you which are the proper sacrifices to make. There are different forms of medicine to ensure that the child doesn't disturb the stable spirits or that, once the child dies, this will be the end of the rebirths. The children that are born this way are given special names like Kokumo ("she will not die again") or Molomo ("do not go again") to illustrate that. So there are different forms of reincarnation, but not in the classical sense of the Hindu tradition.

John Grim

My question has to do with method in your work, Jacob. In a critical, academic setting, no method can claim exclusive rights to uncovering "the truth" about the subject of interpretation. But at some points in your paper I thought you were almost granting privileged status to methods developed in social or cultural anthropology. Let me exaggerate in order to make my point. At times I wondered whether you were going into the field, understanding the people's explanations, but then leaving that behind in order to get on with the "critical work" of "really understanding what was going on." It strikes me that there is a question to be asked here about what you are doing as a historian of religion in relation to anthropological method and in terms of exclusivity of interpretation.

Jacob Olupona

Let me answer by beginning with a specific example. Max Gluckman found among the African people a form of ritual whereby a day of license allows people to say whatever they want about social institutions, about the king, about the big people, about the elders. They are allowed to abuse the king and say all sorts of things. Others have called these rituals of reversal, but Gluckman introduced these as rituals of protest saying that the Africans are protesting against the social order in the rituals of reversal. Further study of some of these rituals confirmed first of all that these are, indeed, rituals of protest; people are protesting against the social order. But those rituals are are also connected with the cosmology. Quite often if you look at the structure of the rituals, they repeat the creation of the universe as perceived by these people. In fact, only one aspect of the rituals was interpreted by Gluckman. This has been demonstrated by comparative work in West Africa and East Africa. It is not that they are wrong; they are correct. But in order for us to have a convincing interpretation, we must incorporate the valid insights of anthropologists and go further.

That raises the question of how the study of religion differs from anthropology. In my opinion, some of the best books in religion are now being written by anthropologists. But the constraints of anthropology as a discipline create limits that I do not want to accept. To be specific, most social anthropologists do not want to talk about transcendence and the sacred, which is at the heart of religious studies. They are quite good at seeing and explicating the connections between religious phenomena and social structure or processes. But they do not want to go beyond "religion as a social extension" and discuss what the subjects of their studies perceive to be essential. These are the kinds of issues I'm trying to get at. We need to take methodology and the analysis we are doing very seriously. It's to our advantage to bring a variety of interpretive strategies to bear on these problems as we try to understand the materials at hand.

Defeating Death and Promoting Life
Ancestors among the Enga, Huli, and Kewa of Papua New Guinea

Mary N. MacDonald

Introduction: On Life and Death

To talk of ancestors in Papua New Guinea is to talk of ideas about life and death. From involvement in such talk and from reading the reports of others, it seems to me that in Melanesia a good life is held to be a life in which a person is healthy and energetic, in which the environment is fertile and fruitful, and in which social relationships are strong and reliable. A good life does not come easily, yet Melanesian traditions maintain that human beings have a responsibility for encouraging such a life through their work, both practical and imaginative.[1] Ritual activities and ceremonial exchanges express a concern with fertility and with wealth, that is, with the continuity and well-being of the human community. Like people the world over, Melanesians must, however, contend with the fact that, despite their hard physical work and dedication to ritual observances, life does not always go well. One of the major disturbances, of course, is death.

If one happens to be at an airstrip in the highlands of Papua New Guinea when the body of a dead person is returned from one of the regional hospitals, one is confronted with behavior that suggests that death is not easily accepted in this part of the world. As soon as the plane is heard, if not before, a loud wailing rises in the waiting crowd. Traditional funeral observances include such wailing as well as bodily mutilation, divination to identify a "killer," and accusations directed at the ghost of the departed for deserting his or her kin.

I shall consider stories that three highland peoples of Papua New Guinea—the Enga, Huli, and Kewa—tell about ancestors, and I shall discuss the ways in which they structure ritual communication with the ancestors. I suggest two things: that death is experienced as an unwelcome interruption in community relationships (that is, it is not accepted as "natural"), and that the institution of ancestors is a way of overcoming death. Over generations, thinking about life and death and thinking about the relationship with those who have died, Melanesians have come to a notion of ancestors who "live" on and who continue to interact with the members of the community in which they once dwelt. These ancestors, it is thought, need the help of the living (who, for example, ritually "feed" them), while the ancestors, it is maintained, can help or hinder the living in their earthly pursuits. Ancestors, in this Melanesian sense, are part of a multigenerational and extensive social network. When clan brothers and sisters die, people continue to interact with them. They tell stories about ancestors, sing of ancestors, perform rituals for ancestors, and expect ancestors to have an ongoing interest, benevolent or malevolent as the case may be, in human affairs. The creation of vital ancestors, who are transformed, not destroyed, by death, is one way of responding to a problem—death—which confronts us all. It is a way of defeating death and promoting life.

The Enga, Huli, and Kewa

In exploring understandings of ancestors and spirituality in the highlands of Papua New Guinea I am focusing on three societies. Similar ideas are to be found in other highland societies, although systems of communicating with ancestors vary. I shall give some background on the three groups and on their notions of sky beings, ancestors, and land spirits. Then I shall tell a story about death from the Kewa, provide an account of a culture hero/mythic ancestor from the Huli, and discuss a cult for the ancestral ghosts from the Enga.

The Enga, Huli, and Kewa are among the larger linguistic groups of Melanesia. They occupy neighboring territories and speak related but mutually unintelligible languages.[2] It is held by linguists that the three languages are derived from a supposed earlier language referred to as Proto-Engan, and it is hypothesized that the Huli and Kewa are descendants of people who, some two thousand years ago, began to move south out of the Enga-Western Highlands region. Today the Enga occupy what is called the Enga Province, and the Huli and Kewa are two of the several linguistic communities which occupy the adjoining Southern Highlands Province. Traditionally, the groups had no overarching political organization and lived in small-scale, relatively egalitarian societies, a situation which has been modified to some extent by the introduction of structures of local, provincial and national government, and by opportunities for greater mobility. Despite some differences the Enga, Huli, and Kewa share a basic outlook regarding death and the ancestors, an outlook which is widespread in Melanesia—namely, that death is an undesirable event, the result of a human mistake or foolishness, and that those who have died retain contact with their living descendants and exercise an influence in affairs of the earthly community.

The Enga, Huli, and Kewa cultivate sweet potatoes and other vegetables, and they keep pigs. They gather nuts and fruits and hunt marsupials, birds, and wild pigs. While the particular patterns of subsistence they pursue depend on local conditions, they all devote considerable energy to the production of the staple, sweet potatoes. Gardening skills are complemented with gardening rituals, many of which make associations between physical and social reproduction and between products produced in gardens and products "produced" by exchange.

From the accounts of anthropologists who have worked among the Enga it seems that Enga social structure is more clearly defined, or that the putative rules of Enga social structure are more often observed, than is the case among the Huli and Kewa. The Enga belong to named and localized exogamous patriclans. A cluster of contiguous clans forms a named phratry, the founder of which is said to have been the father of the clan founders. Each clan has several subclans whose founders are said to have been sons of the clan founders. The subclan is further divided into named patrilineages whose founders are said to have been sons of the subclan founders. Men of the same patrilineage live together and assist each other with wealth exchanges, bridewealth payments, compensation payments, rituals, and building projects.[3]

Like the Enga, the Kewa belong to named patrilineal groups, but the groups tend to be dispersed over several settlements, and only in some cases do the clan names refer to the supposed founders of the groups. Each settlement will have sections of several groups (called *repa* or *rupa*.) Among the Kewa it is the settlement group made up of several clan subsections that acts corporately. It is the settlement group that would, for example, carry out the ritual for the ancestral ghosts. Although there is an ideology of patrilineality, it is not difficult for members of other clans to become incorporated into a Kewa clan and to take on the marriage rules and the rights and obligations of that group.

Robert Glasse, who describes Huli social structure as a cognatic descent system, writes:

> *There are no corporate descent groups in which membership rights and duties are ascribed solely as a consequence of descent, as among the Enga. Nor are there corporate units, ostensibly agnatic, but actually based on patrifiliation and other principles. Instead membership is an achieved status that can be acquired by any member of a cognatic stock. It follows that*

every man is eligible for membership in a number of groups. There are no local groups in a residential sense, but there are well-defined territories in which group members, resident and non-resident, have recognized rights. There are some group members who reside exclusively in one parish-territory. Others commute more or less regularly between two or three. And some men fulfil obligations to a group without residing on its land. It is a complex, mobile society. Individuals have great freedom of choice. High status is achieved by acquiring rights in many groups rather than by winning recognition in any one.[4]

Mythic Ancestors, Sky Beings, and Ghost Ancestors

Today most Enga, Huli, and Kewa are members of Christian denominations; traditional ideas about death and about ancestors have been modified by Christian teachings. Major indigenous rituals honoring and placating the ancestors have largely been abandoned. Nevertheless, the ancestors and "the ways of the ancestors" are recalled in conversation, speech-making, and storytelling. Missionaries, who first entered these areas in the 1950s, saw the cults of the ancestral ghosts as incompatible with worship of the Christian God and strongly discouraged them. Today some Christians make attempts to celebrate the ancestors within the context of Christian worship. For example, in some Catholic communities among the Huli and Kewa the ancestors are recalled on All Saints' Day and All Souls' Day[5] and "spirit stones" from former cult houses, that is, stones which mediate the presence of ancestral ghosts, have been placed in a number of churches. Healing rituals and other domestic rituals continue to be practiced and the telling of traditional tales goes on. In storytelling sessions the South Kewa, among whom I worked for several years, include accounts of rituals practiced in the "old time" before government and missionaries. What was once practice has now become narrative.

Huli myths tell of founding ancestors, human beings who were visited by the *dalaya ali*, or "sky people" (*dalaya* = sky, *ali* = people). The sky people are said to live in a realm above where there is plenty of food and they are said to be kind to earth people. At some time in the past a rupture occurred between the world of the sky and the world of earth so that there is now little contact between the two realms. The earth people tend to idealize life in the sky world as what their life could have been like if some foolish person in the past had not offended the sky people and caused the separation. The Enga and Kewa also speak of sky people and, like the Huli, regard these people as being far away and known more through stories than through actual contacts.

The Huli founding ancestors, some of whom have particular names, and who precede the kind of women and men now on the earth, are said to control the course of nature and to intervene in the affairs of human beings. These nonhuman or prehuman ancestors are called *dama*, a term which is also used for various land spirits.[6] Honabe, the myths tell us, was the first dama woman on the earth and she cooked food by the heat of her own genitals. She married a dama called Timbu and bore five sons and one daughter. Later, seven more children, the first bird, and the first possum came forth from Honabe's menstrual discharge. One of Honabe's sons, Helahuli, married a woman who bore him four sons (Huli, Opena, Dugube, and Duna) who are regarded as the first human beings and the founders of the groups that today bear these names. The Enga and Kewa also tell tales of culture heroes who long ago established the kind of life people now live upon the earth.

Datagaliwabe, who is also called "The One," is distinct from the dama and is said to be present everywhere and to see everything. He is particularly concerned that people fulfill social proprieties and is thought to punish those who fail in this regard. Unlike the forest spirits and ghosts, Datagaliwabe cannot be placated with offerings of cooking meat, from which he could "eat" the aroma, or with displays of dancing, which would give him the opportunity to exercise his limbs and enjoy the sociality of the human community. Glasse says that there are no rituals for Datagaliwabe.[7] Some of my informants have claimed, however, that even though people did not think they could negotiate with Datagaliwabe in the way they could with the ancestral ghosts, pigs were killed for him and prayers offered to him in recognition of his guardianship of the social order. Huli Christians liken Datagaliwabe to God the Father and say that, whereas in the past they thought that he was concerned only with proper behavior within kin groups, the preaching of missionaries has made them aware that Datagaliwabe is concerned with proper behavior toward all people.

The Enga tell of Aitwe, a male creator symbolized by the sun, who resides in the realm of the sky people and is concerned with proper social behavior. Although Aitwe does not usually bother himself with the activities of human beings and ghosts, he can be called upon for help in serious cases of ghost attack. Rituals directed to Aitwe were performed periodically. The Kewa speak of Yakili ("the man above" or "the man of the sky"), who is thought to be remote from daily concerns but to be concerned with the long-term welfare of human beings. In the past, in order to communicate with Yakili, people killed pigs and possums on mountain tops. On these occasions they thanked Yakili for past favors and enlisted his help in ensuring the future fertility of gardens, animals, and the human community.

Whereas in daily decision-making the sky beings and mythic ancestors are not mentioned, the supposed actions and desires of ghosts—*dinini* to the Huli, *timango* to the Enga, and *remo* to the Kewa—are frequently discussed. They are vital to considerations of causality. An aspect of the personality that was present in life is thought to survive death or to be transformed at death. Ideas on how this happens vary. Sometimes, say the Huli, the dinini leaves the body during sleep. One should, therefore, waken a sleeper gently in order to give the dinini time to return before the person opens his or her eyes. At death, the ghost makes its way through an invisible opening in the crown of the skull and does not return. The Kewa call the spirit which goes wandering during sleep *wasupa* (shadow), and distinguish it from remo, the ghost in whom the person has a continuing existence after death. Similar ideas about the continuation of a dead person's interaction with the living after death are to be found throughout Melanesia.

The Huli have varying and rather vague ideas about the "life" and location of ghosts.[8] The Kewa speak of ghost settlements, reached by taking a path through the forest or by following a stream to the south, in which the departed dwell and to which they try to draw their relatives. The Enga locate the ghosts of the long dead in an underground realm parallel to the sky realm and the earth realm. All agree that, before reaching their final destination, ghosts of the recent dead return to the vicinity in which the deceased formerly dwelt. People take precautions to avoid conflict with them. According to the Huli, the ghosts of women, in attempts to have their kin kill pigs for their enjoyment, attack their relatives, but not their own offspring. It is thought that having consumed the smell of the cooking pork and blood from the pig a ghost will be satisfied and desist from her attack. Among all three of the highland groups that we are considering, spouses, both male and female, take precautions to keep the ghost of a husband or wife at bay. Strong-smelling berries or a bright light—things which ghosts are thought to dislike—will, for example, be carried, or placed outside the house, by a person whose spouse has recently died.

The Huli, Enga, and Kewa all hold that ghosts, particularly the male ghosts collectively, are interested in the affairs of their descendants and may be summoned to help them. The relationship of ancestral ghosts and their living kin is a matter of reciprocal benefits. The Huli say that the ancestors continue to age after death and stand in need of help from the living to counteract the effects of aging. The Enga and Kewa say that the ghosts need to be fed and empowered, something which is accomplished by coating "ghost stones" or "ghost eggs" with oil and pig blood and inviting them to consume the smell of cooking pork. If the ghosts are not given the attention which is held to be their due, and the food they need to sustain their ghostly life, then they will seek it by causing problems for their descendants.

In a Huli ritual called *ega kiliapa* pigs are cooked to attract the male ghosts, who will feast on the aroma, and two young men perform a leaping dance in which the ghosts join, thus loosening their invisible limbs. In another ritual, called *teba*, the dama are asked to remove cataracts from the eyes of the ancestral ghosts. The living have a responsibility to carry out these rituals so that the ghosts can continue to "live." If they fail to do so, they can expect their own lives to be diminished. With the decline of traditional rituals since the coming of missionaries in the 1950s, some Hulis have seen Christian rituals as an alternative means of communication with the dead.

Until the time of colonial contact the Huli engaged in frequent warfare, and the dinini of slain warriors were thought to go eventually to a place in the sky called Dalugeli. The Huli say, too, that ghosts reside in pools of water and in a place called Humbinianda, which is hot and lacks water. They claim, however, that they are not too sure where the ghosts of their parents and grandparents might be, and those who are Christian will suggest that the dead are now with God in heaven.

Today, throughout Papua New Guinea, government rules require that bodies be buried, but, after the flesh has sloughed away, the Huli may retrieve the bones of the dead and place them on platforms or in boxes within the family compound. When I first visited the Huli in 1973 platforms were much in evidence; on a 1991 visit boxes painted with traditional designs seemed to be more popular. Huli homesteads are surrounded by ditches and by distinctive fortress-like walls made of pointed sticks that are often painted with red, yellow, and black designs. In the past the Kewa placed their dead on platforms in the forest and after the flesh had fallen away would retrieve the skulls and carry out a ritual of burning the fur of a marsupial in the skull to please the ghost of the deceased. This domestic ritual could be carried out by women as well as by men. In the South Kewa area the larger bones would then be placed in a cave or rocky outcrop. Today the Kewa bury their dead and, as far as I know, leave them buried. However, people often carry small bones of parents or grandparents who died a generation or two ago.

The Huli, the Enga, and the Kewa all make a distinction between ghosts of the recent dead, whose relationships to the living community are seen as an extension of their relationships during life, and long-dead ancestors, whose relationships to the community are collective rather than individual. The ghost of a recently deceased person may, for example, be thought to express his or her displeasure at the failure of a descendant to carry out the expected mortuary rituals on time by causing illness to the offending person or a member of his or her family. If, however, there is a general failure of crops or an epidemic of influenza, the collective ancestors may be thought to be responsible. In the first case it is members of the domestic community (spouses, children, brothers, and sisters) who will act to remedy the situation. In the second case it would in the past have been, and to some extent still is, the adult men of the community, members of male cults, who take ritual action. Today, of course, Christian rituals are also an option in dealing with problems thought to have been caused by ancestral ghosts.

A Kewa Story and the Problem of Death

Death, our own and that of others, is a problem that we confront in various ways—with resignation, with anger, with sadness, with denial. The stories we tell about death do not make it go away or give a satisfactory explanation for it, but they accompany our struggle. They assure us that death is part of the human situation. Although Melanesian stories hold out the prospect of overcoming death by becoming ancestors, it is not a welcome prospect, for the energetic life of the living community is much preferred to the shadowy life of the ghosts.

I would like to relate a tale frequently told among the South Kewa. It is a tale about a youth who turned into a snake. When I first heard it I had no idea what it was about. The story is often told at storytelling sessions, particularly around the time of funerals. Part of the story—an exchange between a youth and his sister-in-law—is sung by the storyteller, and this part will also be sung, interspersed with other mourning songs, following a death. I have heard the story many times in short forms and in long forms and whenever someone dies it comes to my mind.[9] The story goes like this:

> *A man, his wife, and his young brother lived together. The elder brother did not treat his younger brother as kindly as one would expect and the younger brother felt sick in his liver because of this. It was time for a pig kill in another settlement and the man should have gone but he was ill. Since he was sick and could not go himself he sent his brother and his wife to the pig kill at the other settlement. The two of them set out and walked on and on, dragging a pig with them and carrying shells which they were to exchange, until they reached the place where the pigs were being killed.*
>
> *After the youth and his sister-in-law had observed the dancing and killing of pigs and had been fed pork they started for home carrying pork and shells, which they had received from exchange partners. The young man and his*

sister-in-law had planned to take a rest on a mountainside on their way back. The youth reached the place first and lay down to sleep. When the woman arrived the youth was already asleep. She looked at his face and she was astonished to see that he was turning into a snake. Other people came along and they too saw that the sleeping youth's face had turned into a snake's face. In fact his whole body was starting to turn into a snake's body.

The woman cried out, "Your brother will be angry. Get up and come with me." Then the boy woke and spoke up. Actually the boy was singing and his sister-in-law was singing too.

The woman sang:

Brother-in-law, your brother will be angry,

Let us go home,

Get up now.

The youth, however, answered:

No, I have turned into a snake,

I cannot get up and walk back with you.

Then he left her and slithered into the forest. The woman returned to the settlement and told her husband what had happened. He was very upset and cried for his brother and painted himself with clay. It is said that the man who turned into a snake still lives on the mountain. And, as the Kewa say, that is all to the story.

Having declared that "that is all to the story," the Kewa storyteller usually proceeds with another tale that connects with an episode or theme of the one previously narrated. One such story concerns a man from the east and a man from the west who created two different kinds of landscape. These two men had different ideas about the human condition. The man from the east said that people would die but that some of them would return to the human community again, while the man from the west said that people would not die but would periodically shed their old skins and be renewed. They came to blows over their different ideas and, ironically, it is the man from the west who shoots an arrow into the other's stomach, killing him and thus introducing death into the world. Another Kewa tale tells that once it was possible to sing the dead back to life, but one man was so distressed over his brother's death that he cried and from then on it was no longer possible to bring the dead back to life. Then there are stories that tell of one brother killing another and so introducing death.

Once we understand something of the cultural context of the story of the youth who turned into a snake we can probably say that it resonates with some of our own experience of life in the world. When human relationships become unbearable we may well desire an escape that will make those responsible for our misery feel especially guilty and remorseful. We can empathize with the young man who, rather than leave the heightened sociality of the pig kill for the company of an oppressive elder brother, opts to join the fellowship of the ghosts. While the stories that the highland peoples of Papua New Guinea tell about death echo universal concerns, they also say something of the particular experience of subsistence agriculturalists whose life is sustained within kin and exchange partner networks. In this context the cause of death is attributed to unsatisfactory relationships. Although highlanders do not accept death with equanimity, this is not to say that a person might not at the end die peacefully. When death does occur, the mourning is long and loud, both to assure the dead that they are truly missed and to protest something which ought not to be, something an "enemy" has done.

Returning to the story of the youth who is transformed into a snake, let me remark that, among the Kewa, when a person dies those who were with her or him will report seeing a snake, or a possum or even a black cat, depart from the body and vanish into the grass or forest. The mourning songs composed for the occasion may express the sentiment that the person has departed because she or he was unhappy with the way others treated her or him, or they may accuse the dead person of selfishly leaving her or his kin. Usually there will be a process of divination to find who has commissioned sorcery to bring about the death. That is, death exposes problems in social relationships. The diviner may reveal the problem to lie, for example, in a soured relationship with an exchange partner or in the failure to make payments to affines. Anthropologist Roy Wagner, who worked among the Daribi, to the southeast of the Kewa, has suggested that believing in ghosts and interacting with them is a way of overcoming death. Wagner calls the impersonation of the dead by Daribi mediums and dancers "the invention of immortality." He sees ghosts, then, as a metaphoric innovation, by which the problem of death is transformed into the problem of relationship to dead who live on as ancestors.[10] It is possible, of course, to state the matter another way and to see human relationships, including relationships with those who have died, as the fundamental concern.

Pajapaja: A Huli Mythic Ancestor

The Huli, like other Papua New Guineans and other horticulturalists, are concerned with the fertility of their land. According to the Huli, an ancestor, Pajapaja, whose name means "good, good" was an only child who, as a young man, would allow his finger to be cut and thus would shed his blood to make the land fertile. It is said that he was killed by greedy people who were not content to have some of his blood from time to time but wanted it all at once, thinking that they could thereby make the land fertile forever. While in the Tari area of the Southern Highlands in August 1991, I was told by local members of the Catholic Church and the Evangelical Church of Papua that they see Pajapaja as in some ways a "picture" of Jesus.

The story of Pajapaja, as related to me by Huli Catholics in 1991, goes like this:

Pajapaja, whose name means "good, good," was an ancestor who lived six generations ago at the time between the dama and the more recent ancestors. His mother was Tiripi, a Duna woman, and nothing is known of his father. At that time it was customary to carry out a land fertility rite (dindi gamu) *at Pepenete, close to where Dauli Teachers' College is now. This rite continued to be carried out until after the arrival of the missionaries. Tiripi, Pajapaja, and a ritual expert* (gamu agali), *along with men from the various Huli clans, would gather at the site.*

After the men from each clan had killed pigs they would give the intestines to Tiripi for her to wash in a nearby stream and they would proceed to cut up the pork with their sharp bamboo knives. As Tiripi set out for the stream she would say to the gamu agali that he should pretend to let his knife slip and so make a small cut on Pajapaja's finger. Since the knife was sharp he would hardly feel it and only a small amount of his blood would be lost. Then, said Tiripi, the gamu agali should mix the youth's blood with the blood from the slaughtered pigs and sprinkle it over the land to restore its fertility.

On one occasion when the ritual was being carried out at Pepenete and Tiripi had gone to wash the intestines, Kolipa Koli, who was the leader of the Peta clan in Tari, said that Tiripi had told him that they should kill Pajapaja. In fact Tiripi had said nothing of the sort, but Kolipa Koli thought that if they killed the youth and mixed all his blood with the pigs' blood and sprinkled it over the land, then the land would become fertile forever and there would be no need to repeat the ritual. It was greed and laziness which led him to this conclusion. The other leaders fell in with what Kolipa Koli claimed Tiripi had said, and they killed Pajapaja. After sprinkling his blood, they cut up his body and distributed the pieces to the clans.

The Peta clan received pirikini *(waist section).*

The Haro clan received halene *(ears).*

The Habaro clan received habuni *(lips).*

The Tobe clan received tobene *(stomach).*
The Ayako clan received ayuni *(liver).*
The Pi clan received pirikini *(waist section).*
The Wiya clan received wipuni *(genitals).*

The head pieces (hukuane) *were dropped into the Kupame and Narime lakes, which are located in the foothills of Mt. Ambua. The intestines* (tini) *and some bones* (kuni) *were buried in the swamps that are called Hayafugwa, Talifugwa, Kererefugwa, and Mogorofugwa. The leaders of the clans still hold some of the small bones of Pajapaja.*

When Tiripi could not find her son, she wept inconsolably and accused the men of killing him. They chased her out of the Huli area and beat her as she made her way along the road leading to the Duna. Huli people shouted insults and threw mud at her and men raped her as she trudged along weeping for her only child. All the Huli clans except for the Tani mistreated Tiripi. Members of the Tani clan were sorry for her. They wiped her tears and washed her and fed her and decorated her with shells. Two Tani clans, the Yepari and Guari, invited her to stay and rest with them. Tiripi foretold that these two clans would become the largest Huli clans and in fact they did. Today Tani is the largest clan.

Until the Huli killed Pajapaja the Huli did not know fear or shame or suffering. The Huli people brought pain to Tiripi and now they too experience pain. After a few days of rest with the Tani, Tiripi continued her journey toward the Duna but she was never heard of again. People believe she is still alive and still weeping for her son. The descendants of the men who killed Pajapaja know what their ancestors did. The Huli people know that it was wrong to kill Pajapaja and ever since they have been carrying out rituals of repentance. It is said that blood of Pajapaja is kept in a bamboo container at Dapirinite, where there is still a house for the kebe ritual, and that the ritual experts at that place are constantly seeking forgiveness, on behalf of all Hulis, for Pajapaja's death.

When Fr. Berard came and spoke about Jesus, many people thought he was talking about Pajapaja. Some people even collected pigs and went to Fr. Berard and said, "We want to kill these pigs to compensate for the death of Pajapaja." But Fr. Berard said that Jesus and Pajapaja were not the same person.

Most of the information I have on Pajapaja was supplied in the context of discussion with Catholics and Evangelical Church of Papua members in the Tari area about their experiences of Christianity. For them, Pajapaja became a focus for a dialogue between the ways of their ancestors and the ways of Christianity. In a group of Catholics I was asked, "Do you think it is all right for the old people when they come to church to address their prayers to Pajapaja?" I responded by asking for more information about Pajapaja, and there followed a lively discussion tending toward the view that Pajapaja was a good ancestor just for the Hulis, whereas Jesus is an ancestor somewhat like Pajapaja but concerned with the welfare of all people. As with notions of Datagaliwabe and God, it is clear that a merging of traditional and Christian figures is occurring. Pajapaja as ancestor is talked about in connection with a fertility ritual, the dindi gamu. It seems that, given this narrative model, when Huli Christians tell the stories of Jesus they see him, too, as an ancestor and an agent of regeneration. It may not be too great an exaggeration to say, then, that the new religion, Christianity, is being incorporated into the Huli world via stories and rituals which permit people to focus on Jesus as ancestor.[11]

The Enga Imbu Ritual

While many Melanesian stories tell about ancestors, communication with ancestors is mediated in a variety of rituals, some for individual ghosts and some for the ancestors as a group. In *Let Sleeping Snakes Lie* Paul Brennan describes a ritual that is performed by the Central Enga[12] to placate the ancestral ghosts and gain their good will.[13] Some Enga groups call the ritual *imbu*, and there are other names for it. Among the Kewa a similar ritual is called *ribu*. (The medial "b" sounds as "mb.") Ribu can mean "rich" or "poor." The ritual enlists the aid of the ancestors to overcome a situation of poverty and to replace it with a situation of wealth and well-being. Yet, in order for the ancestors to have the power and will to help their descendants, they must first be nourished and entertained by the living.

Imbu is carried out at intervals of several years. The need for its performance is presaged by the appearance of an animal, bird, or reptile associated with the clan's mythic history. Brennan calls this creature "the clan totem."[14] It is thought that the snake, to take a creature that figures in the title of Brennan's book and in the Kewa story we have heard, becomes aroused when the ancestral ghosts are displeased with the way things are going among their descendants. Their displeasure is reflected in the failure of gardens, the sickness of children, the weakness of pigs, and so on. The loss of vitality observed in the environment and in the community may be accompanied by sightings of the "snake" in clan territory. It is then clear that the time has arrived to carry out the imbu ritual for the ancestors.

Only adult males of the particular clan take part in the imbu ritual, but women and children and men of other clans may assist in gathering the animals and vegetables necessary for the ritual.[15] After the performance of the ritual, men of other clans may be given food from it to eat. According to Brennan three to five days are spent hunting possums, gathering pigs, and assembling the sugarcane and vegetables to be consumed in the ritual. The ritual takes place in a grove of tall *pai* trees where the clan stones are buried. The grass in the grove and in nearby areas is trampled down, an action said to frighten away insects, which are seen as possible bearers of misfortune. In a footnote Brennan points out that *sambai* (cane or *pitpit* grass) stands in opposition to *ita* (tree) while *nene* (insect) is in opposition to *endakali* (people).[16]

The food is cooked in earth pits while ritual officiants remove the clan stones from the holes in which they are buried. The stones are then decorated with black ash and red and yellow pigments and placed near the cooking pits. The stones, which are associated with the ancestral ghosts, are thought to inhale or eat the aroma of the feast.[17] In the imbu ritual the living community is said to communicate with the ancestors and to feed them. After the ancestral ghosts have been satisfied, the stones are wrapped in aromatic cooking leaves and returned to their holes. The ghosts, having been nourished and made powerful, are again in a position to help the living. It is said that the "snake" returns to the stones, where he will sleep until roused by an unsatisfactory situation in the clan with which he is associated.

Ancestors and Spirituality: Insight or Alienation?

What do Enga, Huli, and Kewa discourse and ritual performance concerning ancestors tell us about the way that people experience their participation in the cosmos and about the way that they reflect on that experience? I have suggested that, by entertaining the notion of a continued existence as ghosts of the recent dead and as more remote ancestors, Melanesians, and other peoples too, are able to overcome death symbolically and to promote life. We may ask, though, as we might of all religious believers and practitioners, whether they are just deceiving themselves. That is, are ancestors as a religious category a source of insight into our situation in the cosmos or a source of alienation from it?

The early sociologist Herbert Spencer, who read about Melanesian ghost beliefs and "worship of ancestors" in the accounts of Thomas Henry Huxley and John MacGillivray and developed his theory that all religion begins with the worship of ancestors, would probably dismiss ideas about the continuation of life beyond death as false.[18] Others, inclined to see religion as a projection of psychological and social needs, would point to the needs satisfied by the idea of ancestors. Then, in most cultures there are people who claim to have had experiences of people who have died. Can we interpret Melanesian ancestor traditions as a way of dealing with something which may be true for all of us—that the dead continue to influence our lives? With reference to Spencer it should be mentioned that what we see among Melanesians is not so much "ancestor worship," in the sense of reverent veneration, as the continuing of relationships with those who have died and the structuring of these relationships in ways similar to other relationships of social and economic exchange.

The ideas of Sigmund Freud and Meyer Fortes are useful in considering the psychological aspects of relationship to ancestors. In *Totem and Taboo* Freud argued that the belief that the dead can harm the living enables the living to overcome or reduce the guilt that they experience toward the dead.[19] In Freud's view both affection and hostility are present in human relationships, but the hostility, which detracts from the ideal of affectionate familial relationships, is repressed. When such repressed hostility is projected onto the dead it produces situations, so the argument goes, such as we find in the highlands of Papua New Guinea, where malevolence is usually to be expected of the ghosts of the recent dead and sometimes to be expected of the ghosts of the long dead.

As a result of work on Tallensi religion, Fortes made some modifications to Freud's theory and suggested that, at least among the Tallensi, repressed hostility may find its outlet not so much in fear as in acquiescence to the continued authority of ancestors.[20] Among the Tallensi, then, rituals of "ancestor worship" serve to reinforce the traditions of the ancestors as they are transmitted through the living elders and to ensure the solidarity of families and clans. Were one to apply the approaches of Freud and Fortes to the highland groups being considered here, one could say that in all three groups there is a fear of the ghosts of the recent dead, a fear which could be understood as a repressed hostility in familial relationships which has been projected onto the dead. One could also say that there is an awe-ful respect for the collective long dead, a respect which could be understood as a repressed hostility toward figures of authority. I am, in fact, inclined to agree that, at one level, problems in familial relationships and problems of authority within clans or within local settlement groups are highlighted in the orchestration of rituals for the ancestors.

Roy Rappaport's study of the ritual killing of pigs for the ancestors by the highland Tsembaga of Papua New Guinea[21] goes beyond psychological and sociological explanations and uses an ecological model for understanding beliefs about ancestors. Rappaport begins with the competition between pigs and people for yams and other garden produce.[22] According to Rappaport the belief among the Tsembaga that, at intervals of several years, large quantities of pigs must be killed for the ancestors and that pigs must be killed at funerary observances and warfare settlements serves to regulate the pig population and to provide protein (pork) for the living in times of stress. Hence, for Rappaport beliefs about ancestors and rituals directed toward them are, at least from one point of view, a device for regulating the ecological balance.

The Freud, Fortes, and Rappaport theories all shed some light on how and why beliefs and practices concerning ancestors are important to particular peoples. They help us to locate the beliefs and practices of the Enga, the Huli, and the Kewa within their social and ecological contexts. Such beliefs and practices do not stand alone. They are part of more comprehensive religious and cultural systems to which they provide access. Tales about mythic ancestors and rituals by which highlanders of Papua New Guinea relate to "real" ancestors speak to an experience of a world in which life is valued and in which death is to be overcome. The wisdom passed down through the generations suggests that this life, measured from birth to death, is not all there is. Yet, since it is all that is known, the world of ancestors is built in the shade of its image.

Notes

1. In "The Power of Intentions: Thinking about Kewa Ethics" (*Journal of Religious Ethics*, 1992, 331–51) I discuss the notion of a good life within the Kewa context.

2. The three languages are non-Austronesian and belong to the Trans-New Guinea Phylum, West-Central Family, East New Guinea Highlands Stock. On the characteristics of these languages, see Stephen A. Wurm, *Papuan Languages of Oceania* (Tübingen: Narr, 1982).

3. For a more detailed description of Mae Enga social structure, see Mervyn J. Meggitt, "The Mae Enga of the Western Highlands," in Peter Lawrence and Mervyn J. Meggitt, eds., *Gods, Ghosts and Men in Melanesia* (Melbourne: Oxford University Press, 1965), 105–7.

4. Robert M. Glasse, "The Huli of the Southern Highlands," in Lawrence and Meggitt, eds., *Gods, Ghosts and Men*, 28–29. For further discussion of Huli descent and social organization, see Stephen Frankel, *The Huli Response to Illness* (Cambridge: Cambridge University Press, 1989), chap. 3.

5. See also the chapter by Ewert Cousins, above, in this volume.

6. Glasse glosses dama as "deities" in "The Huli," 33ff. From Huli informants contacted in 1991 I obtained varying accounts of the dama. Some described them as ancestors of a culture hero type who settled the land and who control the weather. Others said they were dangerous forest-dwelling spirits of various types, including giants and cannibals and guardians of particular trees and streams. Some Christians described them as "devils." Most people elaborated several kinds of dama.

7. Glasse, "The Huli," 37.

8. For further information on traditional dinini beliefs, see Glasse, "The Huli," 29–32.

9. Several tellings of this story are to be found in context in my book, *Mararoko: A Study in Melanesian Religion* (New York: Peter Lang, 1991). The text given here is my out-of-context retelling.

10. Roy Wagner, *Habu: The Innovation of Meaning in Daribi Religion* (Chicago: University of Chicago Press, 1972), 170ff.

11. In a paper, "Pajapaja and Jesus: Indigenous Religion and Christianity among the Huli," given at the third East-West Center workshop on primal spirituality in January 1993, I provide an extended discussion of the changing religious situation of the Huli.

12. Enga, with some 200,000 speakers, is the most widely used of any Melanesian language. There are nine major Enga dialects, and, as may be expected, some cultural variation from one sociolinguistic group to another. When Brennan speaks of the "Central Enga" he is considering the Layapo, the Kaina, and the Mai.

13. Paul W. Brennan, *Let Sleeping Snakes Lie: Central Enga Traditional Religious Belief and Ritual* (Adelaide, South Australia: Australian Association for the Study of Religion, 1977), 36–40. Another account of the ritual is to be found in Meggitt, "The Mae Enga," 114–20.

14. Anthropologist Mervyn Meggitt and historian Roderic Lacey think that the relationship is not totemic in the strict sense.

15. Among the Kewa several clan sections participate together in the ribu. This reflects a residence pattern in which sections of several clans dwell in the same settlement.

16. Brennan, *Sleeping Snakes*, 56 n. 53.

17. Among the South Kewa such stones are referred to as "ghost stones" and the particular word for "stone" also means egg. The Huli call such stones "bones of the ancestral ghosts." The stones may be smeared with pig fat and blood.

18. Huxley and MacGillivray were aboard the *HMS Rattlesnake* on the 1846–1850 voyage of Captain Owen Stanley, and Spencer made use of their accounts in his work on the origins of religion.

19. Sigmund Freud, *Totem and Taboo* (London: Routledge and Kegan Paul, 1950).

20. Meyer Fortes, *Oedipus and Job in West African Religion* (Cambridge: Cambridge University Press, 1959).

21. Roy Rappaport, *Pigs for the Ancestors: Ritual in the Ecology of a New Guinea People*, rev. ed. (New Haven, Conn.: Yale University Press, 1985).

22. Since an adult pig eats as much as an adult person, increasing pig herds are quite a burden, especially for the women who grow and prepare their food.

Discussion

John Grim

May I ask for a clarification about that boy in the story, the youth who becomes a snake? What is it about the story that leads you to talk about death? The boy doesn't necessarily die, does he?

Mary MacDonald

At first I did not have a clue what that story was about. Then I noticed that people often tell the story around the time of funerals and that the words that are sung in the story are also sung the night before a funeral when people are mourning. Then I started to make the connection. When a person dies, often the people who are with him or her will report seeing a snake leave the body. The snake represents the remo, as the Kewa call it, an animating spirit that is present during life. It can come out of the crown of your head and go out when you're dreaming at night. So you should be careful when you wake someone up; you have to give it a chance to go back in. I get cross now when people wake me quickly because it has been impressed on me that I may lose my animating principle. But at death, it leaves permanently. It goes off somewhere else and is manifested as a snake or a possum or something like that. Now for the Kewa, this ghost first of all goes off into the forest and actually there is a term "forest people" that can apply to the recent dead, or to land spirits. So if you encounter someone you might ask, "Are you a settlement person or are you a forest person?" In other words you ask, "Are you a real person or are you a ghost?"

John Grim

Let me just follow up with one question. What do you see as the relationship of narrative and ritual in this process of defeating death?

Mary MacDonald

First of all, I should mention that the Kewa distinguish between two kinds of ghosts: ghosts that belong to stories, and real ghosts. But there are two different kinds of stories as well. Stories that are called *tida* have to do with the sky people and any other ghosts are story ghosts. Then there are *ramani*, which are supposed to be reliable accounts, and they will often have stories about real ghosts, like those of your uncle or grandfather. The stories are one way of remembering. Through the narratives and through the rituals, you institutionalize the dead. They are remembered through the narratives you tell about them. In this way you've given them life.

The rituals are one way of interacting and feeding the ghosts. It's thought that the ghosts continue to grow older in some way. The Hulis talk, for example, about the hair of ghosts becoming whiter and whiter. They might be gray when they first go and then they get really white. They may even develop cataracts on their eyes. But you can carry out rituals that will help them maintain their vitality. I gave an example in the paper of a Huli ritual, in which you invite the ghosts to come and dance with you. By dancing they loosen up their bones and get energy again. So you're helping to keep them alive.

William Ferea

I agree with Mary that the narratives and symbols institutionalize the ancestors. They are put in a hierarchy that Melanesians in general have. I mentioned in my paper that there were no written texts, so narratives and mythologies form a basis for passing on the knowledge about the relationship with the other world, the spiritual world. Mythologies are also a source of education about the continual confrontation and cohabitation with the spirits. Rituals, as Mary said, are a necessary part of the departure of spirits because going from the physical realm to the spiritual realm requires purification. The spiritual realm is much more pure than physical existence, and so these rituals are an important part of the passage.

Ewert Cousins

When the spirits become a part of the collective ghosts, is that transformation or absorption looked upon as something positive or negative?

Mary MacDonald

That's a hard question. Certainly the people that I worked among didn't like at all the idea of becoming ghosts themselves. Attitudes about this differ across Melanesia, but certainly in these groups in the highlands, the state of being a ghost was thought to be worse than the state of being a living person. In discussing this people would point out especially that the ghosts can't eat the way that we eat, and also they can't engage in sex. Sometimes ghost attacks were thought to be the result of people tantalizing the ghosts by having sex in places where the ghosts were.

Ewert Cousins

That reminds me of some of the Homeric material where Odysseus goes into the underworld where he meets the great heroes and they tell him that it's not a nice existence down there. It's very much like the ghosts that you described.

Jill Raitt

Can they ever join the sky people?

Mary MacDonald

No, the warriors can go to live in the sky, but I don't think they actually live with the sky people. Warfare was an honorable activity among the Huli until the 1950s. There was almost constant warfare. When you go there today you see these wonderful ditches they dug and homesteads they fortified. It's really quite amazing. So the Huli had a special place for warriors. But when the rituals are carried out for the collective dead, I think it's almost as if the collective dead might be in a better situation than the more proximate ghosts.

William Ferea

Generally, the community of spirits—the spirits as a group—are beneficial to society. There are rituals that are performed for ancestors and feasts held for ancestors where we invoke their presence in the community. Only rarely would you hear the individual ancestors called upon by name. I wouldn't call my grandparents' names out. I just say, "Oh, ancestors!" because recent spirits are thought to be much more dangerous and capable of much more anger. They can cause problems for people who are living, for relatives who have not done rituals properly or who have misbehaved in some other way.

II. Intimate Ancestors

Into the Mist

Ulunui Garmon

It was very difficult to find the right word for the title of this paper. The best I could do was "mist" or "veil," and I finally settled on "mist." But the title could be "Into the Mist" or, "Out of the Mist"; it is the same thing. Both refer to the invisible, visible support of our *ʻaumakua,* our ancestors.

A few days ago, after I had chosen the title, my sister Pua and I were at home and she asked me if I had heard the story one of our aunts told about the mist. I said, "No, tell me!" This aunty is our father's sister who lives in Kaʻu up on the slopes of Mauna Loa where it gets very cold. At a certain time of day, mist settles in a certain area and then disappears. She would go to the window by the sink where she washed dishes and look out at that place. One day she went down to that place and looked around. There, where the mist would normally be, was a cave. She went back to the house and said, "They were in there, the mist came, and they left with the mist. They come back home with the mist." She was talking about the spirits of our ancestors. What she meant was that whenever the mist appeared, it was the time when the spirits of the ancestors entered into the mist to go into the earth, or into the land with which they are familiar. The mist brings them back and then disappears.

That is the kind of tradition we were raised in, and I want to share with you what was shared with me as I was growing up in our household, with my brothers and sisters, my mother and father, my grandmothers and my grandfathers, my aunties and my uncles. This is a part of my life and it is so difficult to put it into writing or to talk about it. What happens to your paper once you have written about yourself or about your people? Please keep that story in mind. When we talk about ʻaumakua, we talk about those ancestors that surround us.

What I have to say comes from this particular family, and the same ideas are being transmitted to our children.

My name is Ulunuiokamamalu. The name Ulunuiokamamalu is an ancestral name belonging to my maternal grandmother's father and his family. This name—like many of our names—contains my past, my present, and my future. I chose to start with this particular name because it gives you a better understanding of how I regard my 'aumakua.

In our family, your behavior should fit your name. We are expected to treat our name with respect because it belonged to our ancestor. It doesn't belong to me, it belongs to my ancestor behind me. It is expected that you become the name, listening to what the name means spiritually and to what the name meant to the person who owns it. When you see your name as something to follow, it becomes a major responsibility. So when the old folks give a name, they expect you to become that name, and in our family, the children do become their name.

I have one grandson whose name is Kaleopa'a. "Leo" is voice; "pa'a" is something hard or tight. And he is a little louder than the others; he matches his name. But the name is an ancestral name, so when he does not act in a way that I think he should act, I call him "Robert," or just say "Excuse me?" without the name. He is expected to grow into his name.

One of my daughters, on the other hand, went by her English name for the longest time. But when she decided to go back to school she said, "I'm not going to use my English name. I'm going to use my Hawaiian name." And, you know, she's different now. She looked for the things that are spiritual and she's growing in that way now. It is her real name that links her to her 'aumakua. It gives her protection, but it is also dangerous because the name can be taken away from her. As the living adult, I have the responsibility of taking back that name if she does not deserve to hold it. I am responsible beyond this living earth, responsible to that ancestor who owns the name. And if I were to have to take away that name, it would be immeasurably worse than cutting her out of the family. The name is a link, an honor and a responsibility.

In a sense, you have no choice in the matter. You do not choose your name or your family. But you do choose whether to hold onto that responsibility or not. I have chosen to hang onto that responsibility because it is an honor. I choose to hang onto that because I need my 'aumakua. I need my ancestor, and not just when I am in trouble. I need my ancestors all the time. For as long as I have lived I have needed them.

It seems to me that we need our ancestors even more in these days when everything changes so rapidly. Change is inevitable and we need to accept that.

My mother saw this coming, even though we lived in a rural area. The six of us children were raised in the culture. We lived in a Hawaiian area, we went to a Hawaiian school, we attended church with all Hawaiians. But she saw that changes were happening out there, so she made us get an education. She knew that we would struggle in today's world, but we needed to know how the other side lived so that we could hold onto the way that we lived, the way our ancestors lived.

When I take up that challenge, that responsibility, I breathe the life into that name. I believe that I breathe life into that ancestor, and with that breath she gives life back to me. They need us and we need them. It is give-and-take, give-and-take. I choose to breathe life into my ancestors through the name. At the same time, I place the responsibility on my daughter to take care of that name, but we hope in turn she will imitate us. We always hope. By our choices we can compliment our name or we can tarnish who we really are. But, as Hawaiians, we always have that opportunity to start anew, so there is no excuse. We cannot say it is too late.

My children were raised on the mainland, in California, so the transition in coming to Hawai'i was very difficult. There were lots of things that I needed to explain to them, more things than my sisters and brothers needed to explain to their children because mine were raised elsewhere, with a different kind of lifestyle. I felt I had to help them understand their relationship with their ancestors. For instance, when I was a little girl and I got hurt, I needed the comfort of my mother, or my father, or my grandmother. I would always go to my grandmother and stand by her side, and she would put her arms around me to comfort me. When she died, she was not taken away. I can still go to her and say, "Grandma, I need you! Help me, show me, stay with me until I understand!" Death does not end that kind of comfort. I may still call her, I may still call my 'aumakua, just like I went to them as a child. I do not desert them because they are no longer walking around. When we get together as a family, we are there and our ancestors are always present.

Two years ago our whole family went through a ceremony together: brothers, sisters, children, and grandchildren. We made them all prepare for this particular ceremony that begins to teach them that you can start over again. We wanted them to look to their ancestors as their 'aumakua, their guardians. But you can't just look for help; you have to take care of them, too. You cannot just go to them without preparing yourself. It works both ways; you owe something. That's how it goes: as in life, so too in death.

Now, this particular ceremony has to do with the rising of the sun. The sun is somewhere every minute, but it comes up over the eastern gate. On our island, the easternmost part is known as Kumukahi, which means "the first source," the place where the sun comes up. When the sun rises, it is the new sun, it is a new day, it is the birth of new things. When the sun sets, it dies in the west. Birth in the east and death in the west, everyday.

Putting the children through this ceremony was much more effective than learning from a book. We took them there, we went through it with them, and now I expect them to continue to consider these things and to look into these things. They will not be able to say, "It's too late. Whatever we had is gone. They took it away." There has to be a point where we say, "Okay, we can't deny history. We hate it, we wish it hadn't happened, but it did. So let's do something about it." It's not lost, I know without a doubt it is not lost.

One of the things that the ʻaumakua do is give you signs: visible, invisible things to look at. When we went to Kumukahi that morning two years ago, it was in January. There are two great boulders there and we needed to be in position at sunrise, with the sun coming up between the two boulders. We were thinking, "Where does the sun come up in January? Where are we going to stand?" We stood together awhile, we separated, we tried to think our way through it, we tried to focus ourselves. I was way off to one side asking my ʻaumakua, "Where shall we stand? We need to be in position. This is the first time with all the children, all the grandchildren. This is the beginning of something new." Suddenly, we heard the flutter of wings to the right of Pua and my son Kupaʻa. It was an *iwa* bird. We moved into position where the bird had been and awaited the sunrise. That is what we call a *hoʻailona*, a "message." You have to listen to the voices, look, be aware, absorb. You have to believe it beyond a doubt in the very deepest part of your gut, the *naʻau*.

So, with that experience, we position ourselves, we face each other. There are clouds on the horizon, but we need the sun because the ceremony is very important to our family. We go through the ceremony as an open circle, including the sun and the things between them and us. The sun keeps the places between the clouds open and peeks through. We are so happy because it is all complete. It is *paʻa*, firm. When it was over, we were facing the ocean and there was a different kind of a rain that came, big drops, soft, straight down. It came just to wet us and then it stopped. When we turned around, there were two rainbows—a double rainbow started on one end of the family and ended on the other end of our family.

I believe in my ʻaumakua. I do not just talk about ʻaumakua; I believe in them. As we try to perpetuate our culture, as we try to maintain the names that belong to us, to take care of our *kupuna* (elders or grandparents), we do have a means of starting over. We do have a means of cleansing. We do have a means of giving thanks. All of those things come.

One of the ways that I look at what is visible and invisible is through dreams. I do not look at dreams as belonging to me; they are the means by which my 'aumakua give me messages. Dreams tell me where I am at that particular time in my life. What's happening? What is it that I am doing? What is it that I need to do? Answers come in my dreams.

At this time of my life, I am more involved in my own genealogy than I used to be. I don't really have a choice. I have a choice, but there is actually no choice. We went to a family reunion and I brought some records home to make copies for my children and that was all I was going to do. But, after I got home and put everything away and cleaned up and went to bed, I woke up from a dream. Because of the dream, I knew that I was going to have to do something more than just make copies for my children. So I began. It's been about six months now, and it has been very intense because I feel my 'aumakua, and other people's ancestors as well.

There is a certain kind of behavior that is expected from you when you work on genealogies, so you have to take care just a little bit more than usual. You cannot fight with your husband; you have to take care how you look at things when you deal with these kinds of names. Are these laws written down? None of it is written. Then how do I know this? It is a matter of putting your dreams together. It is a matter of how you were raised. It is a matter of what your parents expected of you. When you put all these things together, you know immediately how to behave.

I cannot begin to tell you how I know these things. I keep coming back to names. Your kupuna stays right on top of you until you have put it together. Then you go into another name and you know where the name belongs. You know immediately when it belongs. How do you know? How does anybody know? I believe that I do nothing on my own. I believe that my accomplishments are really not mine; they are my 'aumakua's. Who gets the credit? My mother? Her mother? Go back farther! The credit belongs there, not here. I am just a vehicle in which this moves, and I go from this point to my children. I expect it to go from them to their children. They will become the vehicle.

My mother died almost thirteen years ago and it's like she's not dead. People talk about her every day, people praise her every day. They do her ceremonies, her songs, her hula, her chants; she lives every day. In the past thirteen years she has become their 'aumakua. If we keep them alive, then they guide us. It is not ancient history; it's happening right here. We continue to uphold a person, we remember what they did, we practice what they left. With that practice, we breathe life into the 'aumakua, and the 'aumakua gives us the guidance we need. Mahalo.

Discussion

Jacob Olupona

In my home in Africa, missionaries have not succeeded in destroying beliefs and practices related to ancestors. They have succeeded in doing away with the deities, but European Christianity has not succeeded in destroying the ancestors. Ancestors have become the one thing that African Christians and traditionalists share, along with the Supreme God, of course. So my question is, how do you as a Hawaiian and a Christian, or I as an African and a Christian, decide who to go to in time of need? In a crisis, how do you decide whether to go to your 'aumakua or to the Christian God? For instance, this morning you were asked to give a prayer and you offered a Christian prayer in English. Why didn't you invoke your ancestors?

Ulunui Garmon

I could have done a chant, but I did not prepare myself for that. In that case, I would have done a chant that belongs to the culture and would have ended it with a prayer, a Christian prayer that includes the supreme Jesus.

Now on the question of how do you decide, let me respond with a question. What do you think about protocol in your family? For us, age is status and death is majestic. I don't particularly want to go to that highest level yet, but I'll take the status of age. In these terms, there is a protocol for handling problems in the family: the youngest child always went to the oldest child, then they went to the mother, and then to the father. I have no problems with my Hawaiian culture, with mixing my ancestral 'aumakua and my Christianity. What I'm doing is using protocol. My blood, my koko, is Hawaiian and it belongs to my ancestors. I also recognize Christianity and the things that belong to God. I'm just using protocol. I go to my mother, my grandmother, or my grandfather for the things that pertain to them.

Pualani Kanahele

I want to comment on your question, Jacob. We come from a line of chanters and dancers. When I want to memorize a chant real fast, I go to the ancestor that was the chanter in my family. If I want to bless my son with the Christian priesthood, I go to the Christian God. If I want to take my children to the beach and be assured of a good catch, I ask the 'aumakua in our family who was a good fisherman for help. That's protocol. Some of us are split and have a hard time with this, but some of us can make the separation and be comfortable with it.

Puanani Burgess

This reminds me of a story about my grandmother. She was a deaconess in a large Hawaiian church in Honolulu, and she also prayed to her ancestors to thank them for the gift of healing that she did through massage. I once asked her, "Isn't that a problem for you?" She said, "Why? I have the Christian Church for the Christian God. I have my own 'aumakua in this room. I keep them separate; they don't fight, they don't meet. Why must I choose?" For her, the Hawaiian way meant including all, having as many as possible. She didn't understand why she had to choose one over the other.

Charles Long

This shouldn't sound too strange to anyone. Almost everybody in the world now is juggling at least two kinds of traditions as a part of their normal life. But there is a little theological problem. Christianity doesn't like for you to have other gods. We may agree or disagree, but Christianity doesn't like all these gods. I just want to remind you all about that.

Jill Raitt

There are a hundred varieties of theological opinion on that subject.

Charles Long

But not one of them says they like you worshiping all these other gods. You can juggle it any way you want, but. . . .

Jill Raitt

The Jesuits in China said veneration of ancestors was fine! [See below, the first page of John Grim's chapter.]

Charles Long

The Jesuits are not the pope, and the pope said they were wrong!

Voyages of Māori Ancestors from Hawaiki
Two Ngāti Porou Traditions

Margaret Orbell

In Aotearoa, or New Zealand, Māori people cherish traditional stories about the ancestors from whom their own particular tribe, or *iwi*, traces its existence as a social group. Usually, these founding ancestors are believed to have lived originally in the homeland of Hawaiki, a fertile land that lies to the east, in the direction of the rising sun. From Hawaiki, the ancestors sail to Aotearoa in ships (*waka*) with famous names—such as *Te Arawa, Tainui, Tākitimu, Aotea, Mātaatua*—and in other vessels, too, which are less well known. Often these ships are laden with possessions, such as birds and plants. Their crews experience many adventures during the voyage, and they perform wonderful deeds. Usually they are threatened with disaster, but always they are triumphant.

In their new home, these first tribal ancestors lay claim to the land and make it ready for their descendants. Their actions create precedents for later occasions; for example, the ritual chants that they recite have been retained by their descendants. They travel throughout the tribal territory distributing people and possessions, and in the process they establish boundaries and bestow names upon features in the landscape. Sometimes they leave behind as rock formations their footprints, their possessions, their dogs, sometimes even their sons or daughters—all of them turned to stone.

Quite often, they shape the land on an ambitious scale. In the South Island a series of great lakes, mostly, in fact, formed by glaciers, were believed to have been dug out by Rākaihaitū, an ancestor who arrived from Hawaiki and set out to explore the country. He dug them at intervals with the digging stick he brought along on the voyage, and his descendants were thus able to catch eels and ducks in the stretches of water he had created. His digging stick is still there today; it is now a mountain, Tuhiraki.

Until fairly recently, most scholars have assumed that these narratives are essentially historical—that they contain a "germ of truth" that, over the ages, has become "encrusted with myth." Using this approach, scholars have excluded from consideration those episodes that have seemed impossible, or unlikely, as historical events. But this is an arbitrary approach and, as more and more episodes in the stories came to seem unlikely, scholars were left with little to consider. In the end, most of them abandoned the attempt to explicate these texts, despite their undoubted importance in Māori tradition.

In my opinion, these narratives are best understood in terms of their ritual, social, and political dimensions. They are primarily religious narratives rather than historical ones, and there is much to be learned from them about the thought and experience of the people to whom they belonged. Instead of excluding the so-called supernatural elements, one should consider the stories in their uncensored entirety and attempt to establish contexts for them in traditional ritual and belief. Voluminous nineteenth-century records of myths, legends, ritual performances, songs, proverbs, and oratory provide an abundance of material for this purpose. These ancient stories will not be diminished by such analysis. Instead, it will reveal something of their imaginative power, their complexity, and their importance to the society that produced them.[1]

Earliest Ancestors, Tribal Ancestors, and Hawaiki

I will discuss in this paper some aspects of two of the stories about the founding ancestors of one particular tribe—Ngāti Porou on the East Coast of the North Island.[2] First, however, the tribal ancestors who arrived from Hawaiki must be briefly distinguished from the earliest ancestors of all, those ancestors who gave the world its present shape.

These earliest ancestors determine the nature of the world in general and the nature of people in general, and their stories were therefore told, with some variation, by all of the tribes of Aotearoa. Everywhere it was believed that the world came into being with the separation of the first ancestors, Rangi the male sky and Papa the female earth. These first parents, along with their children and their children's children, embody and shape the world in most of its aspects: sky and earth, sea, plants, humans, and other living creatures. They establish, too, many of the norms that govern human behavior. People behave as they do now because of these precedents that were established in the beginning.

The fullest account that we have of the traditions of Ngāti Porou—the tribe with which we are especially concerned—is available in the writings of two nineteenth-century *tohunga* (religious experts), Mohi Ruatapu and Pita Kāpiti. Both were teachers in the *whare wānanga* (schools of learning) which, until the arrival of Christianity, were held on the East Coast for the instruction of young men. In the 1830s, Mohi Ruatapu was one of the three main teachers at what was probably the last of these whare wānanga. Much later, in the 1870s, he produced a large body of writings comprising four separate accounts of the history of the world. Pita Kāpiti's writings, while not so extensive, include valuable accounts of ritual performances. In recent years some of the writings of these men have been edited, translated, and published.[3]

Mohi Ruatapu, in each of his accounts, begins with the story of the first parents, Rangi the sky and Papa the earth. He then tells of their immediate descendants, giving the histories and genealogies of men such as Tāne, Māui, Tāwhaki, and Rata and of women such as Hine-ahu-one, Pani, and Whaitiri. Often we are not told where these people live, but sometimes their stories are located in a place called Hawaiki.

This land of Hawaiki has generally been assumed by scholars to be the name of the real, historical place from which the first Māori settlers sailed when, in reality, they colonized Aotearoa. Yet, when one examines the kinds of things that the Māori actually said about Hawaiki in myths, ritual chants, songs, proverbs, and oratory, it appears rather to be a paradisal land of origin broadly comparable to similar lands in other religious traditions. In mythology it is a source of human life, for the first woman is shaped by Tāne from the soil of Hawaiki, and this episode is reenacted whenever a child is conceived and born. Also, Hawaiki is a source of favorite foods, the place where, among other things, the *kūmara*, or sweet potato, the most highly valued of food-plants, grows wild in great abundance, untouched by human hands. Some living creatures came from Hawaiki in the ancestors' ships, while others made their own way to Aotearoa. Certain birds flew from there; some kinds of fish, such as the *moki*, were thought to make a seasonal migration each year; and the mainly herbivorous rats, which were a favorite food, were thought to have swum from Hawaiki in a long chain, each rat holding in its mouth the tail of the rat in front of it.

As the source of life and fertility, Hawaiki is the place of origin of most living things, especially those that are highly valued. Not surprisingly, then, it is also the homeland from which the founding ancestors of the tribes arrive in Aotearoa.

The Māori, like other traditional peoples, attached complex symbolic significance to geographical directions. In particular, the east, being the direction of the rising sun and the rising stars (and therefore the source of light), is associated in many contexts with life and success. For this reason, Hawaiki was usually said to lie in the east. Naturally enough, the tribal ancestors, when they arrive from Hawaiki, generally sail from the direction of the rising sun and land at last on the eastern shore of the country.[4]

The Myth of the *Horouta*

I return now to Ngāti Porou, in the territory on the East Coast of the North Island, and to the leading tohunga, Mohi Ruatapu. In his manuscript books, Mohi Ruatapu begins by writing about the origins of the world. He then goes on to tell of two important ancestral journeys that were made from Hawaiki to his tribal territory. One of these stories concerns the ship known as the *Horouta*, and the other an ancestor called Paikea who rode to Aotearoa on the back of a *taniwha* (water spirit) that took the form of a whale. Sometimes Mohi puts the *Horouta* story first, and sometimes the Paikea one. I will begin with the *Horouta* and will be primarily concerned with it.[5]

Ngāti Porou, like other tribes, trace their descent mainly from ancestors who came from Hawaiki. At the same time, though, they also claim certain ancestors who did not arrive from Hawaiki but who had, quite simply, always lived in Aotearoa. In particular, there is Toi, a very early ancestor who has no knowledge of the kūmara and, in some versions of the story, no knowledge of fire. This transitional figure is therefore forced to live upon wild plants, which he eats raw. Accordingly, he is delighted when a stranger, Kahukura, arrives one day from Hawaiki and, untying his carry-belt, takes from it some preserved kūmara, which he gives Toi to eat. When Toi asks how this delicious food can be obtained, he is told that it must be fetched from Hawaiki.

So the *Horouta*, under the command of Kahukura and with a crew of twice seventy men, sails eastward to obtain the kūmara from Hawaiki. Toi himself is occasionally said to have accompanied them, but he is not mentioned again. Notice that this voyage begins in Aotearoa, not in Hawaiki as in most of the migration traditions.

A ritual chant is recited, and the *Horouta* reaches Hawaiki with extraordinary speed. On their arrival the crew find that the kūmara have already been harvested. So while they are still in the vessel, Kahukura recites a ritual chant and thrusts his digging-stick into the cliffs of Hawaiki. These cliffs are actually composed of kūmara. Kahukura cuts the cliffs down with his digging-stick, and the kūmara tumble down and fill their ship. He then performs another chant, and the kūmara cease to fall.

This episode in the story does not make very good sense if it is regarded as history, but it makes excellent sense when it is interpreted as a mythological, religious tradition. A close analysis by J. Prytz Johansen, a Danish historian of religion, shows that the episode in which Kahukura acquires the kūmara from the cliffs of Hawaiki must have been reenacted each year during the rituals performed among Ngāti Porou when it was time to plant the seed kūmara.

Johansen shows that the cliffs in the myth are equivalent to the piled-up baskets of tubers that in reality lined the (partly underground) storehouse in which the kūmara were stored. These buildings were *tapu*, under religious restriction. It is clear that, as part of the planting ceremonies, the officiating tohunga made his way to a storehouse, and that his actions in acquiring and bringing away the seed kūmara were equated with Kahukura's similar actions in acquiring the kūmara from the cliffs of Hawaiki. Almost certainly, the tohunga would have recited during this event the ritual chant that Kahukura, in the story of the *Horouta*, recited as he thrust his digging-stick into the cliffs of Hawaiki.[6]

Thus, Kahukura provided a role model for the tohunga who was in charge of the elaborate kūmara-planting rituals. Every year, Ngāti Porou reenacted the first acquisition of the kūmara; or rather, I think one can say, that every year this crucial event was believed actually to occur once more. In some sense, it seems the tohunga did not merely *imitate* Kahukura; instead, through this ritual he actually *became* Kahukura. Quite literally, history repeated itself.[7]

To return now to the *Horouta*: Kahukura has achieved his purpose, which is to acquire the kūmara for the people of Aotearoa. He remains, therefore, in Hawaiki, while the crew of the *Horouta,* led by another tohunga named Pāwa, set out upon their return voyage. Since the *Horouta* approaches from the direction of the rising sun, it makes landfall, as do most of the ships in such traditions, on the eastern shore of the North Island.[8] More specifically, it lands initially in a region—comprising a very large bay, or bight—which lies some distance to the north of Ngāti Porou territory. The area is usually known today as the Bay of Plenty; its Māori name is Te Moana-a-Toitehuatahi.

In this respect, too, the *Horouta* is following a common pattern: in many of the traditions about voyages from Hawaiki, the ancestral ship lands in this particular region. I think there is a special geographical reason why they do so; and I would like to leave the *Horouta* for a moment, as it sails across the ocean, and consider this question.

The rising sun, as we have seen, is a manifestation of power. We come now to a second manifestation of power. It so happens that an extensive area of volcanic activity, with hot springs and mud pools and active volcanoes, is located in the Bay of Plenty and in a large region that stretches inland from it. Since this volcanic region, with its extraordinary fires, is on the eastern side of the North Island, and since Hawaiki was thought to lie across the eastern ocean, it was assumed that volcanic fire had itself been brought from Hawaiki. The belief was that these fires had been summoned from there by an especially powerful tohunga named Ngātoro-i-rangi, one of the tribal ancestors who had arrived on the ship named *Te Arawa*.[9]

In the southern Bay of Plenty, the island of Whakaari (or White Island) is a highly active volcano. It is clear from references in songs and myths that this island, along with a small neighboring island called Paepae-Aotea, was thought to lie close to Hawaiki.[10] Partly for this reason, I think, the *Horouta* now makes landfall in the Bay of Plenty. However, it lands first far north of the Bay of Plenty, at a place called Ahuahu, then sails southward. And presently there is a near disaster.

The Māori believed that the kūmara had always to be stored away from the fernroot—that these two food plants must never be brought into contact—for the kūmara represented peace and the fernroot represented war.[11] For this reason the crew had been told by their tohunga not to carry any other food apart from the kūmara. But, at Ahuahu a woman named Kanawa broke this tapu by secretly taking on board some fernroot. So when the *Horouta* was close to Whakatāne in the southern Bay of Plenty (this is a region immediately opposite the volcanic island of Whakaari), the gods who had charge of her became very angry, and they caused a great wind to arise. To appease the gods, Kanawa was thrown into the sea; but she rose to the surface and caught hold of the bow of the vessel. She would not let go, and the ship capsized. (Among other things, this episode in the myth provides a salutary warning against the breaking of tapu.)

The *Horouta* was damaged; its bowpiece was broken. All the people wept for the damage done to their ship. Then they held a meeting and decided to obtain another bowpiece. Their tohunga, Pāwa, divided the people into two groups. Seventy men stayed to guard the vessel, while the others, under Pāwa's leadership, went inland to obtain timber for a new bowpiece.

In these myths of voyages from Hawaiki, it is in fact common for a ship to be wrecked. This usually happens after the crew has reached its destination, and the vessel then turns to stone. In this way the ship becomes a sacred landmark, in the form of a reef or some other rock formation, and it remains forever with the tribe that traces descent from it. In the present instance, though, the *Horouta* has not yet completed its voyage. It is lying on the coast near Whakatāne, and not yet in Ngāti Porou territory. Therefore, it is not permanently wrecked. In due course it is repaired and sails on.

First, however, Pāwa and his men make their way inland. While Pāwa himself, with some companions, goes looking for a suitable tree to fell for timber, others set off under the leadership of a man named Awapaka to catch birds to feed the workmen. These huntsmen catch their birds, reciting the appropriate ritual chants, and they preserve them in their fat in calabashes—and in this way, they establish for the first time the patterns of behavior relating to bird hunting, which their descendants subsequently followed. That is to say, Ngāti Porou believed that when they hunted birds, they were acting as Awapaka and his men had done in the beginning. Moreover, the ritual chants they recited in this connection were thought to possess their efficacy because they had been recited by these first huntsmen.

Pāwa, meanwhile, had found a suitable tree and felled it. He now needed a river in order to float his tree to the coast. So he recited a ritual chant, he urinated, and by this simple means he created the Waioeka River. In the same way he created three other large rivers: the Mōtū, the Waipāoa, and the Waiapu.

It turned out, however, that the tree Pāwa had felled was not required. Word came from the coast that the *Horouta* was not as badly damaged as had been thought: the men who remained to guard it had raised the vessel by means of a ritual chant,[12] they had patched it, and the *Horouta* was now sailing around the East Coast, stopping at intervals to distribute the kūmara in the places it passed. Accordingly, Pāwa and his companions continued on by land, traveling in the same direction as the *Horouta*. Since it was too late to take their potted birds back to the *Horouta*, they themselves feasted on their catch. They left untouched just one calabash of birds, carrying it with them so that those on board the *Horouta* could taste the delicious food.

On the journey overland, Pāwa created many landmarks. For instance, near a place called Wharekahika he left his son Maroheia, turned into a rock—and he is still to be seen there now. He stirred up the sea nearby—and that is why there is still a strong ocean current there. In another place, near Awatere, an echoing cliff is known as Te Reo o Pāwa, "Pāwa's Voice," because when people called to him, Pāwa answered. In this manner, creating landmarks as he went, Pāwa made his way right around the territory of Ngāti Porou and the closely related neighboring tribes.

In the Waiapu region, where Pāwa had planned to meet up with the *Horouta*, the ship had once more sailed on without him; but it had left behind—turned to stone—its anchor and bailer, and the kūmara which it had brought for the Waiapu region. So the men on board the *Horouta* did not get to taste the calabash of birds that Awapaka had brought all that way. The calabash was abandoned there, and it is now a rock. Its name is Toetoe, or "Left-over."

As for the *Horouta*, none of the accounts I have seen say what finally happened to it. Some writers describe it as sailing right down to the South Island, distributing kūmara all the way. The kūmara, of course, were forever associated with the *Horouta*. So, too, were Pāwa's landmarks and, in the Waiapu Valley, the anchor and bailer of the *Horouta*, which were now rocks.

The Stone Calabash and Kahukura's Belt

We have glimpsed something of the importance of the myth of the *Horouta* in traditional, pre-contact Ngāti Porou religion and thought. Other examples of its traditional roles could be given. However, the *Horouta* remained of great importance to Ngāti Porou throughout the nineteenth century and into the early years of the twentieth century, and it is still important to orators today. I should like to describe two occasions on which skilled orators spoke of the *Horouta* in order to sway the sympathies of their audiences.

When the Māori became Christian, which they mostly were by the late 1840s, belief in the *earliest* ancestors—universal ancestors such as Rangi, Papa, Tāne, Tāwhaki, and Whakatau—began to diminish. This happened gradually, over a long period of time, but Christian teachings inevitably had this effect. Though poets still spoke of these figures, they did so less often and in less complex and varied ways.

On the other hand, the traditions relating to *tribal* ancestors were much less affected by missionary teachings. The Bible, after all, had nothing to say about Māori *tribal* origins;[13] and since the missionaries generally assumed that the stories telling of origins in Hawaiki were essentially historical, they did not recognize them as part of the traditional religion. So the poets and orators of Ngāti Porou, like those of other tribes, were free to continue to think in terms of their tribal myths of origin, and to refer to them as appropriate.

The first of the two occasions I mentioned occurred in June 1872, when the leading *rangatira* (chief) of Ngāti Porou, Major Rōpata Wahawaha, brought together all the subtribes (*hapū*) of Ngāti Porou, along with some neighboring tribes, at a place called Mataahu, just north of Waipiro Bay. The purpose of this great meeting was to unite the East Coast tribes and demonstrate their loyalty to Queen Victoria and the British Crown.[14]

In the previous years there had been much fighting in the region, for many men had accepted the Hauhau faith, which promised victory over the Europeans. The adherents of this Hauhau faith had taken up arms against the Crown, both in their own tribal territory and elsewhere, while others, including Rōpata Wahawaha himself, had fought strenuously on the side of the government.

Eventually the government troops had won, and by this time there was peace. But the East Coast tribes were still greatly divided, for the fighting had split families and subtribes, and relatives had sometimes fought against each other. And there was another matter. Although Rōpata Wahawaha had been honored by the queen for his military role, he feared that the government might use the fighting as an excuse to seize tribal lands in retaliation, as it so often did on such occasions.

So, Rōpata Wahawaha held a great meeting with much ceremony and symbolism. After the preliminary speeches and dances of welcome and reply, Mohi Tūrei, an Anglican clergyman who was also steeped in Ngāti Porou tradition, asked God for guidance and deliverance and sang a long song making appropriate reference to the recent events. Then, after a speech by Rōpata, there was a public, ceremonial collection of donations for the funding of schools and churches. The table where the money was placed stood on the *marae* (ceremonial courtyard) alongside a tall flagstaff from which flew an enormous flag that had been presented to Rōpata by the government. As they made their donations, all those present walked beneath this flag, and in this way they reaffirmed their loyalty to the Crown. Some were former enemies of Rōpata, rebels he himself had taken prisoner. When they walked beneath the flag, they were forgiven.

On the following morning, when the tribes and subtribes were seated around the marae in the places assigned to them, 170 calabashes of potted birds, and more calabashes containing pork, were carried onto the marae. The bearers, as they brought them forward, recited the appropriate ritual chants (which, as we have seen, were believed to have been recited for the first time by their ancestor Awapaka and his men, when they landed in the *Horouta* and initiated all the practices associated with bird hunting). Carried onto the marae with these calabashes, and prominently displayed among them, was a rock that was draped with fine garments. This was "the stone calabash."

After the food for the feast had been consecrated and blessed by the Reverend Mohi Tūrei, Major Rōpata Wahawaha rose to his feet. In a masterful speech, he gave a detailed account of the story of the *Horouta*. He recalled, among much else, that Pāwa's party, when they failed to meet the *Horouta* at the mouth of the Waiapu River, had left there the calabash of potted birds they had intended to present to the crew of the ship. He remarked that this calabash, named Toetoe (Left-over), "is still standing there now; it's a rock." Next, Rōpata described how the *Horouta*, which was thought to have been wrecked, was in the end raised up, hauled ashore, and mended, and how it then sailed off once more.

Then, coming to his main point, he made a detailed comparison between the fate of the *Horouta* and the unhappy circumstances in which his tribe had found themselves. "As for this broken vessel, it is you yourself, Ngāti Porou."[15] Just as the crew of the *Horouta* had been warned to take only one kind of food on board, so "for this vessel also the law was laid down: there was to be one God . . . and the law [of the land] was alone to be the source of proper conduct and well-being." Yet, many men had turned away from the one true God and followed the Hauhau faith. As a consequence, "the God who guarded this ship turned right away, and his people were left to experience trials. And that was how our vessel came to be broken."

God did not allow their tribal "ship" to be entirely broken, however. Rōpata continued:

> And that indeed is the reason for our gathering. All the peoples have gathered here to bind up the broken parts of our ship. And that is the reason for the stone calabash which has been brought forward here: it is in memory of the breaking of that ship, the Horouta. The stone calabash did not then achieve its purpose. But on the breaking of this vessel [that is, Ngāti Porou's recent tribulations], it has been made to achieve its purpose, being brought to the workmen [that is, the present meeting] so that they could eat. We, in like manner, have fully achieved our purpose, accepting God and the law.

In this way Rōpata identified Ngāti Porou both with their damaged ancestral ship and with the workmen who mended it: they were the ones who had been "broken," and at the same time they were the ones who could fix this problem. And he did this in the context of the feast he was presenting to his guests.

In his long speech there are many more parallels between the trials suffered by those who came on the *Horouta* and the circumstances in which his tribe found themselves. While his identification of Ngāti Porou with their ancestral ship was certainly conventional and traditional,[16] the ways in which he developed this idea to fit his people's new circumstances show much ingenuity and originality. Yet, this approach is in itself traditional. Orators have always been flexible and ingenious in the uses they have made of myths, songs, and proverbs.

Ngāti Porou, like other tribes, were familiar with such analogies, and so responded to them strongly. The Māori-language newspapers published in the latter decades of the nineteenth century are full of references to the vessels to which the different tribes trace their origins, and these references very often occur in the course of reported speeches.

I should like to mention, briefly, a second occasion in which the migration traditions were recounted for specific purposes. Again it relates to the *Horouta*, and to Ngāti Porou. This was not a speech exactly, but a published letter inviting the readers of a Māori-language periodical to be present at the ceremonial opening of a new meetinghouse in the Waiapu Valley. The conventions, however, are those of oratory. The year is 1902.[17]

Having greeted their readers and issued their invitation, the writers of the letter request their guests to bring with them donations to help pay off the debts that remain after the building of the meetinghouse. Appealing to tribal sentiment, they do this by recalling the first episode in the story of the *Horouta*, the one in which Kahukura unties his carry-belt and takes from it the preserved kūmara that so pleases Toi. In translation, their remarks are as follows.

> *Tread as you come, in the footprints of your ancestor, Kahukura, which lie before you in every place. And bring also his belt, which had preserved kūmara inside—and so it delighted Toi's throat, and he went across the water to the other side. Enough: the food inside that belt is now silver, gold, and notes.*

In this way the speakers are identifying their guests with Kahukura and themselves with Toi, who needed and welcomed what his honored guest had to bring. Here again, we see that orators could be secure in the knowledge that their audience was familiar with this famous story, and familiar too with such reference to it. The tradition of the *Horouta* unified and energized the people of Ngāti Porou. Although some of the uses previously made of the story must have been disappearing by 1902, its power survived in oratory.

The Story of Paikea

Last, there is the second of the ancestral journeys from Hawaiki that the tohunga Mohi Ruatapu records in his writings. I must deal with this more briefly than with the *Horouta*, even though Paikea is one of the most celebrated of the ancestors of Ngāti Porou. As much as any, he is the one who represents their *mana* (prestige, power) and unifies their subtribes.

The story begins back in Hawaiki, where the powerful rangatira Uenuku has seven score sons.[18] A ship has been built and is to be taken out to sea for the first time. All the sons adorn themselves for this voyage, and Uenuku anoints their tapu heads. But when one of the sons, Ruatapu, presents himself to Uenuku, he is rejected: his head cannot be anointed because his mother is only a slave woman, a captive taken in battle.

Greatly shamed, Ruatapu plans a spectacular revenge. He goes weeping to the new ship, and he bores a hole, then plugs it. Later, the seven score sons take the ship out to sea, and Ruatapu keeps urging them to go further out. Then when the land is lost to sight, he pulls the plug from the hole. The vessel fills with water, and the young men look in vain for the bailer: Ruatapu has hidden it. They bail with their hands, but it is no use. Their ship sinks, and they are swimming in the ocean.

Ruatapu by this time has assumed a demonic aspect. He pursues his brothers and he drowns them, one by one, until in the end only Paikea is left.[19] The two brothers are swimming around in the ocean, each trying to drown the other. But in the end, Ruatapu acknowledges that he cannot kill Paikea; his mana and the mana of the ritual chants he recites make this impossible. So Ruatapu bids farewell to his brother, and Paikea sets out to swim to land. As he swims, he recites a long and famous ritual chant to strengthen and warm himself. When this chant ends, a taniwha appears and he is carried on its back. This taniwha takes the form of a whale.

Paikea finally lands at the northern end of the Bay of Plenty (where the *Horouta* also made landfall). He names this place Ahuahu, after a place in Hawaiki; or rather, he thinks at first that he has returned safely to Hawaiki and is now in the place of this name. He then makes his way southward, and settles for a while in Whakatāne, marrying a woman of that place. But he does not like it there, no matter how much he tries, and after the birth of two children he moves further south.

Eventually, he reaches Te Kautuku, which is in Ngāti Porou territory and north of the Waiapu Valley. There he comes across Huturangi, the daughter of an early ancestor named Whiro-nui, bathing in a pool called Te Roto-o-tahe. He marries her, and for a while he lives there with his father-in-law. Then he again continues south, searching for a better place. He takes with him his wife and his father-in-law.

In the end Paikea comes to a place which satisfies him, because it resembles almost exactly a place he has known in Hawaiki. He names it Whāngārā, after this place; its full name is Whāngārā-i-tawhiti, "Whāngārā-in-the-distance" (or perhaps "Whāngārā-from-the-distance"). He stays there, and he names each of the hills after the ones in the original Whāngārā. In this way, the region known as Whāngārā is very closely associated with the homeland of Hawaiki, almost identified with it.

Paikea is perhaps the most important early ancestor of Ngāti Porou. The mana which he revealed in surviving Ruatapu's attack in the water, in swimming across the ocean, and in calling up the taniwha has been a source of great pride. His marriage to Huturangi, daughter of Whiro-nui, provides a link between subtribes in different parts of the region; and the lineages that go back to him and his wife include many famous people, not least Porourangi himself, after whom Ngāti Porou take their name.

Because of his mana, Paikea was conspicuously placed upon a large carved house which was built in about 1860 at Ūawa (Tolaga Bay). This house honored, and was named after, one of Paikea's descendants, a leading rangatira named Te Kani a Takirau who had died a few years previously. Paikea was chosen as the *tekoteko*, the figure which stands above the bargeboards at the front of the house, a visual reminder of the ancestor who validates the chiefly lineages and unites the community.

A famous *haka* (or dance song) celebrating Paikea was composed for the opening of this house. This haka recalls how he swam in the ocean, quoting from the chant he sang as he did so, and it speaks of his encounter with Huturangi. It is still often performed today; and it celebrates not only Paikea's exploits, but everything that followed from them. I will bring his story—and this chapter—to an end with this haka. The words sung by the chorus are italicized.[20]

> Uia mai koia, whakahuatia ake, ko wai te whare nei?
> *Ko Te Kani!*
> Ko wai te tekoteko kei runga?
> *Ko Paikea, ko Paikea!*
> Whakakau Paikea,
> *Hei!*
> Whakakau he tipua,
> *Hei!*
> Whakakau he taniwha,
> *Hei!*
> Ka ū Paikea ki Ahuahu,
> *Pākia!*
> Kei te whitia koe—
> *Ko Kahutia-te-rangi, auē!*
> *Me awhi ō ringa ki te tamāhine*
> *A Te Whiro-nui, auē!*
> *Nāna i noho Te Roto-o-tahe, auē, auē,*
> *He koruru koe, e koro ē!*

> Oh ask and you'll be told, "Who is this house?"
> *It's Te Kani!*
> Who is the tekoteko up above?
> *He's Paikea, Paikea!*

Make Paikea swim,
Hei!
Make him swim, he's supernatural,
Hei!
Make him swim, he's a taniwha,
Hei!
Paikea landed at Ahuahu,
Pākia!
You've crossed over,
Kahutia-te-rangi!
Let your arms embrace
Te Whiro-nui's daughter, alas—
She who was in Te Roto-o-tahe, alas, alas—
You're a tekoteko [now], old man!

Notes

1. For an initial examination of the migration traditions from this point of view, see my *Hawaiki: A New Approach to Maori Tradition* (Christchurch, New Zealand: Canterbury University Press, 1985).

2. The East Coast, as a capitalized expression, is a term referring to one particular region on the eastern shore of the North Island.

3. Both writers have been edited and translated by Anaru Reedy. They are: *Ngā Kōrero a Mohi Ruatapu: The Writings of Mohi Ruatapu* (Christchurch, New Zealand: Canterbury University Press, 1993); and *Ngā Kōrero a Pita Kāpiti: The Teachings of Pita Kāpiti* (Christchurch, New Zealand: Canterbury University Press, 1997). My discussion draws upon these works.

4. The significance of Hawaiki in traditional Māori thought is discussed in Orbell, *Hawaiki*, 13–20.

5. For the first part of the *Horouta* story, down to the birdhunting episode, I have mainly followed the account in Mohi Tūrei, "Te hui ki Mataahu," *Te waka Maori o Niu Tirani* 8 (17) (1872): 109–18.

6. J. Prytz Johansen, *Studies in Maori Rites and Myths* (Copenhagen: Munksgaard, 1958), 112–28. This analysis makes use of a number of texts relating to the *Horouta* story and to kūmara planting rituals, in particular some early translations that were published from the writings of Mohi Ruatapu and Pita Kāpiti.

7. Elsewhere in his writings, Johansen stresses this important point. See, for example, his *The Maori and His Religion in Its Non-Ritualistic Aspects* (Copenhagen: Munksgaard, 1954), 147–84. In this respect, and in many others, I am indebted to his work.

8. Since most of the population was in the North Island, most of the traditions concerning migrations from Hawaiki have the tribal ancestors landing on the North Island rather than the South Island.

9. The tribes tracing descent to the ship named *Te Arawa* belong to this volcanic region. See Orbell, *Hawaiki*, 118–19.

10. For example, see Margaret Orbell, *The Natural World of the Maori* (Auckland: Bateman, 1985), 51, 54. In Māori thought, small things in many contexts were tapu. It must be for this reason that Paepae-Aotea, rather than Whakaari itself, was highly tapu. Paepae-Aotea was a home of taniwha, water spirits, which sometimes were the spirits of ancestors. Its name means, literally, "Threshold of Aotea," and Aotea was an old name for the North Island; Andrew Sharp, "New Zealand, naming of," in A. H. McLintock, ed., *An Encyclopedia of New Zealand* (Wellington: R. E. Owen, 1966), vol. 2.

11. In other ways, too, they represented different symbolic spheres; Orbell, *Natural World*, 38–40.

12. In the writings of Mohi Ruatapu, this same chant was recited by Tāne when, in the beginning, he separated Rangi the sky and Papa the earth.

13. Many Māori saw parallels between their experience and the experiences of biblical peoples, and there were those who decided that the Māori were the twelfth tribe of Israel.

But nothing in the Bible actually contradicted the Māori traditions concerning their tribal origins in Hawaiki.

14. A full account of this meeting was published by Mohi Tūrei in a Māori-language periodical (Tūrei, "Te hui ki Mataahu"), and my account comes mainly from this source.

15. This remark and those quoted below are my translations from Rōpata's speech, as reported by Mohi Tūrei ("Te hui ki Mataahu").

16. Similar identifications of a tribe and their ancestral ship were frequently made in oratory in other areas also, and still are today.

17. See N. Kopuka and R. Tawhiwhi, "He pānui kawanga whare nui . . . ," *Te Pipiwharauroa* 58 (1902): 8.

18. I am mainly following Mohi Ruatapu's writings here.

19. Paikea, it is generally claimed, is a name taken at this point by Kahutia-te-rangi, the eldest and highest-ranking of Uenuku's sons. There is also a rare word, *paikea*, which apparently refers to a sea monster, or to a whale.

20. Information about the house and the song is taken mostly from W. J. Phillipps, "Carved Maori Houses of the Eastern Districts of the North Island," *Records of the Dominion Museum* 1 (1944): 107–8. A few words in the song are of uncertain meaning. The word "whitia" may be a pun, meaning both "crossed over" (from Hawaiki) and "transformed" (from Kahutia-te-rangi to Paikea).

Discussion

Diane Bell

Margaret, I'm very interested in following up on something you alluded to as you were talking about the various kinds of ancestors. There are the original ancestors that all Māori people acknowledge in genealogies as being ancestors, and then there are these tribal ones who give identity to specific areas of land and specific facets of their local, social organization. Do they all appear in genealogies?

Margaret Orbell

Each tribe has its own collection of genealogies, and the tribes are fairly well distinct from each other. Obviously, there are intermediate regions and so on, but basically each tribe, each people, has its own genealogies. So each tribe will begin with these universal figures and then, as you go down the genealogies a little bit, you come to the ancestors who came from Hawaiki and established the tribal identity.

Diane Bell

So how is the link made from those universal ancestors to the tribal ancestors in the genealogy? What's the narrative that connects those two?

Margaret Orbell

That's a good question. The connection is rather vague. Sometimes it can be traced back. The father of Paikea was Uenuku, a powerful man. This was in Hawaiki, and Uenuku's genealogy could be traced back there. But in other cases the distant ancestors are just known to have been in Hawaiki and no direct connection is made. Their origin in Hawaiki must have been felt to be sufficient.

Jacob Olupona

I'm interested in the discussion of myth and history in your paper. Your point is well taken that the episodes in the stories do not make good sense if you regard them as history, but the narrative makes excellent sense when it is regarded as a religious tradition. What I would like to know is how the Māori themselves deal with history. It seems to me that they do regard those myths, those old traditions, as history. The reason that I am asking this question is that for a long time Africans could not reconstruct their pre-colonial history precisely because the oral traditions that are so important were regarded as nonhistorical, as very illogical, as total nonsense. So when the Europeans were dealing with African history, and dealing specifically with these oral traditions, it was impossible to write history. But as soon as the African historians came in to recover these oral traditions and to say, "This is history for us," then of course you had a lot of history textbooks coming out based on these oral traditions. Is that process going on now in your country?

Margaret Orbell

May I ask a question first? What did—or do—your historians do with episodes that could be characterized as supernatural? How do they cope with them?

Jacob Olupona

Most of them would accept them as real. Because they take them from the perspective of the storyteller, they regard them as real. Some of those stories even incorporate Islam and Christianity in ways that those two religions were not able to describe themselves.

Margaret Orbell

There's no problem, of course, when people can still accept supernatural episodes. There, you have people functioning within the religious tradition, and there is no problem. So they can be regarded as history in that context. The situation is rather complicated in New Zealand because some people have this unquestioning, uncomplicated attitude to stories like that of Paikea on his whale, and others do not. I was reading something the other day where somebody was saying, "Well, clearly what happened was that Paikea left Hawaiki in a ship which was called the Whale." So attitudes vary on this point, but it is now difficult in Aotearoa for many Māori people to accept the story with its supernatural aspects. It's a fluid situation.

Jacob Olupona

So that means that it is not going to be history in the strict sense?

Margaret Orbell

It's a history of ideas, though, isn't it? It's a religious history. There are those who are very much involved with it on this basis because it's a powerful unifying force. Many people do still feel the power of the myth without quite . . .

Jacob Olupona

. . . believing it?

Margaret Orbell

Yes.

Laurel Kendall

I was struck by this business of Christian definitions, by the power of ideas that come in with certain political power behind them that then shape how people choose to think about their tradition for many, many years. In Korea the process was somewhat different. You had a generation of missionaries coming out of theology schools where they were told that behind their indigenous religions were mistakes and perversions of a primitive monotheism, that people had it right once but that it had been corrupted. So things were written about Korean religion in the early twentieth century on that premise that led to some distortions that were perpetrated once Korean Christians found their voice. A highly dubious cultural history is privileged over actual religious practices, and particularly women's practices, on the ground. My point is that these histories are very complex, that the Christian filter is nowhere uniform, but it's certainly a crucial factor.

Margaret Orbell

Absolutely. The Māori were lucky that the missionaries did not think of the stories about tribal ancestors and voyages from Hawaiki as religious. It was much easier for the Māori to accept Christianity because they only had to distance themselves—though not completely—from figures like Tāne, the very earliest ancestors. There was no need to distance themselves, at least in the nineteenth century, from the early tribal ancestors who were just as powerful and important, because these were considered "historical" figures.

Enlightenment, Ancestors, and Primordiality
A Note on Modernity and Memory

Charles H. Long

I would like to make three moves in this paper. First, I want to say something about how the meaning of primal traditions and ancestors came to be a part of my intellectual ancestry. I then want to move to the phenomena of ancestors in those cultures where this meaning is venerated. Finally, I should like to say a word or two about the intellectual and existential impact of these two kinds of ancestry.

The Story of a Friendship

Now to the first point. I begin with the story of a friendship of two Parisian intellectuals, Maurice Leenhardt and Lucien Lévy-Bruhl. Leenhardt was a Protestant missionary who spent more than three decades in Melanesia; Lévy-Bruhl was a professor of modern philosophy at the Sorbonne. The friendship was rich; it expressed regard for the personal as well as the intellectual dimensions of the two men. This friendship also defines a moment in the study of religion. Maurice Leenhardt has left us an important legacy in his work *Do Kamo: Person and Myth in the Melanesian World*,[1] and Lucien Lévy-Bruhl is remembered best by his books on the primal traditions, *Primitives and the Supernatural, How Natives Think,* and *The Soul of the Primitive*. An abiding meaning of this intellectual friendship and an important document in the study of religion was the posthumous publication of Lévy-Bruhl's *Carnets*, which is partly due to his conversations and associations with Leenhardt, and in which he modifies his former notions of a "primitive mentality." Though there have been relationships between the scholar and the missionary before—and in some cases the scholar and missionary have been the same person—in this case the relation-ship is more complex. While both men are concerned with religion, they ap-proach the matter from very different perspectives. Leenhardt was a confessing Protestant missionary in the field, while Lévy-Bruhl, who was from a Jewish background, was part of that sociological tradition in France that included Marcel Mauss, Emile Durkheim, Henri Hubert, and Marcel Granet; the tradi-tion is still carried on in the brilliant analyses of primal traditions by Claude Lévi-Strauss. In addition to the sociological and anthropological contexts, Lévy-Bruhl lectured and wrote major treatises on modern philosophy, dealing especially with Leibniz, Jacob, Comte, and the English empiricists. His fame is based, however, on the six volumes devoted to the analysis of the notion and meaning of the "primitive mind"; he is the philosopher of primitive mentality par excellence.

As rare as this relationship was in Paris between the Great Wars, it is equally complex. It is Lévy-Bruhl, the philosopher, who created the Institut d'Ethno-logie at the Sorbonne and it was the missionary, Maurice Leenhardt, who pre-ceded Claude Lévi-Strauss in the Chair of Comparative Religions of Non-Liter-ate Peoples at the Collège de France! This relationship, this criss-crossing of orientations, vocations, and disciplines, raises one of the central problems re-lated to the meaning of the study of religion in the modern period. The seeming confusion of disciplines, with a confessing missionary becoming a professor in the neo-positivistic tradition of French ethnology and a professor of modern philosophy devoting most of his career to the study of primitives, bears closer scrutiny, for it evokes questions about modernity, religion, and the primitives.

From an academic point of view we are accustomed to keep separate the advocacy of a particular religion from the more "objective" study of religion, yet it is the missionary, Leenhardt, who spent more than twenty years in the field, and the scholar, Lévy-Bruhl, who was the armchair propounder of theories about the nature of the "primitive." It is precisely this curious relationship that might shed some light on the study of religion at this time. I leave this story for the moment; I shall return to it at the end of this presentation and evoke certain nuances from the story of this friendship.

Who Are the Ancestors?

Professor Max Gluckman observed in 1942 that in "Zululand, on the whole, the ancestral cult has largely died out while beliefs in sorcery and magic have sur-vived."[2] Subsequent critical studies have shown that Gluckman was only partly right in this assessment. For the most part he was referring to those urbanized Zulus who had been subjected to some form of western schooling.

It is clear that the meaning of the ancestors is closely related to the structure of the Zulu cosmos. While the ancestors are in the place of the dead, they are equally present in the mundane details of the living and not simply evoked or remembered in funerary rites and ceremonies. Axel-Ivar Berglund has wisely suggested that we should avoid the term "ancestor" and the phrase "ancestor cult," for they give the wrong impression of what is really taking place in cultures of this kind. He suggested the use of "shade" instead.

> *One reason for not using the word ancestor is that the English idiom suggests ascendants who are dead (according to Western concepts) and, as a result, there is a distance between them and the living. There is, in other words, a separateness between the living and the dead. This is not descriptive of Zulu concepts, which . . . assume a very close and intimate relationship and association within the lineage between the departed and their survivors. To quote an informant: "My father is departed, but he is," the idea being that the father is present and active although he is no longer living as the speaker was."[3]*

Berglund's work on the Zulu shows how the shades are expressed in a direct and indirect way throughout the society of the Zulus. They have a force and power in the determination and structure of gender, in healing practices, in divination, and in the understanding and possession of the Zulu land. The notion of the role of ancestors or shades in the possession of the land is equally strong among the cultures of West Africa. Jack Goody's *Death, Property, and the Ancestors* is a monograph dedicated to the funerary rituals among the LoDaaga. He shows how the rituals of death are directly related to inheritance and to the continuation and integrity of the lineages and how property as land and the power to influence is made a responsibility for the community in the midst of the breaking of the lineages by the fact of death.

Peter Metcalf has remarked about what almost every casual observer from the modern west notes when, in commenting on the Berawan, he says,

> *Nowadays, the Berwan speak of their religion as* adèd luna *(luna = old), or in Malay* adat lama. *But this is a new term designed to distinguish traditional religious practices from Christianity, which has secured many converts in the last twenty years. The concept of* adèd *is wide but precise, and I*

*can find no exact English equivalent. It is simply "the way of doing things,"
and the* adat lama, *the traditional religion, is the old way of doing things.*[4]

With this statement Metcalf introduces us to the entire round of funerary rites and what he refers to as the eschatology of the world of the dead and its bearing upon the living.

1) The natural and the supernatural world are inseparable; each is intrinsically a part of the other.

2) Natural entities are endowed with spirit and with spiritually based power.

3) Humans and natural entities are involved in a constant spiritual interchange that profoundly affects human behavior.

4) The spiritual interchange between humans and nature is dominated by hostile forces.

Let me conclude this section at this point, since we have already heard detailed discussions of the meaning of ancestors from our colleagues. We had the advantage of hearing from many colleagues who were members of the cultures that they discussed. I shall attempt to make an analogy to that of my colleagues by trying to evoke my ancestors, intellectually and personally, out of the cultures of which I am a part. At this juncture I return to some of the echoes of the first section.

Ancestors and Modernity

For all sorts of reasons the brilliant group of scholars centered around the Durkheimian school were from a Jewish tradition. They were not practicing Jews, most of them being agnostic or atheistic in their orientation. They had accepted the modern intellectual option outlined and carried through in the Western Enlightenment, thus establishing a record of scholarship in the study and analysis of other cultures, other places, and other times. Their work was, however, contextualized within the problematics of modernity itself. This problematic was not of their own making. In the French tradition it can be seen as early as the work of Alexis de Tocqueville in his *Democracy in America,* where in the midst of his querulous admiration and wonder about the new democracy in North America, he constantly reflected upon the long-term viability of a people or a culture that had no ancestors, who had nothing old, who had no memories, who could evoke no supernatural meanings in their habitation of the land. In reflections of this kind, de Tocqueville had reference not only to the practices of the Americans but equally to the ideological position of the Jeffersonians, who were most radical in their position regarding the ancestors. They in fact carried on a war against the ancestors—and this is not simply in reference to the Revolutionary War. It was equally a war against setting up and institutionalizing a cult of ancestors. They were against inheritance; the dead should have no power or influence over the living! These Jeffersonians would turn over in their graves if they knew that they were being venerated in their country by being referred to as Founding Fathers![5]

But back to the sociologists. Durkheim, in his scholarly work, was concerned with this same sort of issue. In *Anomie* he raised the issue of the relationship of meaninglessness as a modern cultural phenomenon to the issue of tradition and memory—the locus of religion. One might read his work, as well as those of the Durkheimians, as an attempt to evoke within the structures of modernity some echo of the meaning of tradition by introducing the world of modernity to their imaginative reconstruction and to the sources of the religious sentiment in other cultures. Lévy-Bruhl attempted to decipher the primitive mind vis-à-vis the mind of modernity as expressed by Kant, Hume, or Hobbes. Was there another kind or type of mentality, or did human mentality constitute a universal order of being? If the latter, where has the capacity of our memory gone—the ability to know the ancestors, the presence of them in our lives, and the constitutive meaning of power?

This is not simply an intellectual problem. The modern world is a world that is simultaneously a world in which millions of people have been displaced from their ancestral traditions. Now, this displacement has not been as other displacements, wherein one culture had the option of accepting the ancestors of the new culture or cultures. The world has been displaced by a culture of modernity that denies the efficacy of all ancestors. The Christian tradition, as part of this spread of modernity, has presented several cultures with the option of being "born only from above." The adjudication of the issues of the land, kinship lineages, the world of the dead and their well-being and influence in the world of the living—all of this is left to chance.

For my culture, a part of the African diaspora in the modern world situated in the United States, a country with a decidedly Calvinist and Enlightenment orientation, the meaning of ancestry has always been a social, political, and religious problem. Unlike the situation in the Caribbean and South America, there was a conscious effort made to destroy the efficacious meaning of the African ancestors in North America. Our ancestry was directed to that of the country of our enslavement, with little space or time given to the imagination or creation of meaning for that space that the ancestors formerly occupied. For different reasons this situation is becoming the lot of several other peoples and cultures in the world. In my case I cannot, in any simple or directly authentic way, attach myself to the African ancestors; the ancestors must be truly my ancestors, related to the intimacies and existential structures of my life, and not simply ideological contructions.

What can ancestors mean in the anti-ancestral traditions of modernity? It is clear that even in the cultures of modernity and displacement there is still a yearning for the ancestors. This yearning expresses itself in sentimental and demonic forms, through recourse to racisms, jingoisms, and nationalisms of various sorts. These modes attempt to use the valuation of the ancestral orientation to set forth the most virulent forms of modernity. Nevertheless, the space for the ancestor in the human mode of being still remains.

What meanings may be gleaned from the cult of ancestors? Ancestors define a primordial and existential structure of intimacy. In traditional societies they are ritualized at the times of creation, initiation, marriages, and death, and the many other mundane relationships surrounding the extensions of these events into the ongoing life of society. All of these situations define the necessary exchanges that must take place among and between human beings. Ancestors prevent us from forgetting the vulnerable but necessary risk involved in all human exchanges. They also remind us of the death of the flesh and the perduring values of the bones that become the datum and our trace, and in this sense the literal meaning of "datum" as the *giveness* of the mystery of human community and generation.

While the modern period has been anti-ancestral, it has not been devoid of exchanges. It is out of the order of these exchanges that a new meaning of ancestry must emerge, an ancestry that must take account of the mixture of exchanges, the negativity of these exchanges, and the ambiguity of the ancestry of this tradition. We cannot deal with the meaning of ancestors as simply a sentimental survival of a former period. Our ancestors may no longer be those beneficient shades and elders who have presided over the well-being of our communities; they are no longer the unambiguous *la donne* described so well by Marcel Mauss in his classic text of the same title. But neither should we allow them to be trivialized and voided of their value by the ideological interpretive schemes of either Marxists or the capitalists, who evacuate the seriousness of exchanges into the sterile language of commodities. There are, indeed, ancestors of modernity. They need our help to be, and we their help to survive.

"We are what we remember, so the historian and his [sic] art of remembering are of paramount importance to all societies. They are especially important in our societies which are modernizing madly."[6] What does it mean to have ancestors today, and what does it mean to exercise a critical act of memory in regard to the past? We are, all of us, products of several strands of memories, traditions, ancestries. Our pasts, individually and collectively, do not define singularities and purities; our ancestral traditions are composite, mixed, contextualized. All of our ancestors have undergone the complexity of exchanges of goods, services, bodies, meanings—that entire complex that is the heritage of the world of modernity.

We can do no better than to honor all of our ancestors with a critical account of their sojourns as living actors in the world. As scholars and historians this means that we must create the possibility of memory so that a new kind of history can emerge for our future. To return to the first part of this essay, we must combine the evangelism of a Maurice Leenhardt with the critical skepticism of a Lévy-Bruhl or Marcel Mauss. We must revere our specific traditions, not simply by preserving them in their purity, but seeing them equally as modes of intimate imagination of that chaotic past through which all our immediate ancestors lived.

Notes

1.See Maurice Leenhardt, *Do Kamo: Person and Myth in the Melanesian World* (Chicago: University of Chicago Press, 1979). Note especially the introduction by Vincent Crapanzano. For a biography of Leenhardt, see James Clifford, *Person and Myth: Maurice Leenhardt in the Melanesian World* (Berkeley and Los Angeles: University of California Press, 1982).

2. Max Gluckman, "Some Processes of Social Change Illustrated from Zululand," *African Studies* (Johannesburg) 1 (1942): 258ff.

3. Axel-Ivar Berglund, *Zulu Thought-Patterns and Symbolism* (London: C. Hurst, 1976), 29.

4. Peter Metcalf, *A Borneo Journey into Death: Berawan Eschatology from Its Rituals* (Philadelphia: University of Pennsylvania, 1982), 5.

5. See "Introduction: Modern Ancestors," xix–xx, above.

6. Albert Wendt, "Novelists and Historians and the Art of Remembering," in Antony Hooper et al. eds., *Class and Culture in the South Pacific* (Auckland: Centre for Pacific Studies, University of Auckland; Suva: Institute of Pacific Studies, University of the South Pacific, 1987); quoted in Vilsoni Hereniko, *Woven Gods: Female Clowns and Power in Rotuma*, Pacific Island Monograph Series, 12 (Honolulu: University of Hawaii Press, 1995), 131.

Discussion

Rubellite Johnson

Those of us who know what it is like to practice ancestor worship have not said much about the immense obligation that is entailed, especially in the practice of rituals. Hawaiian children often have to make a decision when they get to school about whether they are going to continue all those *kapus* or let them go. Many simply decide that they are not going to go back home again. They run away.

Charles Long

The fact that it is ritualized means that you don't always have to have a powerful sense of meaning every time you perform the ritual. That's the whole point of ritual, to keep you from having to invest all your time in producing meaning. In my paper I mentioned Lévi-Strauss and the Jewish intellectual group in Paris. It's very important, I think, to realize they were all Jews, and that they were a certain kind of atheist or agnostic Jewish intellectual. They grew up in a ritualized culture right within modernity. They later gave it up, but they never forgot it. Among the essays that Lévi-Strauss wrote was a piece on table manners. He wrote about his grandfather who was a rabbi and all the rituals they had when they sat down to a meal. Lévi-Strauss gave all that up years earlier, but he was able to come back to it in his writing and ask, "What was my grandfather doing? What was that all about? Why do human beings find it necessary to live a ritualized life?" In the process, he was able to address a whole range of other important issues. So the question is not whether to give up a practice. The crucial questions are how we want to think about the practices we engage in, and what can be evoked from a practice as a basis for thinking. It seems so wrong-headed to suppose that we think about things first and then go out and do them. Ritual is one of the things that prevent us from thinking that we have to produce meaning all on our own. That's the power of the ritual, or the power of ancestry that provokes the ritual act.

Rubellite Johnson

Your comments earlier about the displacement that has occurred in recent historic times seem to me to be related to the tensions that exist today within the Hawaiian community. The present political situation is very difficult and you find a lot of different responses to it even among the Hawaiians here in the room. For me there is appeal both in my cultural heritage and in the Jeffersonian project. New avenues of thought and action have opened up to me because of my western training and education. Yet there is always this pressure for Hawaiians—and for most native people these days—to be completely pure, to be true to our aboriginal religion. But you can't actually return to the past, and most of us probably don't really want to do that. I don't want to give up all the other things I have gained through contact with other societies of the world.

Charles Long

I have a curious way of seeing the world I was born into. There are no pure traditions as far as I can tell. To put it another way, it's not an issue of purity and danger; purity is danger. When purity is invoked in relationship to a people or society or culture, you are already in danger. What is being denied there is the fundamental, historical materiality of the modern world, which has to do with displacements and with a wide variety of exchanges. So if there are "primal traditions," they are traditions that must come to grips with the traditions of modernity before they do anything else. There is no way to jump over that and get back to some original tradition. In that sense, you simply can't go home again. To go home again means going through the traditions that separated you from home and, unless you go back through those traditions, you will never get home. Maybe it is clearer if I change metaphors and say you can't fly home. You can't simply start here and jump back over there. I always have this argument with my friends who are African Americans, who feel that if they get on an airplane and go to Africa, they have become a part of Africa again. I tell them, "No, we have to go back to Mississippi, Alabama, Georgia, New Orleans, and all those other places first and work through that." That's the hard way home. If you don't go home the hard way, then the place you get to will not really be home.

It's in that sense that I am looking in a critical way at modernity and trying to move away from the temptation to think that there is an easy way of dealing with ancestors. My ancestors lived very ambiguous, mixed up, strange, almost unrecorded histories. I know about it and it's in my culture and in my bones. That's the only resource I have for doing anything. I can't act as if that doesn't exist, but I find that it's a great temptation for people who have been colonized or oppressed during the modern period to think that there is an easy way out. I don't think there is. It's an extremely difficult problem. But at the same time, it's the only way out for them, and possibly for everyone else on the planet as well.

Encounters with Korean Ancestors
Rituals, Dreams, and Stories

Laurel Kendall

"You must waste quite a lot of time bowing and apologising to the family spooks," said Peter. "You should just walk slap through them as Gerald does. It's much simpler, and doesn't seem to do either party any harm."

"You needn't talk," Peter," said the Duchess. "I distinctly saw you raise your hat to Lady Susan one day on the terrace."

"Oh, come, Mother! That's pure invention. Why on earth should I be wearing a hat on the terrace?"

—Dorothy L. Sayers, *Busman's Honeymoon*

There is method in so frivolous an introductory quotation. From another time and place, Lord Peter Wimsey and his mother strike some of the notes that will be sounded in this paper. Their behavior would probably be comprehensible to a Korean shaman who might be horrified at the notion of "slap walking" the ancestors without provocation, but would immediately empathize over time spent "bowing and apologising to the family spooks." The terms of the relationship between ancestral Wimseys and their still quick descendants are cast according to notions of proper and improper behavior among living Wimseys—Lord Peter would not tip his hat to the deceased Lady Susan on the terrace because Lord Peter would never wear a hat on the terrace. This, too, has Korean resonances, as does a process whereby ancestral appearances become the stuff of family stories, sometimes with an element of playfulness. I am concerned here with the ways in which the presence of the dead is realized among the living, less with the formal rites of ancestor veneration than with the memories, dreams, and appearances in shaman seances that enable the living to construct particular remembered dead as "characters" in the stories they tell about themselves.

The Korean term for "ancestor" (*chosang*) is not fixed. In formal rites (*chesa*) performed according to the ritual manual, the ancestor is a shadowy presence somewhere beyond the curling incense smoke, the object of ritualized demonstrations of filial piety as the source of virtue, family reputation, and life itself. The ancestor who speaks through the shaman's lips is an immediate presence, sobbing, complaining, and often accusing the living of neglect. These are the ancestors whose troubled touch brings illness, whose anger causes misfortune. These discrepant images of "ancestor," derived from the very different contexts of their ritual realization, have caused some scholars to posit that men, who perform rites of ancestor veneration, and women, who participate in shaman rituals, have utterly discrepant views of the ancestors.[1] Anthropological studies of Korea have also varied in the manner of their defining "ancestors" as the objects of social inquiry, agreeing only that the ancestors—and by extension, restless ancestors and ghosts—are a proper subject of study in a society that values kin ties as a locus of social and moral worth.

Following and complementing the work of China anthropologists, anthropologists of Korea have described who the proper ancestors are and who is entitled to claim them, and how notions of "ancestor" and "descendant" map lines of kinship and inheritance and validate status through privileged antecedents.[2] We have some sense of how these notions, and the Confucian ritual idioms through which they are expressed, took root in Korea during the Choson period and how they were manipulated in the creation and maintenance of national and local elites.[3] We know that at the island and coastal boundaries of the Korean world, where inheritance in land is not the primary determinant of status and survival, notions of "ancestor" and "descendant" are manipulated to foster local solidarity and distribute the burden of ritual feasts among a greater number of kinsmen.[4] We have learned that ancestor veneration is being transformed in the crucible of contemporary urban life[5] and reinterpreted in Christian practice.[6] And we know something about the unofficial ancestors, the ancestors (chosang) so named but not so properly categorized, who emerge from outside the tidy boundaries of agnatic kinship to exert claims upon daughters, sisters, mothers, spouses, and successor wives during shaman divinations and full-dress costumed seances (*kut*).[7] We know that, as elsewhere in East Asia, those who died young, violently, or in the throes of unsatisfied resentment are likely to become restless ancestors and ghosts, inflicting illness and strife upon the living.[8]

In anthropological writing, the ancestors of Confucian rites stand as essentially Durkheimean metaphors of a particular social order, the links through person, time, and place that confer moral identity in the name of family and lineage. Consider then, the metaphoric power of a press photograph portraying family elders bowing in the snow beside the barbed wire fence of the DMZ, giving New Year obeisance to ancestors left behind in North Korea.[9] Here, the particularistic metaphors of family and lineage are transmuted to that of a nation, its integrity ruptured by war, its division cast in barbed wire. But if the notion of "ancestor" were only that of a mechanical totem, the photograph would lose its power. As an ethnographic representation of a divided nation it appropriates meaning from more particularistic suffering, from the grief, longing, and guilt of those who left kin behind in the North, feelings assumed to find their resonance in the ancestors themselves.

That the dead feel, that they continue to express emotions appropriate to a mother, father, child, sibling, or spouse, is affirmed in stories, dreams, and seance appearances. The restless ancestors of shaman ritual have been seen to measure stressful and problematic social relationships among the living: the feelings of wives toward their husbands' kin;[10] dead first wives toward their successors, or successor wives toward their stepchildren;[11] or brothers' wives and married sisters.[12] Such studies, my own included, present shaman rituals, kut, as a functional mechanism for airing, placating, and exorcising the sources of social and spiritual discontent. Anthropologists have assumed that shamans assume that daughters-in-law bear ambivalent feelings toward deceased mothers-in-law or that second wives find the malice of a dead first wife to be a logical and compelling explanation of distress. Such are the relationships that are dramatized in a shaman's stock portrayals of the dead during the ancestors' segment (*chosang kori*) of a kut.[13] This emphasis upon structure, upon the replication of social relationships projected onto both the living and the dead, has been useful. It assumes a meaningful tension between Korean social life and the often denigrated rituals of women and shamans, and it lends us a female vantage point from which to view Korean kinship. But it does not convey the immediacy of ancestral encounters, how the dead are realized among the living, and how this process unfolds over time.

A Dream about Grandmother

Let me begin with a story that was already a story a few months before I happened to record it. I ended my ethnobiographical account of the shaman "Yongsu's Mother" in 1985 with mention of her anxiety over her son's courtship with a young woman from a Christian family.[14] The daughter-in-law of a shaman's household would undertake weighty obligations to the spirits, and any dereliction would bring harm to her husband's house. The young couple persisted and the marriage took place in 1987, a few months before the birth of a grandchild. Yongsu's Mother told me that her daughter-in-law had stopped attending the Christian church. The daughter-in-law, walking me to the bus stop as an opportunity to speak in private, asked me if I really "believed" in the spirits. In the intervening years, I have watched the daughter-in-law's skepticism give way to an engaged curiosity about Yongsu's Mother's work and the premises of her world.

In 1989, Yongsu's Mother's own mother died. When I returned to Korea for a brief visit in the summer of 1991, the household was preparing for a shaman ritual to send the dead woman's soul to paradise (*chinogi kut*). To my surprise, the timing of this ritual had been prompted by the daughter-in-law, or within the logic of the household, by the dead woman who appeared to her grandson's bride in a dream. The grandmother, an occasional resident in the household before her death, had come to the door seeking food. The daughter-in-law had told her, "Grandmother, I can't let you in, I'm a Christian," but that had not stopped the dead woman from entering the house. "Her face was all pinched and drawn," the daughter-in-law provided a detail that emphasized the dead woman's need for sustenance from the living and underscored the family's urgent obligation to her. The dream quite literally brought the dead grandmother into the house; the family would sponsor a kut where, speaking through a shaman, she would address her children, grandchildren, and acquaintances.

By the time I heard the daughter-in-law tell it, a few months after the dream, her story was a brief but polished recitation. By telling it, I assumed her to be saying several things. She identified herself as a Christian and so resisted the claims of a restless ancestor, but by her own admission she was ineffectual. How, after all, could she deny her husband's grandmother access to the house? As a daughter-in-law of the house, she necessarily acknowledged the relationship, and in acknowledging the relationship, she accepted obligations to the ancestor. By telling her dream, not only did she capitulate to the demands of restless ancestors, she became an agent in their realization. The new bride became a matron teller of family stories, a witness to the family's continued interaction with its dead.

Perhaps the most immediate model for the daughter-in-law's dreaming was Yongsu's Mother's own story of her husband's dead first wife, who barged into the house seeking food to satisfy her hunger on the day that she was entitled to receive ancestral offerings. It was through Yongsu's Mother's stories, collected as ethnobiography that I learned to appreciate the continuing and emergent nature of relationships with the dead.[15] In Yongsu's Mother's life—as described, as experienced, and as subjected to anthropological investigation—ancestors claim a compelling presence. Their behavior is predictable, within the logic of behavior imputed to the unquiet dead, but their presence is more than metaphorical, their representation more than stereotypical. They are characters in the construction of her own story, characters with whom she continues to wrestle and whom she occasionally refashions in the telling. The dead appear in her tales with a logic of presence that recalls the novels of Gabriel Garcia Marquez, Toni Morrison, or William Kennedy. Like Phrancis Phelan of William Kennedy's *Ironweed*, who takes a sentimental journey through Albany on Halloween night, she encounters the ghosts of a former life along the way. And like Phrancis Phelan, or Lord Peter Wimsey of the lead quotation, she accepts the appropriateness of an encounter with a particular specter on a particular occasion, much as her daughter-in-law dreamed the dead grandmother into the house looking pinched and hungry when the family was overdue for a ritual to send her soul to paradise. As an effective plot device in Kennedy's novel of recollection and reconciliation, the specters from Albany's past make a claim for their time in Phrancis Phelan's memory. The dead, as apprehended presences, make similar claims upon Yongsu's Mother, both in the stories she tells about the past, the stories that explain who Yongsu's Mother is and why she became a shaman, and in the present, in enduring and still troubled relationships. The ancestors are among the links between "then" and "now," not literary devices, neither hers nor mine, so much as Yongsu's Mother's autobiographical material. What was, for the novelist, an act of creation and inspiration, was for the anthropologist a matter of listening, observing, and recording, through which I encountered Yongsu's Mother's ancestors in numerous guises.

Ancestors in the Telling of Yongsu's Mother's Life

Like many other anthropologists who found themselves recording a life story in the field, I was seduced by a compelling storyteller into listening and recording.[16] But while the *book* is the product of a classical anthropological encounter, the *stories* are a product of Yongsu's Mother's world, told and retold before I met her. The nature of our particular relationship might be suggested through the text itself, in the relative weight given her voice as against my hesitant questions, and by the tone (insofar as I could render it into English) of our conversations. Following Vincent Crapanzano, whose much remarked-upon *Tuhami: the Portrait of a Moroccan* shifts focus from the life story itself to the context in which the story came to be told, I was interested in the motivation and circumstances that trigger particular kinds of autobiographical texts.[17] Unlike Crapanzano, I did not see these tales as gifts intended for me alone.[18] Telling tales of past hardship is a meaningful act among the women of Yongsu's Mother's world. Within that world, stories about the dead are evoked to explain how the thorny hand of the dead still meddles in the affairs of the living.

As ancestors, the two most significant characters of her tales are her own dead husband and her husband's first wife, both of whom meet the predictable criteria of restless ancestors: they died young, at least relatively young, before their children were grown, and with unfinished business in the world. Strictly speaking, neither of the two is Yongsu's Mother's ancestor, although both are ancestors of her house for whom she must unfailingly provide a chesa feast and goad the children into an awkward approximation of correct ritual procedures. Indeed, the story of a missed chesa day provides the climax to her story of the dead first wife. When their common husband lay ill in the hospital, the dead wife appeared seeking her chesa rice, barging most inauspiciously into the hospital via Yongsu's Mother's dreams.[19]

Dead husband and first wife appear in the portentous dreams of Yongsu's Mother's stories, and Yongsu's Father provides significant communications through Yongsu's Mother's current dreaming. Deceased husband and wife appear during the ancestors' sequence of kut for Yongsu's Mother's household. As the Spirit Warrior of Yongsu's Mother's shrine and as the shaman's personal Body-governing God (*Taesin Momju*), Yongsu's Father assists her in all her work as a shaman.[20] Of the two ancestors, he is far and away the more significant presence, an intimate acquaintance with whom she enjoys a working relationship as shaman and guardian god. The dead wife was only glimpsed in dreams, although her hand is still seen in more recent acts of malice. She has been the subject of more than one exorcism.

My own acquaintance with Yongsu's Father and the dead first wife comes from stories, but not only from stories. I have attended the first wife's chesa, seen her in kut, and was once an accomplice in an attempt to exorcise her baleful presence.[21] Yongsu's Father speaks to me when he appears in kut and when I make offerings in the shrine.[22] I never fail to fill his special wine cup; when I neglected him just once, he punished me, then reported my plight to Yongsu's Mother in a dream. Lately, he has taken to asking me for beer, since this is considered an American drink.

To summarize material presented elsewhere at greater length, Yongsu's Mother blames the dead wife for her own early widowhood and her subsequent difficulties in raising three stepchildren. The dead wife snatched away their common husband, as jealous dead wives are said to do.[23] Tales of portentous dreams are offered as confirmation. As a newlywed, Yongsu's Mother saw the dead woman lurking about outside the nuptial chamber. A few years later, she argued with her when the dead woman intruded into the husband's hospital room. Her husband dreamed of the dead wife attempting to crawl in between them under the quilt. One of her new sisters-in-law dreamed of the dead woman on Yongsu's Mother's wedding night; she saw her surrounded by flames but clearing a path to the door. As final confirmation, Yongsu's Mother claims that once her husband died, the dead woman no longer appeared in her dreams. "He always appears alone; they don't go around together." "That's because he likes you better," I suggested, and she smirked.

The story of the dead first wife is important to Yongsu's Mother and often retold. As a measure of its importance, Yongsu's Mother has worked with her material over the years. In the hospital, the first wife snatched the cake that Yongsu's Mother offered to her husband, or the husband woke up, saw his dead wife, and screamed. The two versions were produced within a month of each other.[24] In 1985, Yongsu's Mother had elaborated upon the story of the first wife crawling under the quilt to include a description of how the dead wife had puckered up her lips in anticipation of a kiss from the living husband.[25] In this version, the husband was ashamed; he did not reveal his dream to the bride, but told his sister-in-law. Yongsu's Mother heard the story when she confided her own uneasy dreams to this same source, asking if the dead wife had a bulging forehead, deep-set eyes, and sparse hair. I thought this the very image of a female ghost, but Yongsu's Mother claims that her sister-in-law readily acknowledged, "She looked exactly like that."

Yongsu's Mother's relationship with her dead husband is difficult to characterize, or perhaps, by its nature, steeped in ambivalence. He is "that man," "that old guy," who lied about his age and circumstances to claim her as a bride. He drank, they quarreled, he died. They continue to quarrel. He appears in her dreams and she argues with him. He appears at her kut and she argues with him. In her characterizations, he was vain of his traditional elite (*yangban*) origins, stubborn, and given to extremes of violent drunken behavior. She says, "I married very badly," and considers the match one of the great injustices of her life.

There is a second husband-voice in some of the stories, though, a consoling voice when she sobs on her way to her wedding and a remorseful voice that apologizes, between bouts of drinking, for the hardships that he has inflicted upon her.[26] Planning her second stepdaughter's wedding in 1977, she conjured a cozy image of herself and her husband planning the first stepdaughter's wedding, an image at odds with her usual portrayal of a time of great domestic turmoil.[27] In the summer of 1983, when I returned to Korea newly wed, she surprised me with a story of her husband's kindness, buying his bride a package of commercial soap from the market to spare her hands the lye soap then still made from cinders in country households. In all of her stories, whether the husband be wrathful or kind, she insists that he was profoundly attracted to her; he deceived her family because he desired her and curtailed her freedom because he feared that she would run away.[28] The jealousy, too, persists beyond the grave. When she followed the anthropologist in having her ears pierced, she claimed that Yongsu's Father tugged on the earrings and kept the incisions from healing. He thought that she was fixing herself up to get another husband.

Yongsu's Mother chuckles when she talks about his jealousy, which, like his solitary appearance in her dreams, is not only a mark of pride but also a measure of the spiritual cooperation she commands as a shaman from the powerful attachment of her guardian god. As she expresses it, her husband helps with her work. He told her in a dream to turn out her boarders and use her spare room for a shrine; he promised to give her the rent money.[29] When business fell off in the fall of 1977, she suspected that he was angry with her. When she found that the dead first wife was the true source of her distress, she considered this more plausible; why should her husband "prevent his wife from making a living"?[30] How well he provides for her is a matter of contention when they banter with each other during a kut. She threatens to find herself a better husband unless he brings her more clients.[31]

I have described his appearance in a kut, manifested by her friend and colleague, the Songjuk Mansin.[32] Songjuk Mansin's portrayal assumed a knowledge of Yongsu's Mother's stories, assumed that not only Yongsu's Mother but the rest of us would respond to the appearance of a man we had never met but of whom we had heard so very much. He reminds everyone that he was a yangban, and Yongsu's Mother snaps at him, "You're always going on about your noble origins, 'yangban, yangban.'" He laments that if it weren't for his drink-bloated belly, he would be alive today. "Well, you drank." (She gives him no quarter.) He suggests they take their socks off, an allusion, perhaps, to her story of their wedding night when she adamantly refused so much as to let him help her remove her padded socks from her blistered feet.[33] She says, "What's the point?"

Yongsu's Father is not quite one of those restless ancestors who, by force of discontent, has become a local tutelary god and whose story has passed into local legend.[34] But neither does he appear in kut as a generic dead husband. Songjuk Mansin gave voice to a particular character with a particular history, a character who had come into being for Songjuk Mansin, for the anthropologist, and for many others through Yongsu's Mother's stories. Songjuk Mansin recreates him in a manner that is both compelling and also a little bit amusing for Yongsu's Mother. He exists (if one can call it that) within the cultural logic of a restless ancestor, but he lives through a process that is both personal and shared, autobiographical and creative.

Return of Another Drunken Spouse

The appearance of Yongsu's Father at a kut suggests the interactive quality of ancestral realizations, of stories told to shamans and then returned by shamans in the unfolding of a ritual drama. Because Yongsu's Mother is herself a shaman, it could be argued that her stories have a special and public quality. She tells them to entertain her clients (and the anthropologist) while underscoring the power of supernatural machinations. As I have acknowledged elsewhere, she is a particularly gifted raconteur. The shaman called upon to manifest the dead husband in kut was a close colleague and intimate friend. How typical, then, is this process of telling and returning stories? Let us consider another appearance by a dead husband, this time to a wife who is not a shaman, although her daughter was about to become one.[35] Like Yongsu's Mother, Chini's Mother suffered grievous hardship when her husband died in his prime, leaving the widow to provide for their children. He left the world with a reputation for heavy drinking. When Chini's dead father appears, he affirms his role in the family's misery, first by neglect, then by dying and abandoning them.

> **An Hosun as Chini's Father:** *You think I died away from home because I was too fond of friends, food, and spending money? You think that's why I died, don't you?*
> **Chini's Mother:** *Yes.*
> **An Hosun as Chini's Father:** *And because I died, look at how much pain you've suffered. All because I died, you've had reason to cry* [sobs]. *I can't ask you for money. That would be shameful.*[36] *When I was alive I thought only of my own pleasure, I didn't provide for my family at home. I used what was in my pocket to entertain my friends. This is what's become of me.*
> [Chini's Mother fills his cup, and the dead husband expresses his gratitude.]
> *Ahyu! Today I drink. You know dear, I haven't been able to drink like this for a long time.*
> **Chini's Mother:** *Drink your fill.*
> **An Hosun as Chini's Father:** *This good stuff, and this money, (I'm so*

grateful). I'll settle my account, I'll pay you back with good fortune. Have a glass. I haven't seen you for such a long time.

[The dead husband hands his wife an empty wine cup and fills it with drink for her. When Chini's Mother has emptied the cup and handed it back, the dead husband gestures to the attending shaman for a refill. The shamans giggle at An Hosun's in-character carousing.]

Chini's Mother: *Ahyu! Still drinking.*

An Hosun as Chini's Father: *You used to say I drank too much. Even now that I'm dead that's what I hear, grumble, grumble, grumble deep in your heart.*

As in any kut, the appearance of the ancestors gives voice to a larger family history of pain, recrimination, and reconciliation in the ancestor's promise to help the family. The behavior of the husband, the tears, cups of wine, self-blame, and expressions of joy at reunion are the stuff of both a stock character ancestor and an intimate family history: "You think I died away from home because I was too fond of friends, food, and spending money. . . . You used to say I drank too much." Let us consider how these shreds and patches of experience and memory became part of the shaman's portrayal.

Shamans commonly learn client histories when clients come to them for divinations. On the strength of visions, the shaman asks questions intended to trigger a story and find the root cause of present trouble: "I see an ancestor who died dripping blood, was there someone like that? I see someone who died young." Divination, as a process of the shaman's concentrating while she shakes her bells and then casts rice grains into suggestive configurations, gradually gives way to a conversation in which the client tells her story and the shaman offers her diagnosis, sometimes capping the client's experience with other stories.[37] Among clients of long standing (*tan'gol*), not only the family but also its particularly potent gods and potentially restless ancestors are known to the shaman. In some instances, she knew the ancestors in life.

Thus, Chini would have revealed some of her family's story when an elder sister brought her to the young shaman, Kwan Myongnyo. The family's assumption, that Chini was a destined shaman in need of an initiation, both prompted the consultation and led logically to stories of past hardship as diagnostic of a supernatural calling. Kwan might already have been familiar with some of the particulars through her prior acquaintance with Chini's sister. Kwan Myongnyo introduced Chini to a more experienced shaman, Kim Pongsun, who would train her and officiate at the initiation kut as her "spirit mother." By the time I met Chini, her "spirit mother" was thoroughly conversant with the particulars of her past life. In the kut a third shaman, An Hosun, performed the ancestor sequence, giving back as ritual drama what had already been told as story. It is possible, but not necessary, that one of the storytellers was Chini's Mother, the restless ancestor's interlocutor. The mother's pain was bound up in a larger history of family pain that would be told in her daughters' stories.

The shamans, for their part, do not claim a one-on-one possession. Rather, they are seeing visions, feeling sensations appropriate to the spirit—such as Chini's father's desire for alcohol—and interpreting divine or ancestral will through inspired speech (*kongsu*). Their practice bridges inspiration and skill as significant stories become compelling performance, what Chungmoo Choi describes as "the art of distilling the information collected into an emotionally affecting subtext."[38]

Ethnographers have noted that many of the ancestors who appear in kut are unremarkable, that sometimes their identities are not clear either to the participants or to members of the officiating shaman team. The women with whom I worked, aware of the direction of my own interests, would sometimes shout out to the wailing ancestor on my behalf, "Who are you?" and supply me with the appropriate term of kinship. Roger and Dawnhee Yim Janelli suggest that ignorance over the ancestor's identity is "functional," that it engages several participants in the projective possibility that a complaining mother-in-law might turn out to be the shade of their own mother-in-law. The Janellis also acknowledge that some of the performances they observed included specific references to the lives of remembered ancestors.[39] The sequence of ancestral appearances is hierarchically structured. Senior generations appear first and generally have the least to say; the portrayals become more vivid as the remembered dead emerge. Chungmoo Choi sees in the sequencing of ancestral appearances, from distant to recent and compelling, a process that draws the participants into the performed reality of ancestral encounters and leads them toward an emotionally therapeutic confrontation with the remembered dead.[40]

Her analysis has great merit in unraveling the theatrical and psychological dynamics of a kut, the manner in which shamans evoke the ancestors through dramatic portrayals. However, it must also be acknowledged that the members of client families participate in the construction of the ancestral presence not only in their dialogic encounters during kut but, as I have been suggesting here, by the dreams they dream and the stories they tell. Their own constructions of ancestorship weave through the shaman's portrayal and continue long after the kut. Yongsu's Mother's stories recount more than twenty years of her posthumous relationship with her dead spouse, and she continues to tell stories.

The pivotal role of those who grieve in the construction of "ancestor" may be illuminated by situations of their absence, where idioms of ancestral invocation are removed from the domain of kinship and transposed as political metaphors. Let me round out this discussion with some examples of ancestral construction from the frontiers of Korean popular culture.

Ancestors as Idioms beyond Kinship

I have mentioned how a photographic representation of an act of ancestor veneration, performed for kin lost in the North, could stand as a metaphor for a divided country, drawing emotional power from its image of sundered families. The idiom of aggrieved dead, those who died violently, far from home and in their prime, has also been made manifest in rituals and imagery that evoke the pain and injustice of Korea's national history. One male shaman, active in Seoul, has gone to the banks of the Imjin River to hold kut for the war dead who perished there, many of them school children conscripted by the People's Army. He claims that one family heard through the lips of a shaman the confirmation that their son had been among the dead; for years they had not known his fate. Here, the victims of history are still known to those who mourn. Far vaguer are "[t]he ghosts of an estimated 126,000 Koreans killed during the Japanese invasion of Korea in 1592 [who] were brought home in an elaborate Buddhist ceremony . . . after haunting Japan for 400 years in search of their ears and noses [taken as trophies by Hideyoshi's armies]."[41] The Buddhist ceremony, the culmination of a Buddhist nationalist project, made its point, but in a manner that was necessarily more symbolic than evocative.

Recently, the Popular Culture Movement (Minjung Munhwa Undong) has crafted dramas of social protest around the cultural logic that the aggrieved souls of historically oppressed persons may be summoned to bear witness through the lips of a shaman. Dr. Chung Hyun Kyung, in her memorable address to the World Council of Churches in Canberra in 1991, invoked "Joan of Arc and other women burned as witches, all the victims of the crusades and of Western colonization, Jews killed in Nazi gas chambers, Vietnamese napalmed and boat people starved, those 'smashed by tanks in Kwangju, Tiananmen Square and Lithuania'. . . ."[42] Like the commemoration of Koreans killed in the late-sixteenth-century invasion, the aggrieved dead invoked in Canberra are known only as the subjects of history. The act of invocation was, in Canberra, a plea for the common humanity of all victims of oppression, a global vision that borrowed upon the particularistic idiom of kin who mourn.

When those who participate in these reconfigured rites are complicit in their construction and conversant with their symbolic intentions, performance may yield a moving experience that bridges the boundaries of ritual and theater. Public rituals, performed either by professional shamans or performers who take the shaman role, have been held to propitiate the souls of those who died resisting state oppression—students and workers who were killed during demonstrations, tortured, or who committed protest suicides. The protest dead fall well within a Korean cultural logic of unquiet souls. They died in their youth with lives unfulfilled, they died violently, and they died carrying urgent business with the living. At least some of the participants in their public commemoration knew them in life, and martyrs' stories are known and retold among the community of protestors.

Kwang-Ok Kim provides vivid accounts of the public rituals performed to purify and release the souls of Park Chongch'ol, a university student who was killed under police torture in 1986, and Yi Hanyol, a student who suffered a fatal injury during a demonstration in the volatile spring of 1987.[43] Dance professor Aijoo Lee performed the role of shaman, dancing her portrayal of Chongch'ol's tortured body or of Hanyol's life as part of a "history of humble and poor Koreans who have been oppressed and exploited successively by traditional feudalism, Japanese colonialism, American imperialism, and the succession of 'fascist' regimes in alliance with foreign superpowers."[44] The crowd "called back" Hanyol's soul through the fervor of their commitment to his cause. The emotional impact generated by these evocations was intense. Kim reports that when Professor Lee portrayed the death of Chongch'ol, "[a]ll the participants were moved, weeping, shouting in anger and fury against their imagined enemy. At that moment all present, including the secret police and foreign news reporters, shared the ethical message of the ritual."[45] When the shaman/dancer tore through the long white cloth bridge that marked Hanyol's passage into paradise, the dead youth's mother and sister collapsed in the street.[46]

Professional shamans have also been hired to console the victims of oppression. Some confusion of intentions is inevitable where the sponsors have taken literally the ideological assertion that shaman rituals are about giving voice to the oppressed and expressing their grievances in the name of social justice. Soon Hwa Sun interviewed a young shaman who had initially been willing to work with students in creating a kut that would respond to contemporary needs.[47] The shaman's enthusiasm cooled, however, when she felt that the students were insincere in their desire to lead the dead to peace in the other world, or in finding their own consolation through this act, the object of the ritual in her eyes. Rather, she came to feel that her efforts had been manipulated for political ends by those who had little respect for the shaman tradition she represented.[48]

The feminist group Alternative Culture (Ttohana ui Munhwa) sponsored a kut for the dead to console those Korean women who were forcibly conscripted to provide sexual services for the Japanese Imperial Army, a gendered victimization retrieved from the history of colonial domination. The officiating shamans, however, experienced great difficulty in summoning the souls of dead "comfort women," claiming that it was almost impossible to invoke the dead in the absence of their grieving kin (Cho Oakla and Kim Eunshil, personal communication). The dead had been absorbed into a generalized history of "comfort women"; their own stories had been obliterated by those same forces that took their lives and dignity. Neither horror nor pity were sufficient to call them into a circle of symbolic sisters they might never have imagined in life.

Conclusion

The shaman rituals for the dead are the most public and consequently the best studied expression of ancestorship as a dynamic force among the living. The emotional power of these confrontations between the living and the dead is widely recognized and appropriated into contexts that blur the boundary between ritual and political theater. But the ritual alone, the performing shaman alone, does not construct the restless ancestor. This, rather, is a process begun in the bosom of the family, and continued there once the kut is done. Ancestors intrude into dreams and are summoned through the stories the living tell about them. They exist in the assumption that living and dead continue to regard each other with both positive and negative feelings, an assumption that lends its power to and is affirmed in the power of dramatic appearances by ancestors in kut.

Notes

My initial fieldwork in Korea in 1977 and 1978 was made possible by fellowships from the Institute for International Education (Fulbright) and the Social Science Research Council, as well as by a grant from the National Science Foundation. A grant from the Eppley Foundation for Research allowed me to return to Korea in 1985 to complete this project. With the generous permission of the University of Hawaii Press, this paper elaborates upon material initially presented in my *The Life and Hard Times of a Korean Shaman: Of Tales and the Telling of Tales* (Honolulu: University of Hawaii Press, 1988). I alone am responsible for the shortcomings of this effort.

1. Roger Janelli and Dawnhee Yim Janelli, *Ancestor Worship and Korean Society* (Stanford: Stanford University Press, 1982), chap. 6.

2. William E. Biernatzki, "Varieties of Korean Lineage Structure" (Ph.D. diss., St. Louis University, 1967); Roger Janelli and Dawnhee Yim Janelli, "Lineage Organization and Social Differentiation in Korea," *Man*, n.s., 13 (1978): 272–89; Janelli and Janelli, *Ancestor Worship*; T'aek-kyu Kim, *Tongjok purakui saenghwal kujo yon'gu* (A Study of the Structure of Social Life in a Lineage Village) (Seoul: Ch'onggu, 1964); Kwang-Kyu Lee [Yi Kwang-gyu], "Ancestor Worship and Kinship Structure in Korea," in Laurel Kendall and Griffin Dix, eds., *Religion and Ritual in Korean Society* (Berkeley: Institute for East Asian Studies, University of California, 1987), 58–59; Matsuhiko Shima, "Kinship and Economic Organization in a Korean Village" (Ph.D. diss., University of Toronto, 1979); Sunhee Song, "Kinship and Lineage in Korean Village Society" (Ph.D. diss., Indiana University, 1982).

3. Martina Deuchler, "Neo-Confucianism in Action: Agnation and Ancestor Worship in Early Yi Korea," in Kendall and Dix, eds., *Religion and Ritual*, 26–55; Lee, "Ancestor Worship." For similarly functionalist interpretations of Chinese shaman ritual, see Emily M. Ahern, *The Cult of the Dead in a Chinese Village* (Stanford: Stanford University Press, 1973); David K. Jordan, *Gods, Ghosts, and Ancestors: The Folk Religion of a Taiwanese Village* (Berkeley and Los Angeles: University of California Press, 1972); and Jack M. Potter, "Cantonese Shamanism," in Arthur P. Wolf, ed., *Religion and Ritual in Chinese Society* (Stanford: Stanford University Press, 1974).

4. Lee, "Ancestor Worship"; Kyung-soo Chun, *Reciprocity in Korean Society: An Ethnography of Hasami* (Seoul: Seoul National University Press, 1984), 98–104.

5. Lee, "Ancestor Worship," 69; Ton-hui Im [Dawnhee Yim Janelli], "Han'guk chosang sungbae ui pyonch'on sa" (A History of the Transformation of Korean Ancestor Worship), *Chont'ong Munhwa* 8 (1986): 47–53.

6. Youngsook Kim Harvey, "The Korean Shaman and the Deaconess: Sisters in Different Guises," in Kendall and Dix, eds., 164–65.

7. Laurel Kendall, *Shamans, Housewives, and Other Restless Spirits: Women in Korean Ritual Life* (Honolulu: University of Hawaii Press, 1985), chap. 7.

8. Kil-song Ch'oe, *Han'guk ui chosang sungbae* (Korean Ancestor Worship) (Seoul: Seoul National University Press, 1986); Roger Janelli and Dawnhee Yim Janelli, "The Functional Value of Ignorance at a Korean Seance," *Asian Folklore Studies* (Nagoya) 38

(1979); Janelli and Janelli, *Ancestor Worship*, 148–176; Laurel Kendall, "Caught between Ancestors and Spirits: A Korean *Mansin's* Healing *Kut*," *Korea Journal* 17, no. 8 (1977): 8–23; idem, "Wives, Lesser Wives, and Ghosts: Supernatural Conflict in a Korean Village," *Asian Folklore Studies* (Nagoya) 43 (1984); idem, *Shamans*, 99–102.

9. *Newsview*, 3 February 1991, 11.

10. Janelli and Janelli, "Functional Value of Ignorance"; and *Ancestor Worship*, 148–76.

11. Kendall, "Wives"; and Kendall, *Life and Hard Times*, chap. 7.

12. Kendall, "Caught between Ancestors and Spirits"; Mayumi Shigematsu, "Saishin ni mirareru josei no shakai kankei" (The Women's Social Sphere in Korean *mansin's kut*), *Minzokugaku Kenkyu*, 1980, 93–110.

13. Alexandre Guillemoz, "La dernière rencontre: Un rituel chamanique coréen pour une jeune morte" (The Last Encounter: A Korean Shaman Ritual for a Dead Young Woman), *Transe, chamanisme, possession: Actes des deuxièmes Rencontres internationales sur la fête et la communication* (Nice: Editions Serre, 1986); Janelli and Janelli, "Functional Value of Ignorance"; Kendall, *Shamans*, 7–8, 147–148.

14. Kendall, *Life and Hard Times of a Korean Shaman*.

15. Ibid., 112–13.

16. Following a venerable tradition in ethnobiographies and oral histories, the scribe establishes the background and circumstances in which the life was recorded (cf. Ruth M. Underhill, *Papago Woman* [1936; reprint, New York: Holt, Rinehart, and Winston, 1979]). In more recent work, the description of the encounter between anthropologist and informant is expanded, in acknowledgment of the inevitable subjectivity of fieldwork, but also to enhance the human interest of the work. See, for example, Margaret B. Blackman, *During My Time: Florence Edenshaw Davidson, a Haida Woman* (Seattle: University of Washington Press, 1982), Marjorie Shostak, *Nisa: The Life and Words of a !Kung Woman* (Cambridge, Mass.: Harvard University Press, 1981), and Pat Ellis Taylor, *Border Healing Woman: The Story of Jewel Babb* (Austin: University of Texas Press, 1981), works that skillfully weave the story of a project around the story of its subject.

17. *Tuhami* (Chicago: University of Chicago Press, 1980) describes an encounter between a Moroccan and a stand-in from the world of a departed colonial patron and explores the psychological consequences of this history, both for Tuhami and for his anthropological interlocutor. More than any of these other works, *Tuhami* suggests the tension between stories told and the dynamic process of their telling but, in the end, gives us more of Crapanzano than of Tuhami. Although Tuhami is also a valued storyteller among his own people (pp. 60–61), we do not encounter him in that milieu, and we hear very few of his tales. *Tuhami* is as much a logical consequence of as a refinement upon an anthropological tradition of recording life stories that has confused the opportunity and act of *recording* data, an event circumscribed by the presence of the anthropologist, with the business of *telling stories*, which is far more open-ended.

18. On one occasion, when the boys were still young and bashful, she herself declaimed the congratulatory address, falling into a wicked imitation of a staid Confucian elder while her neighbors and the anthropologist tittered in the background.

19. Kendall, *Life and Hard Times of a Korean Shaman*, 109–13.

20. Ch'oe (*Han'guk ni chosang sungbae*) notes that it is the unquiet, discontented dead who achieve the status of gods in the shaman world, an interpretation that would account for Yongsu's Father's elevation, and for others among the guardian gods who enjoyed close, if infelicitous, relationships with their chosen shaman.

21. Kendall, *Life and Hard Times of a Korean Shaman*, 103–4.

22. Ibid., 129

23. Kendall, "Wives"; and Kendall, *Life and Hard Times of a Korean Shaman*, chap. 7.

24. Kendall, *Life and Hard Times of a Korean Shaman*, 113.

25. Ibid., 111–12.

26. Ibid., 96, 107.

27. Ibid., 108–9.

28. Ibid., 25, 108.

29. Kendall, *Shamans*, 56.

30. Kendall, *Life and Hard Times of a Korean Shaman*, 103.

31. Ibid., 120.

32. Ibid., 120–21.

33. Ibid., 24–25.

34. Ch'oe, *Han'guk ui chosang sungbae.*

35. For a detailed description of this ritual and more of Chini's story, see Laurel Kendall, "Initiating Performance: The Story of Chini, a Korean Shaman," in Carol Laderman and Marina Roseman, eds., *The Performance of Healing* (New York: Routledge, 1996), 17–58. This particular ritual is the subject of a film, *An Initiation Kut for a Korean Shaman*, by Diana Lee and Laurel Kendall, distributed by University of Hawaii Press.

36. Requesting "travel money" for the ancestors is standard business in this ritual. One of the daughters coaches her mother to "give Father some money" but indicates that a small bill is sufficient for an ancestor. The father continues his sobbing lament.

37. Chung-moo Choi, "The Artistry and Ritual Aesthetics of Urban Korean Shamans," *Journal of Ritual Studies* 3 (1989): 236–39; Kendall, *Shamans*, 71–74.

38. Choi, "Artistry," 241; Kendall, *Initating Performance*. Choi discusses the specific techniques that shamans use to make these evocations emotionally compelling.

39. Janelli and Janelli, "Functional Value of Ignorance."

40. Choi, "Artistry."

41. *Newsview*, 28 April, 1990.

42. *New York Times*, 16 March 1991.

43. Kwang-Ok Kim, "Rituals of Resistance: The Manipulation of Shamanism in Contemporary Korea," in Charles F. Keyes et al., eds., *Asian Visions of Authority: Religion and the Modern States of East and Southeast Asia* (Honolulu: University of Hawaii Press, 1994), 195–219.

44. Kim, "Rituals of Resistance," 35.

45. Ibid., 30–31.

46. Ibid., 36.

47. Soon-Hwa Sun, "The Work and Power of Korean Shamans" (unpublished ms.).

48. Ibid., 140–45.

Discussion

Jacob Olupona
You told us something about the context of this study and made a distinction between the earlier ancestor cult, Confucian ideology, and the rituals you studied. Would you like to elaborate on that?

Laurel Kendall
Neoconfucian ideology was adapted as a social blueprint in Korea about five hundred years ago, and Koreans on that basis constructed lineages based on male-linked kin. At the apex of many of these lineages were family ancestors, ancestors who held high position, and the commemoration of those people was a way of asserting status in the world. You can read descriptions of Korean society where you get no sense of restless ancestors or the active dead at all. Standard historical treatments say, "Confucianism came in, they took over and shamans and women weren't involved in the cult of the dead anymore." There are actually two problems here: Confucians didn't like shamans because they were women and they danced in public; and modern Koreans didn't like shamans because they had come to think this was all "superstition." It's now quite clear that women were and still are involved in the cult of the dead, but they were beyond the pale of official discourse about what Koreans are supposed to do. If you read the Ministry of Culture and Information's handbook on Korea for 1990 you learn that "shamanism" has all but died out, except maybe in a few rural country villages. To the contrary, shamans have been very active in urban centers for as long as I have known Korea. The women I've worked with have more business now than they ever did. Shaman practice seems to have adapted well to a clientele who are petty capitalists in a high-risk market economy. What was once a religion for peasants now addresses chance and risk in a small-time, petty capitalist economy.

John Grim
I'm struck by the different image of ancestors in comparison to some of the other discussions we've had. The ancestors in people's papers have generally been very benevolent, helpful, and someone that you evoke and carry with you. But here we have ancestors who are problematic. Is this an issue in the sociology of knowledge? Is it a gender issue? Is it related to the issue of *han*?

Laurel Kendall
You find this ambivalent appraisal of the ancestors throughout East Asia. Some people remain solidly within Confucian discourse and the ancestors are sym-

bols of virtue, sources of virtue, and inspirational abstractions. If ancestors are problematic, they write it off to the doings of superstitious women. But in ethnography you find the ancestors occurring as the dead who cause problems, maybe because the relationship between the living and the dead is problematic, maybe because of unfulfilled need, or desire, or love, or something else that is unresolved and consequently keeps the dead around. Roger and Dawnhee Janelli found such a great discrepancy between what some of their male informants were saying and what some of their female informants were saying that they suggested that men and women conceptualize the dead differently based on their different kinds of experiences. Men seem to be talking about their own immediate forebears in the family into which they were born and raised, whereas women's experience of the dead seems related to their experience of entering a hostile environment—their in-laws' home—and their most immediate problematic ancestors are the ancestors of the husband's house. I don't think this holds completely. First of all, the Janellis also cite men who claim to have had trouble from the ancestors. Second, women's ancestors are bilateral. In the initiation kut that I mention in my paper, most troublesome ancestors were matrikin ancestors. I don't think gender really draws a full stop on how you see the ancestors.

William Ferea

There are some interesting parallels to practices among my people. The recent dead will often come back to visit the family through a person who has been initiated and can receive the dead. That person's own spirit will be pushed aside, leaving space for the spirit of the dead to come in and then pass on messages about matters like land disputes. Often someone sings songs that are inspired by the ancestor, and these songs are then passed on to the living.

Laurel Kendall

Do these songs come from the ancestors?

William Ferea

Yes, they are composed by the dead people and brought back for the living to sing. My grandmother came back once and sang her song to one of my elder sisters, but we didn't pick up the song. It was a mourning song about how she had died, why she had died, and so on. Unfortunately, my sister had never been initiated into this kind of song because she was too young for that, and the tone of the song was in the old language that we younger people couldn't catch. An older person would have taken hold of the song. When my sister recovered, we asked, and she could not remember the song. The spirit had gone, she was her normal self, and the song was no longer there. I've collected many such songs from the old people in the villages that were divinely inspired. A very different situation resulted in a song when the jungle caught fire. A banyon tree, which is a place where spirits live, was burning and a voice came out of the fire and sang a song that has been continued. My own grandfather passed on his song to an older man from the next village and it's still sung now. So Korean shamanism seems to me to be similar to the movement of spirits of the dead to the living, to console, to pass on messages.

Laurel Kendall

I'm interested in the songs that can and can't be remembered. Are there prohibitions against tape-recording or writing down these songs? Or is that something you just would not do with an ancestor's song?

William Ferea

You can't record the songs at an initiation of a shaman, but other songs can be recorded. The problem is that the spirit of the dead doesn't warn you when it is coming. It comes at a party or family gathering and then suddenly someone falls down and starts weeping. The spirit catches everyone by surprise, and then she starts singing or starts talking. People ask, "Who are you?" and the spirit makes the ordinary sounds that the dead person used to make in life.

Laurel Kendall

A sudden appearance like that would be very rare in Korea. If it happened to someone, it would be a sign that she was destined to become a shaman. Once she became initiated it probably wouldn't happen again because the person would have sufficient control over the spirits she was calling.

These are powerful experiences. In writing my paper and in listening to these presentations and discussions, I've been thinking about how we try to translate experiences into scholarly papers. Clearly, there are some things that we can't translate: the quality of listening to a story or listening to a song. Even videotapes are a pale shadow of what it's like to be there when a shaman is presenting an ancestor. You're not there with the smells and the sounds and the sweat. I'm wondering, is there something more we ought to be doing as scholars to translate, to transmit these experiences? Or maybe we should leave them alone.

Jacob Olupona

I think I've noticed a dialogue going on here between those who are telling their stories as experienced by them as participants in their own culture and those who are telling the stories as various kinds of participants from another culture. That makes me want to ask a question that may be difficult to answer. Do you really believe that the ancestors are present during the performance of a Korean shaman? Or does such a question require you to leave your role as an anthropologist for the realm of personal feelings?

Laurel Kendall

No, I think my personal feelings and my anthropology are so close that I wouldn't know how to pull them apart. It's very hard for anthropologists to deal with the "Do you believe?" question, because if, on the one hand, one says, "No, I don't," then one is just a skeptical exploiter of other people's beliefs. If, on the other hand, you say, "Yes, I do," you are suspected of being some sort of academic charlatan, or fool.

I would say that I think this is a process whereby the dead are made real in ways that I wish my dead could be made real. Dreams are whatever dreams are. Whatever these appearances are, the shamans claim that they are hearing voices, they are getting sensations, and their role is something like that of a translator—more than that, of portrayer and evoker of experience. In that evocation there is an emotional exchange that is real in its effect. "Are they really, literally, there?" is pretty much a western question. "Do I feel they are there?" That's a question about the emotional satisfactions we get from an evocation of the ancestors. I can say that I have been brushed by the wings of an ancestral presence because I've been allowed to share in these events. I'm struggling to find a way to express this that is neither an uncritical acceptance of all experiences nor a very distanced, "objective," scholarly writing. As a strategy, I attempt to convey the vividness of people's stories as they were told to me. I'm trying to present them honestly, because their story is far more important than my story. I'm a medium, as it were.

Rhythms from the Past Beating into the Future

Pualani Kanahele

[The session began with a Hawaiian prayer.]

That was a prayer to our *'aumakua*, wherever they may be, behind us, close to us, far away from us, guiding us from the east or from the west. It is a way to attract their attention, to call on them, to include all of them.

My mother was a great woman and she was a great teacher for many people. At one of the conferences we did for students, we talked quite a bit about my mother, but we did not talk much about my father. Afterward one of the women said to me, "I expected you to talk about your father, but you only talked about your mother." So I said, "Well, my mother was a very public person and a teacher. What she shared was for everybody to know and to learn. My father was a very private person. What he and his family had was for us and it was not for us to share."

So I want to talk today about my mother. She was a good mother, a great person, a good Christian. She was interviewed many times and once she was asked, "When do you compose?" Her eyes lit up and she said, "Oh, I wake up at two or three o'clock in the morning and that's when I compose." The interviewer asked why, and she replied, "Because it's quiet and peaceful. That's when I can reach out. And more importantly, that's when they can reach back to me." This is the attitude that has been instilled in us. She did not sit us down and say, "This is the way it is, this is the way it is, and this is the way it is." It was a way of life, a way of life that we learned. It was a rhythm for us and we followed it. Hopefully, our daughters will imitate their mothers as well. We also follow our father, but in our culture it is the mother that we tend to imitate.

One of the senses that we utilize is the sense of feeling. We feel from our *na'au,* from our gut. Maybe this starts at birth, maybe it starts before. This sense of feeling is something that we must cultivate because it is the pulse that makes us sensitive to the unseen world. It gets us going toward adulthood and leads us, hopefully, to become one with the 'aumakua. But because we live in this world, somewhere along the way people eliminate this sense of feeling and become very logical. There's always an explanation for it, but we forget about this fundamental sense called feeling.

As we grew up in our family, we were not allowed to forget our sense of feeling. Whenever we went to a new place where we had never been, our na'au would tell us whether we belonged there or not. If we felt bad about being there, we had to leave or ask permission to be there. In either case we found out more about that particular place, but we cultivated this sense of feeling. We were not allowed to forget it or to become caught up in this other world to which we belong. Both worlds—logic and feelings—have to work side by side in order for us to maintain our identity, and in order for us to be good members of our society.

When I told my husband that I was coming here to take part in this conference, he chuckled to himself. I asked him why he was laughing and he said, "You know it's really funny that you should be going to speak about 'aumakua at that conference." When I asked why, he said, "Oh, because you [and Ulunui Garmon] were both raised in the Christian environment." That is true. We were raised in a Christian setting and we are Mormon. But the people around us were Hawaiian and spoke in Hawaiian. People went to school and learned Hawaiian; we went to the ranch in the summer and everyone there was Hawaiian. And even if they were Christians, they still had their *pu'olo,* and their pu'olo told them how to take care of their ancestors. Pu'olo are bundles by which they could send out to do evil or to get revenge or to hurt someone. They kept their pu'olo and they talked about spirits and about night marchers.[1] They had all of this knowledge and they handed it down to us. So even in this environment of Christianity, we also grew up with a Hawaiian heritage, and it is not foreign to me as a Christian.

For me, this feeling is the thing that sends pulses and the pulses make us move our arms as Hawaiians. I like to think of it as rhythm, because we are from a dancing tradition and the dancing tradition has to do with rhythm and pulses. When we play our drums, the beat of the drums ends the way it began. There is a cycle, a rhythm. As the drum beats, we also do a step in our family's tradition that ends where it begins. It comes back to the center. Your senses tell you where you are and how you started. It allows you to go out and it brings you back.

The rhythm as we know it in hula does not only apply to hula itself, it applies to our life. It defines who we are. Ulunui mentioned one of the most obvious rhythms, the rising and the setting of the sun. First you have birth and then you have death. And once death comes, there is another birth and the cycle continues. You have to have death in order to have birth.

When my father died two years ago, we held a ceremony because it was a new time in our life. Both our parents were gone and now we were the parents, the *makua*. Up to that time, we were not the parents even though we had children. Now the parents were gone and a ceremony was needed to begin the new cycle. My daughter was pregnant and near her due date when my father died. On the day that we were going to bury my father, my son-in-law saw a large black boar walking up the driveway to our farm. This had never happened in the ten years that we had lived there. The boar walked up the driveway, crossed in front of our house, stopped in front of our house and looked inside. My husband started looking all over, saying, "Where's my gun? Where's my gun?" But we wouldn't let him shoot the pig. It had never come before, and it would leave the way it came. The boar stood around for awhile and continued on its way. For us, that was a *hoʻailona* (sign) that my daughter was going to have her baby. That night, she went into labor after we buried my father; she went into labor and she had a son the next day. We named the child after my father.

My family is from the island of Hawaiʻi and we are hula people. Because we are from the island of Hawaiʻi, Pele is foremost in our minds, in our hearts, and in our pulse. She lives in the rhythm of our island, in the rhythm of birth and erosion. Last Friday was the ninth anniversary of the continuous eruption of Pele at Kilauea Volcano and so we began another workshop with our families. The story of the migration of Pele is interesting to us because it tells us that Pele and her siblings started off on this journey to a land they had never seen before. They jump into a canoe, get onto a wave, and ride it. The first land that they reach is Nehoa, then Lehua, and then Niʻihau. They do not stay long in any place until they come to the island of Hawaiʻi. Pele is there for a while and then she makes a spiritual trip. She comes out of her body, travels to Kauaʻi, and then back to Hawaiʻi. The next to follow her in this cycle is her younger sister, Hiʻiaka. The story is very, very long, but there is continuous movement, back and forth, east and west. Pele is the deity of land, she is the one who is born from the womb of her mother. Her responsibility is to go back into the womb of her mother and bring out the magma—the lava, or the "Pele" as we call it—to allow for the extension of the land. The first trip that she made eastward tells you that the land was built and extends eastward. Today when we look at the movement of lava and how the land is being made, it moves southeastward. That was the movement of Pele in her initial migration and she continues to move eastward. But Pele is also destructive. She has covered a lot of homes of loved ones that we know, a lot of land of people who have lived there for a hundred years, people whose ancestors have lived there for hundreds of years. She has covered that land within this last eruptive cycle. So people look at Pele and see destruction.

Her sister, on the other hand, is looked at as being the deity of birth, the deity of new growth, who follows her sister in this cycle to the east and comes back to the west. While Pele is thought of as being the maker of new land and a destructive force, Hi'iaka is known as the benevolent sister who allows things to grow. The two sisters play on each other, a negative and a positive that are both necessary for new growth. When we begin the hula, we come out with a chant. This particular chant brings the dancers on the stage, symbolizing the rising of the sun. When they arrive on the stage, the dancers do the dances of the gods and then they do the dances of the *ali'i* (chiefs, rulers). Before they leave the stage they do a dance in praise and in honor of the genitals, because from these parts will come more Hawaiians. Then they finish with a dance symbolizing the setting of the sun. So the whole performance is done in praise of life, Pele and Hi'iaka, the cycle.

In an interview, someone asked my mother, "In the older culture, they would usually pick somebody to carry on a particular tradition. Who do you pick to carry on your tradition?" My mother laughed, and she said, "I don't pick anybody. Many of them learn and one of them will come forward and will continue." I was sitting in the room when I heard her say that and it hit me that it was my responsibility. I heard her say it with my own ears. And I know that somebody in the next generation of our family will carry on as well, maybe a daughter, a nephew, or niece. The cycle will be continued because it has been instilled. It's not so much that we carry it on from generation to generation; the process that we go through to instill the rhythm is more important.

Now, what does all this have to do with 'aumakua? What we do comes from our ancestors. My personal connections for 'aumakua are my parents, my grandparents, my great-grandparents. They are my 'aumakua; they are the ones I'm going to depend on if I need help. And they depend on us to allow this rhythm to move forward and to be carried on. If the rhythm does not move on, if we do not carry it forth, then we are brown *haole* (Caucasians) and have none of our culture left in our family. Our culture is our dance tradition. Our culture is our chanting tradition. If we allow the dances to die, then we are brown haole.

This weighs heavy on those who carry tradition, but we also take great joy in that tradition. I enjoy going out to chant, I enjoy playing my drums, and that makes the difference. If we enjoy it, then we have the guidance of our 'aumakua.

But we always have to rethink our rhythm, rethink the cycle. If I'm going to the crater to do a ceremony and they tell me it is for a particular reason, I'm not going to do a generic chant that has nothing to do with that crater. I'm going to think of a chant that I sense would fit the moment. As I make my way from my house up to the crater, I'm thinking of the chant that I should do. This is when I will call on my ancestors, and especially on my grandmother. My mother was a good chanter, but my grandmother was an excellent chanter and so the one I'm going to choose would be my grandmother. She would be the one that I would call on to come forward and to help me, and when I get there I will do it without flaw. That is the connection to our 'aumakua. We keep them alive because we carry on the tradition.

How do we know that the 'aumakua listens to us, that the 'aumakua is there to help us? We look for her sign. Not everything we do is wonderful. Sometimes there is no sign and we wonder, "Shall we do it or not?" When we went to the Smithsonian to bring back our Hawaiian bones that were taken there for scientific analysis, there was a lot of disagreement among Hawaiians about the situation.[2] There was a lot of uneasiness between groups about the idea of going to get them, how they should be brought over, how they should be wrapped, how and where they should be buried. So we had to pool our resources in order for this to come about.

One young Hawaiian went to the Smithsonian to see the bones. He asked if he could see the Hawaiian bones, so they showed them to him. He was so moved by the bones that he left something of himself—something that was personally his and had part of his *mana*—in one of the boxes of these bones as a promise that he would return. There was an urgency in his voice when he came home to Hawai'i and said, "We have to bring them back!" Because of his urgency, we paid attention. We had to pay attention because it came from his na'au. We felt his concern. You need to realize that there are still strong disagreements to this day about the reburial of the bones, even among the people in this room. But we felt we had to listen because of his urgency.

Within several months, the bones came back. Amid the hoopla and the *hakaka*, we brought them back. People on each island were responsible for replanting the bones of their island. On our island, the island of Hawai'i, we kept them in a cave for awhile. We had to prepare ourselves with care, with rituals and with prayers asking our 'aumakua for guidance. You see, there aren't any records of ceremonies for reburial. These bones had been exhumed, taken far away, and studied by scientists. So we had to do a lot of praying, we had to call on a lot of *kupuna* (elders). Many people wouldn't touch the bones because we don't know whose bones they are. And they were right. We don't know who they are and they could have a lot of negative mana in them. Nevertheless, they are kupuna and they belong to our island.

When we finally went out to replant the bones in the proper cave, a rainbow appeared. This was our first positive ho'ailona. Up to that time, we had seen nothing but negative responses from everyone. But our gut feeling told us that we had to put them back into the ground. We brought them back to the vehicle, we rewrapped them in *tapa* cloth, and there were two claps of thunder. No rain, just two claps of thunder. The men rewrapped the bones and reburied them.

That night, we drove the bones from Ka'u back to the people who were waiting to take care of them. They dug a place for the bones and replanted them. After all of this was over we did our cleansing bath at a place where the ocean is usually very rough. That night, the ocean was calm and there was just enough moon so we could see where we were stepping to get into the water and back out. Just before we said our prayers, a number of falling stars appeared toward the west and after our prayers were done, the moon set in the west. To us these were all good ho'ailona, ho'ailona that were an affirmation of what we were doing.

So this is a rhythm from the past that beats into the future. The bones of our ancestors give mana to the ground where we live. That mana eventually becomes a part of us and we impart it back into the ground. The mana then becomes a part of our children, our grandchildren, our great-grandchildren. This is the rhythm, death and birth, the life of the land.

Notes

1. Night marchers are spiritual beings from Old Hawai'i who are seen in groups after dark.

2. See also the chapter by John Grim, below.

Discussion

Rubellite Johnson

Pua, you mentioned people who opposed the return and reburial of the Hawaiian bones. Why did some Hawaiians feel it was inappropriate to bring back the bones?

Pualani Kanahele

Hawaiians did oppose it, and that's what hurt the most. Many were hesitant about bringing back the bones because they felt that there was no longer anyone left with the right to rebury them.

Rubellite Johnson

That's true, but for me a different issue was paramount. I respect the fact that the bones should be returned, but I opposed reburial because of the tremendous outlay of money. I agree that we need to care for our dead, but there are such great needs among our living children. I think the money is better spent on future generations than on those past. Yet, those of us who wanted to allocate that money for the living were not heard.

Pualani Kanahele

Maybe we were heard because we were taking care of the dead and the dead were taking care of us.

Rubellite Johnson

I think it had more to do with political power, but it's important to get these issues out on the table, to show why Hawaiians are divided on these matters. I just can't see committing so much money to the dead when there aren't even enough funds to care properly for our children.

Sam Kaai

I guess the question is whether we believe in abundance, or in the idea that heaven has dealt us a measured portion to be spent. In these islands, many things thought to be valuable are slipping away.

Jill Raitt

The issue of exclusivity came up in your presentation. I want to note that people are often more exclusive in their words than in their lives. The real problem may be at the level of rhetoric. When you talk about the na'au, I understand that as a way of expressing yourself in terms of what is actually happening to you, instead of in terms of a language that colors what is happening to you. Too many people describe themselves in terms of what they've been told or what they've read, instead of examining what they actually feel.

John Grim

It's true that exclusivity is an important question that has generated a lot of energy around this table. We need to keep asking, "Can traditions exist side by side in one person? What is the nature of that internal dialogue within the individual?" For me, however, there is a more important issue. I am wondering whether we can hear the voices of the spirits, the voices of the species, rather than just the voices of the religions. These presentations and discussions are lessons for me in my own cultural autism, in the training that has cut me off from the world around me. You have challenged me from your tradition to examine my own na'au. Am I hearing something I've been taught not to listen to?

Pualani Kanahele

Let me respond in this way. In earlier times, when our men went up to the mountains to cut down an important tree, they also took somebody from their race and killed that person in exchange for the life of the tree. They understood that a person has an everlasting self that we sometimes call "spirit" and a physical self. They knew that the tree that they cut down also had an everlasting self because it grew like a human grows. They exchanged spirit for spirit out of respect for that particular tree, so that the spirit of the tree and the spirit of the man would respect each other in their respective realms. We do the same thing with the fish in the ocean. We believe that the fish in the ocean, the trees in the forest, and humanity all have their own spheres. We were not put here to dominate one over the other; we were put here to live in harmony with each other, to exchange, to use each other respectfully when necessary.

You may have heard about the current controversy regarding the government's practice of hunting down sharks after someone is attacked at the beach. Some Hawaiians oppose the hunting of sharks because they are an important 'aumakua. I have mixed feelings about this. Not every single shark is an 'aumakua, but all of the sharks have spirit and they possess great mana. In fact, at one time the sharks were considered the ali'i of the sea, parallel to the human ali'i who lived on the land. When I see people going off to hunt sharks, I think, "The shark is killing in his own environment. Why are we intervening in that environment to kill the sharks?" Whether it is an 'aumakua or not, that is his world and he doesn't come out of his world to kill us. We are the intruders. So, when we talk about understanding primal people who live in balance with nature, we have to recognize these limits, these containers. Humans are the ones who are trying to climb out of these containers, trying to dominate everything else. We're succeeding in this, and it has created a great imbalance.

III. Ancestral Land

Aloha 'Aina
Love of the Land in Hawai'i

David Ka'upu

Aloha to the gods. Aloha to each and every one of you for your aloha, and for allowing me to be here to share my thoughts with you. I am an ordained Christian minister, and have been for thirty-three years. I am also a Hawaiian and I consider myself a culturalist. The thoughts I will be sharing with you come from David Ka'upu as a Hawaiian. I do not see any sense of confusion or confinement in my development as a Hawaiian Christian. If this seems to some of you to be a very different Christian—or perhaps even unchristian—style, then I make an apology in advance, so that we may discuss these things together.

I would like to begin by sharing some experiences that have impacted my life with regard to the topic of ancestors. My ministry took me to the island of Kaua'i in 1963 where I was pastor to two churches within the Kaua'i Mokupuni of the United Church of Christ. One was a Japanese church and one was a Hawaiian church. The two congregations shared a lot of things, including our educational building. One of the uses we had for that educational building was a weekday program for the Association of Mental Retardation on the island of Kaua'i. The primary teacher for the class of fifteen to twenty retarded students was a member of the Japanese church. Her assistant was part Hawaiian, but not a member of the Hawaiian church.

In 1967 there was a series of accidents on the island, most of which occurred in Waimea Canyon. This happened over a period of three or four months. Experienced hunters and hikers who went out into the canyon region were injured or killed in unusual circumstances. Some of them got lost and rescue teams had to be called in. The assistant teacher of the retarded students had a seventeen-year-old son who had just completed his junior year at Waimea High School. That summer he was hiking with a friend on the trail at the top of the ridge to go down into the canyon and, for some reason, that young lad tripped on the ridge and plunged to his death. All of this, as I said, happened within a period of three to four months.

Then one day—I believe it was September of 1967—a golden eagle was sighted flying in Waimea Canyon. Those who know the area expressed surprise about the presence of the golden eagle. Why was it there? It was totally out of its natural habitat. It did not belong there and people could not understand why the eagle happened to be in that canyon. Someone asked an elderly woman who lived in the foothills of the canyon for an explanation of why the eagle was there in Waimea Canyon. Her simple explanation was, "It is the god Lono who has come back to bless the canyon." After the eagle was sighted, no more "accidents" happened in the canyon. After that first sighting, the eagle was not seen again for fourteen months.

I would like to thank Sam Kaai for reminding me of the second incident that I would like to relate to you. I participated in the first launching of the Hokule'a, a traditional Hawaiian ship built for sailing with ancient navigational methods. The first voyage of the Hokule'a down to Tahiti and back was successful. The second voyage met some stormy conditions. During the storm the Hokule'a was located, but for a period of about three or four days there was no communication whatsoever with the ship. The escort ship was to stay beyond the horizon so that the Hokule'a could sail according to the ancient tradition of the sea. So when the Hokule'a encountered this storm, there was no communication at all. For three or four days, none of us knew whether the ship was still afloat or whether the crew was safe.

The first mate of that crew was a young man whose father is a Hawaiian historian and culturalist. When the swamping happened, and during that period when there was no communication with the Hokule'a or the crew, his father was asked how he felt about the situation. He responded, "The 'aumakua of our family is the mano, the shark, and if there is any place that I feel comfortable for my son to be at this point and time, it is on our seas." Communication with the crew of the Hokule'a was finally restored and they said that when the canoe was swamped, they could see sharks circling them for the days of the storm, but the sharks did not bother them at all. This was an affirmation of the father's knowledge that the son was protected by their family 'aumakua.

The purpose of the 'aumakua system, as I understand it, is two-fold. The 'aumakua system allows our Hawaiian people to affirm the family relationship, both for family members that are physically present and for those that are no longer physically present. Those who are no longer physically present provide family guardianship. This guardian role of the 'aumakua is seen in the story about the Hokule'a. But there is another purpose to the system. We also consider an 'aumakua to be a god or goddess—or whatever term you prefer—that affirms the sense of spiritual energy to which we give the name God. The 'aumakua are the agents who connect our world with the other world. Hence, our affirmation of the ancestral gods, or ancestors in the sense of 'aumakua.

My understanding of the 'aumakua in my own spiritual development leads to two or three conclusions that are crucial for my understanding of life. One is the affirmation of all creation. As I understand it, according to my culture, everything that exists in creation—all the tangible things that we see, feel, smell—these are without question the handiwork of the gods. There is a spiritual energy that provides the necessary foundation of all that there is in life. And to affirm that, my culture allows me to relate to gods or goddesses that have primary responsibilities for each living thing, human or otherwise. For example, when I want to go fishing I affirm Ku'ula, and in affirming Ku'ula I can accept the fact that I'm going to have a good day at fishing. But my affirmation of Ku'ula is a recognition that this is his realm. When I go into that realm, I need to affirm this so that I can be responsible to the ocean, its creatures, and the harvesting of fish. This releases me from any fear of the ocean and its inhabitants. I am at ease on the ocean as long as I have affirmed the god that cares for the ocean.

The island of Molokai is the land of my birth, and La'ama'oma'o, the goddess of the winds, was a part of my earliest experiences. The remotest part of the island was the east valley, called Halawa. The legends of our land teach us that there are forty winds that have been identified as being present in that valley. La'ama'oma'o controls all these winds and she decides when certain kinds of winds should wash over the people and the land. It is her *kuleana*, her affair, to send them out. Now, I am not a meteorologist and I do not know specifically why the winds blow in certain directions or at certain velocities at certain times of the day. But I do accept that there is a spiritual energy in the winds.

There are also very simple but very beautiful explanations of how the valleys and rivers of our lands were formed by the 'aumakua Kamapua'a, the pig god. At the very beginning of creation Kamapua'a went looking for food. In digging the land with his paws the valleys were shaped, and the saliva of his snorting resulted in the streams and rivers of our land. We also have stories that explain the changes in the lengths of the days and nights throughout the year. One day, the mother of the demigod Maui washed her hair and it was not dry by evening. So Maui kept the sun out longer than usual in order to allow his mother's hair to dry. These are not just primitive stories to be replaced by recently developed scientific explanations. These stories connect us simultaneously to the land, to our ancestors, and to the gods. The valleys and the rivers are not simply random processes of erosion, nor are the seasons of the year simply a cosmic accident. The stories teach us about the spiritual source, about the spiritual energy responsible for the earth and creation. This is crucial to my Hawaiian spirituality. It recognizes the affinity between the physical and the so-called metaphysical, between the natural and so-called supernatural reality.

A second way the 'aumakua system is helpful to me is as a Christian minister and theologian, because it enables me to connect the Jesus of history with the Christ of faith. The continuity between the Jesus who lived a historical life and the Christ in whom we Christians believe would be difficult for me to understand without the model of the 'aumakua system. But my Hawaiian spirituality allows me to see Jesus as my 'aumakua who has passed from physical presence to spiritual presence.

Third, the 'aumakua system ties together the gods, the ancestors, and the living by the practice of 'ohana. The simplest definition of the term 'ohana in the Hawaiian language is "family." In our culture, however, there is a much deeper meaning than simply family. I grew up in a family of fifteen children, all with the same parents. The first experience of the day was for us to come together and to have devotions, to acknowledge our sense of spirituality. And the last thing that we did before we went to sleep was to come together for the affirmation of our spirituality in devotion. The call that brought us together was simply the two words, "'Ohana kakou!" When we heard that, we affirmed the ancestors' understanding of 'ohana. The phrase was not confined to, "Come let us make family!" The word *kakou* means togetherness; it is the plural that includes everyone. So, "'Ohana kakou!" also means that we come together to pray and to affirm this relationship with our god or our gods, as the case may be.

So, the cultural foundation of the 'ohana is spiritual. Without this spiritual understanding, the 'ohana relationship is very difficult to practice or even to affirm. The beginning of all family relationships is the acknowledgment of 'aumakua, the spiritual source. And, conversely, 'ohana is the tie that binds us with our 'aumakua.

Hawaiians like to get together as families, and there has been a lot of encouragement for family reunions in recent years. When my own family started to reunite, we began by honoring my great-grandmother on my mother's side. We went to the place where we believe she is buried, even though we have no proof of the exact location; we simply know that she lived in that area. We went to the burial ground and the celebration of our first family reunion took place there. Affirming my great-grandmother was necessary for us to secure our genealogical relationship with each other; but it was also a means for us to revitalize our sense of spiritual relationship with her, our ʻaumakua now buried there in that particular place.

To conclude my presentation, I want to go back to the title, "Aloha ʻAina." In our family, as for all Hawaiians, the ʻaina has *mana*, or "power." We are endearingly known as "keiki hanau o ka ʻaina." *Keiki* means "child"; *hanau* means "born, to give birth to"; and ʻaina is the "land." We are "children born of the land." For us, it is literally the land that gives us life, both spiritual life and physical life. That is why it was necessary for my family to begin the reunion process by going back to the burial ground, the land where our ancestors are.

In this way, you might even say that the ʻaina is our ʻaumakua. In the ʻaina there is that sense of spiritual force, spiritual energy, spiritual awakening. Aloha ʻaina in this sense means respect for the land and its traditions, for all that there is in the land. When I officiate in burial services, I often make the point that when we die here in Hawaiʻi, we will be referred to as "keiki make no ka ʻaina" (approximately, "children who have died belonging to the land"). By that we mean that our spiritual life begins in the land. Our children commit us to the land for the afterlife. We recognize that the land is our spiritual home, the home where we connect with our ancestors who are also there in the land. There is a saying, "Mai kaulai ia na ʻiwi o kou kupuna," which means, "Do not dry out the bones of your ancestors, your *kupuna*." They have begun their spiritual life in the land. So I affirm the ʻaina as our ʻaumakua, the land as a vital source that connects us to the life of the spirit.

Discussion

Jill Raitt

Thank you for speaking openly and insightfully about your Hawaiian faith. I'd like to pursue the question of the relationship of your culture and your faith, because these are often considered to be at odds with each other. How exactly do you see the connection between your Hawaiian heritage and your Christian ministry?

David Ka'upu

Let me respond to that question in this way. As the chaplain at a school for Hawaiian children, I am responsible for about three thousand students. We just completed a new chapel that makes three distinctive statements. One is cultural: we at Kamehameha Schools have a responsibility for Hawaiian culture and for the traditions of our culture. Second, we are a religious Christian school. And third, we have a unique commitment to the education of Hawaiian children.

If you come to our chapel, 95 percent of what you see in there is Hawaiian culture. Perhaps the most distinctive examples of Hawaiian culture are four panels that we had designed and carved. These are panels with symbols of the "old Hawaiian religion." The panels include the *kahili*, the shark, the ocean, and the idols that were in the religious places of Old Hawai'i. Some people get very disturbed by those panels being in a Christian chapel. The reason we had those panels carved was to help us be sensitive to our culture's means and methods that allow us to celebrate our new faith, Christianity. For example, the kahili symbolized royalty in Old Hawai'i and now becomes for us the affirmation of the royal character of Jesus, who is called the Christ. The shark reminds us of our people's acceptance of 'aumakua. For those of us who have become Christians, Jesus Christ is now our "family god," our 'aumakua.

The ocean affirms creation. I often use Psalm 24 in ground-breaking ceremonies. It says, "The earth is the Lord's, and everything in it, the world, and all who live in it; for he founded it upon the seas and established it upon the waters." In seminary I once wrote an overly bold paper claiming that the Hebrew author of Psalm 24 must have known Hawaiian. I guess the point was really that we Hawaiians are an ocean-culture people and we can identify with that psalm. Our land literally came out of the ocean; it is founded upon the sea. This island depends on the waters that flow from the Ko'olau Range and from the Wai'anae Mountains.

The fourth panel depicts the idols of the old Hawaiian religion, and this allows us to affirm the use we make of our own Christian symbols. In the chapel there is an altar, a Bible, and a communion cup. Those are all symbols that allow us to affirm our new Christian faith. We want the panels to speak to us also, to affirm our faith, as those Hawaiian symbols did in the old days for our people.

Jacob Olupona

I want to follow up on that question because it is related to issues I deal with in my own cultural context as an African. Granted, the Hebrew Bible is not that different in some ways from primal traditions, as you have suggested. But is it really that simple to reconcile foreign Christianity with indigenous worldviews? Can the centrality of Christ be reconciled to primal religions that encourage us to talk about ancestors, about all these other gods, about the sacredness of the land?

David Ka'upu

I have no problem affirming the fact that Jesus Christ is the Son of God and that there is indeed salvation through him. My ordination vows as a Christian minister remind me of that and I have no problem with it. What does bother me, however, is the Christian notion that people are the supreme part of creation. What I affirm is that all creation, including humanity, is supreme. Jesus Christ brings a new dimension as the savior of all creation, and for that I need to see the Bible in its wholeness as the Holy Bible, as one book rather than two different testaments. When I see it as one book, then I can affirm Jesus Christ as being the savior of creation, and not only the savior of people.

Ewert Cousins

The technique that was used within the New Testament itself to assimilate elements from the Old Testament was allegorizing, especially in liturgy. For example, in one New Testament text John the Baptist sees Jesus and says, "Behold the Lamb of God." That image assimilates all that "lamb" meant in the Hebrew Bible and focuses it on Jesus. I once spent a year in Jerusalem and we read the Psalms everyday. It was there I realized in a personal way that when we Christians read the Psalms, we do not read them the way Jewish people read them. For us, the shepherd and the king are symbols of Christ. What Christians have done is assimilate the great traditions under the rubric of the cosmic Christ. I don't think Christian missionaries have consciously used this technique very often, even though it often occurs unintentionally and even though it is the one that is used most within scripture itself. We could enrich the Christian theological tradition by doing this in a systematic fashion, by including the truths of the symbols of primal people throughout the world.

Living the Dreaming
Aboriginal Ancestors Past and Present

Diane Bell

The Law of the Land

If one asks: Why do you call out before approaching a sacred site? Why do you sweep the paths clean the first time one visits the camping site of a deceased relative? Why do you click your fingers to move rain clouds? Why does the hunter not get the best part of the catch? Why do you never look directly at or speak to your mother-in-law? Why do you marry a classificatory matrilateral cross cousin? Why do you kill a goanna by hitting it behind the ear? Why is a baby carrier rubbed with red ochre? Why do you always ask a particular relative if you can go to a certain place to hunt or gather? The first answer will most likely be, "because that's the Law," or "that's the Dreaming."

Although Aboriginal beliefs and practices are not consistent across the continent, at the core is the concept of the Dreamtime, a moral code that informs and unites all life. The dogma of Dreaming states that all the world is known and can be classified within the taxonomy created by the ancestral heroes whose pioneering travels gave form, shape, and meaning to the land. Here a rocky outcrop indicates the place where the ancestral dog had her puppies, there a low ridge the sleeping body of the emu; the red streaks on the cliff face recall the blood shed in a territorial dispute; ghost gums stand as mute witness to where the Lightning Brothers flashed angrily at their father Rain; the lush growth of bush berries is the legacy of prudent care by two old grandmothers; the clear, sweet water holes, the home of the rainbow serpent, remain pure only if approached by those schooled in the "business" (the term used for the work necessary to maintain the Law of the Dreamtime). This concept of law as organizing the human, supernatural, and natural world, as allocating responsibilities for the maintenance of order, and as resolving disputes can be generalized for the continent.

The Law is inscribed on the land and encoded in the relationships that are testimony to the continuance of the Law. The Law of the Dreamtime binds people, flora, fauna, and natural phenomena into one enormous interfunctional world. It is the responsibility of the living, who trace direct relationships to these ancestors, to give form and substance to this heritage in their daily routines and their ceremonial practice: to keep the Law, to visit sites, to use the country, and to enjoy its bounty. It is in the living out of the Dreamtime heritage, particularly in the ceremonial domain, that we see how the past is negotiated in the present, how women and men position themselves vis à vis each other and vis-à-vis the Law. The common core of knowledge of the Dreamtime concerns knowledge of ancestral activity (the major sites and their spiritual affiliations), the rights of living descendants, and the responsibilities of the ritual bosses of the business. It is a structural grid onto which people, place, and relatedness are mapped. It is through ceremonial activity that men and women give form to their distinctive interpretation of this heritage.

In much of the Central Desert country Aborigines trace their relationship to the land through both their mother's father and father's father. Other considerations are also important. Some are specific and individualistic: there are special qualities about the place where one's forebears are buried and the place where one was born or conceived. The latter is usually reckoned by the first sensation of movement felt by the mother-to-be, the quickening, approximately the sixteenth week of a pregnancy. Both birth and conception sites are open to a degree of manipulation in that one can plan to be in a particular area when a birth is imminent, or one can choose not to acknowledge a pregnancy until near a site with which one would like to have one's child affiliated. Others are more general and communally based, centering around ties of kinship and ritual sharing or exchange. People also have sentimental ties to places where they worked and lived. These are the places they know, and in Aboriginal society, it is only with knowledge of the ways of the land that one may assert a right to use that land. These links are critical to the structure of ceremonies and to the Aborigines' rights and responsibilities in land and have been the subject of spirited anthropological debate for some time.[1] It is only recently, in the course of presenting land claims in the Northern Territory, that Aboriginal voices have been given any primacy in discussions about land. However, the constraints of the Australian law, which seeks to "recognize" traditional ties to land, specifies that to be granted title to the land of their ancestors, Aborigines must meet the criteria of traditional ownership enshrined in statute (see below, the section "A New Land

Law"). In a sense, Anglo law fixes what was once dynamic, negotiable, accommodating, and integrative. The seamless web woven by Aboriginal narratives is asserted to be unchanging. This assertion, the dogma of Dreaming, has been taken as a lived reality by Anglo law.

In an oral culture, the Law can only be given meaning through the expressions of the living. As long as one has contact with the land and control over sacred sites, the Dreamtime, as the ever-present, all-encompassing Law, can be asserted to be reality. But land, as the central tablet, as the sacred text, is no longer under Aboriginal control across the continent. Accounts of ancestral travels reflect these altered circumstances, and in the accounts of contact with the colonizers and the changing use of land, Aborigines attempt to contain the changes, to assimilate the intruders, and thus make them amenable to their Law. The narratives of travels through the country of the ancestors, of family, and of outsiders, now meld details of the ruptures in relations to land with those of the continuity of connectedness asserted with the past. The Aboriginal narratives I am presenting here were recorded in various contexts and take us from the first contacts with whites in the late nineteenth century through to the post-1976 land rights era.[2] They tell of the struggles of Warlpiri, Warumungu, Alyawarra, Kaytej, and other peoples of the Central Desert region of Australia to maintain the Law of the land of their ancestors.

Narratives of the Land

Charlie Charles Jakamarra, the close classificatory "brother" of a woman I called "sister," was in his late sixties in 1978 when I recorded this account of the journeys taken by his family when the land was still under their control. While explaining his relationship to his land, now worked as a heavy metal mine, he sketched in the sand the orientation of one site to the next, and made the symbol for water (be it soakage, water hole, rock hole, or creek bed), a most precious resource for desert peoples.

> We would begin at Kupurla after dinner and then travel to Lurrpa (now Black Angel Mine). We went backwards and forwards. If we went to Pawurrinji it took three nights to get there. There were soakages in the mulga but there is too much scrub to see that now. Watijiparnta, south of Kuparla and Ngarladu, north of Pawurrinji, are two I remember. . . . Jukurtayimanjimanji was a place where all people could sit down during big rain time. We would go along Pawurrinji and, in the dry time we would come back, and in the dry time at Jukurtayimanjimanji. It was eleven miles

from here that my father died. He was going north, following the water flat.
We left after that. We were too sorry to go back.

The centrality of sacred sites in the Aboriginal system of land tenure finds an interesting correlate in the use to which the land has been put by the colonists. Often, sacred sites encode information about an anomalous physical feature, and often, these sites are of significance to miners, the builders of towns, roads, to graziers, and so on. Although the rationale may be very different, both cultures have found significance in certain sites (one sacred in the religion, the other sacred to the economy), and it is this common focus that generates many conflicts over who has rights in land. Accusations that Aborigines "invent" sacred sites to thwart development reflect fundamentally different value systems and modes of recording information.[3] Codes of secrecy protect Aboriginal sacred sites, but to gain protection under Anglo law, sites must be sign-posted and made public. Disputes only occur when alternate land use is proposed and by then there is a developmental price tag on the site.

The stress on place names in narratives is one way in which people affirm their rights in land: in calling the names they evoke the mythology of the place and their responsibility to keep that knowledge alive. This can be done without having to live continuously on the site. Here Charlie spoke about the death of his father. At the death of a close relative all things associated with that person become taboo. But because people can trace ties to various parts of the country, it was possible to move away and assert a right to another area. There are other reasons why Charlie cannot return to the land of his grandparents. Extensive grazing has destroyed many of the natural watercourses in the desert regions—the waters are muddied, and the banks eroded, plus many of the best permanent water holes are now within the boundaries of pastoral leases of cattle stations (ranches).

When telling of the Dreamtime, people rarely distinguish between what is now vacant crown land and what has been alienated. They are careful, however, not to speak of things beyond the bounds of their country. Here Mollie Nungarrayi, a woman in her late fifties, a revered ritual expert, spoke of the activities of the kangaroo ancestor in the country of Jarrajarra, the land of her deceased father. She was giving evidence of traditional ownership in a land claim hearing in 1981:

The big father kangaroo was staying at one place, and two kangaroos
came up from the east, his brothers, to visit him. They told him, "Get up. Get
up." He could not get up, he still stayed there. They tried to wake him up, get

*him up to rouse him, but they could not get him up. He stayed there. . . . The
fire came down. He was still there and the others were telling him, "Get up!"
The fire was coming closer and closer and his brothers were telling him, "Get
up old man. The fire is coming closer, it's coming right up." But he couldn't
get up because he had injured his back and he still stayed there. He couldn't
get up and the fire was coming closer and his brothers were telling him,
"Come on you've got to get up now. It's going to burn you now." The fire was
coming closer. The two kangaroo brothers are sitting down now. The fire got
really close. Then they did something magic, something special. They took
him under their arm and they were asking which way will we go of each
other, and then they went through the fire. They put the old man somewhere, some magic way. They went to Ngapawulpayi, Nyirrawirnu,
Larrara, Ngapawulpayi and Jarrajarra. . . . Yes Nyirrawirnu, then they
went to see them to Yalukarnti. . . . Yes, right through to Yalukartni. The
Dreaming went right through, but we leave it there . . . at Yalukarnti.*

Although, in speaking of her father's country, Nungarryi referred to times
past, the retelling brought the activities of the ancestral heroes into the present.
The exploits of the kangaroo at Jarrajarra, a range west of Tennant Creek, were
of immediate significance. Their travels validated the close links between persons associated with the sites named in the narrative and provided clues for
reading the significance of the physical features of the landscape. This is land
that until recently people have not been able to visit with any ease, but the stories, the ceremonies, the paintings, and songs of the place have allowed the
knowledge to stay alive. Once access to the sites became possible, the unity of
mythological account, ritual activity, and daily practice is again a lived reality
and, in the narratives, the intervening periods of dislocation are expunged. The
web is again seamless. If the gap spans more than several generations, the relational rents are more dramatic and the fabric of the Dreamtime less easily
mended.

Particularly important sites are located where the travels of the ancestors
meet. Pawurrinji, a clay pan west of Tennant Creek, where the willie wagtail
people (*jintirrpiri*) meets with the diamond dove people (*kurlukurku*), is a site
important to many Central Australian people. In 1976, my close "sister"
Nakamarra, a woman in her mid-seventies, told of Pawurrinji, the country of
her father.

*One day Jintirrpiri was cooking jungunypa [a species of mouse] for his
supper and as soon as he cooked it and got it out of the fire, he started eating*

it. Some was left over. He left that in the tree. He went to sleep after that. He heard someone crying and saw some Kurlukurku people coming. The sound kept coming closer and closer. He got up and got a spear, and shook it in anger. They were hungry. As soon as the Kurlukurku people got closer, he recognized them. He put down his spear, called out to them. They had a feast. The Kurlukurku people came and sat around. They all had a feast. Some went into the ground and their spirit still remains at Pawurrinji.

Today the descendants of these Dreamings cooperate in the ceremonies that maintain the country. The designs the dancers wear, the songs they sing, and the patterns they trace in the sand with their feet encode information about the willie wagtail and diamond dove people. Nakamarra, my sister, taught me the songs, designs, and stories for the place. She was determined to see Pawurrinji once more before she died and to be buried at her place, so that when the new generation visited and called out to the ancestors, she would hear. We did get back to Pawurrinji, and it was just as depicted in the Dreaming knowledge I had seen and heard in her ceremonies. In accordance with Anglo law she was buried in the local cemetery. Only very rarely do old people elude the authorities and manage to die and be buried on their own land.

The travels of the ancestral heroes form a grid that links living individuals and groups together and joins them to the past. Although people may trace a relationship to a number of countries and be able to use the resources of a number of areas, there is a clearly defined limit to how much one may say about the places of another. To presume to speak would be like trespass: both dangerous and improper. This does not mean that people do not have knowledge of the activities of the ancestral heroes on the country of others, but that they cannot assert it as their own. They may hear the narratives but not repeat them. Here, during a land claim hearing in 1980, Nampijinpa, Napurrula, and Nungarrayi, experts in women's knowledge, cooperated in the telling of a Dreamtime narrative of the travels of Yaakiyi, a wild blackberry, which links a series of sites into a hierarchy of older and younger brother. These sibling relationships are in turn reflected in the seniority of the lineages that today assume responsibilities for the particular sites.

Yaakiyi comes from Waake and went to visit his brother at Wakulpu, the other one comes from Yanganpali. He stopped at the soakages all along the way . . . at Warnku he was just sitting in the shade . . . there is a creek there. . . . Then he got up and went straight through to Wakulpu. . . . The one

from Waake, he stopped at Jajilpernange, Wulpuje. His brother at Wakulpu
told him to go straight back. There was one Yaakiyi who was sitting by him-
self at Wakulpu; he was sitting there by himself. His name was Amberanger.
He was the oldest brother. That was his secret name. That is the Dreaming's
own name.

This other Yaakiyi came and was asking this one, "What name are you?"
"I am food. I am vegetable food, I think. What about you?" He refused to
answer. He made a sign which means, "I don't know. I don't want to let on."
"I said mine. I'm hungry." What they were doing [Napurrula explained], is
calling each other's secret names. Another name was Yarriranti. "You can be
Yarriranti." He answered, "What about you?" He then said, "I'm
Wakuwarlpa," which is fruit like yaakiyi. . . . They were asking each other
[Napurrula explained], these two Yaakiyi were asking each other for their
secret names and also for the secret places they held. That is all and then he
went back from Wakulpu . . . to Waake . . . back to Waake. The one who was
at Wakulpu stayed living there permanently. He stayed there and that is it
. . . and the one who came from Wauchope . . . he was staying there . . . where
that house, that hotel is now at Wauchope. . . . He went from there, from
Wauchope. He went to Warnku from Wauchope. He went from Warnku to
where there is a swamp and he slept there, at Wirlilunku, that is the name of
the swamp where the Dreaming camped. . . . Then he went to Wakulpu
forever. He entered the ground.

The soakages of Wakulpu, Kurlartakurlangu, Wirlikunku, a swamp,
Jarnapajinijini, . . . [she names another twenty places] all Yaakiyi places,
Kuunali, Kulalje, Kurlalkinyje [she names a further fifteen places] that
Dreaming just goes around in a circle from Wakulpu [another twelve
places] to a soakage, a rockhole, to the north, around to the west, and on its
way to Ngarnapirlapirla. Stop there! We're getting too close to someone
else's country.

The similarities between this narrative of the ancestors and Charlie's telling
of his family's travels indicate the importance of certain knowledge to desert
people and the style in which this will be transmitted in an oral culture. The
narratives are repetitive, emphasize place, relatedness, obligation, correct behavior, and remark on the search for food and the location of water. When the
stories are written down, much is lost. We do not hear the voice, or see the inter-
actions between narrator and audience. It is well to remember that audience
can be controlled within an oral culture: only those with a right to know will be

told, and one does not ask unless one has a claim on the knowledge. Control over audience is lost once the narratives pass into print. They may be read by anyone who is literate.[4] In oral presentations, there is no absolute chronology, and the characters are not static personalities or moral stereotypes. However, when "tidied up," these stories have become bedtime tales for Australian children: they have a beginning, middle, and end and tell of "how the kangaroo got its black mark," but that is incidental to the telling in context.

These accounts of the ancestors are most often communicated in a ceremonial context and then the dancing, song, and participants contribute to the structure of the story. Here I am drawing on women's ritual activities. I worked with women and these are the narratives to which I have most immediate access. But I am also concerned to give voice to women who too often are not included as cultural authorities. In women's narratives there is an attention to detail, the fine-grain interrelations of person to place, and through their ceremonial reenactments of the travels of the ancestors, knowledge is refound, renewed, and revitalized in ways that address current needs. Through women's narratives new items are incorporated into known frames.[5] In ceremonies Aboriginal women work to ensure harmonious relations between people and land, and to ensure that the land will come up green. They perform ceremonies in which they celebrate this rich heritage; some are exclusively female, some cooperative endeavors with men. In each, women take care to explicate their responsibilities, a central one being to nurture the land. Nungarrayi explains:

> We do that yawulyu [land-based women's ceremony] for Wakulpu all the time. We make the country good . . . so it will grow up well, so that we can make it green, so that we hold the Law forever. My father told me to hold it always this way, so I go on holding yawulyu for that country. . . . Sometimes we dance man and woman together, for Wakulpu, so we can "catch him up," "hold him up."

This is graphically portrayed as the sacred boards, on which are painted the ancestral designs, are held high above the heads of the dancing women.

For some old people in Central Australia, the first experience of white settlers is within living memory. The establishment of the overland telegraph line, with its stations at regular intervals brought small—but permanent—encampments of white men to remote areas in the 1870s. The stations, such as the one at Tennant Creek, became sites for ration distribution and a focus of contact between the intruders and local Aborigines. Today, people recall how the availability of white goods brought them into telegraph stations and ration depots.

Nakamarra recalls traveling from soakage to soakage and her first visit to Tennant Creek in the 1920s.

> When I was a little girl we wore no clothes. We carried babies in the paraja [a wooden dish] and slept on the ground with no blankets. We ate bush potato. When we woke we had a drink, and we liked to eat bush honey. We keep water in a big round dish and stayed two or three nights at each water hole. . . . I was about nineteen when I first visited the old telegraph station at Tennant Creek and was given rations of clothes and tucker—meat, flour, jam, sugar—by the policeman.

Some stayed at the telegraph station, but others remained mobile. As the following statement of Nampijinpa, a woman now in her eighties, illustrates, government departments brought children into the reserves for schooling.

> I was born at Waake. I was walking all around there and that is where I grew up. I became a mother there. I only came to Alicurang [a government settlement established in the 1950s] when I was big. I was walking to all those places, soakages where I lived: Jajilperange, Wirliilunku, a swamp, Kurlulkinyje, Milpajirrame, Mantakarri, Wanjimarange, Wilyaninye, Jurujuparnta, Pajipajile. Wakulpu is the right place in the center of a lot of soakages; in a way it holds the soakages.
>
> My mother took me around when she was alive. We walked around, my father was in the same place with us. My father, whose country was Waake, passed away at Bullocky Soak, Yamarku, on this side of Ti-Tree. . . . My father did not work. He was a bushman. We got rations there, my parents and myself. When that mine started [wolfram at Wauchope] a lot of people went there but we only went for rations. We used to come where the wolfram was, get rations and then go back and eat them, back in our own country. We stayed really at Wakulpu. . . . We got rations at Wauchope. The old people used to get rations, our mothers and fathers used to get rations and tobacco. Then we would go back bush again. . . . Now when I had big grown-up children, I was coming this way to Alicurang, when it was a new place . . . they were getting the children ready for coming to school. People were asking us to come here . . .welfare . . . welfare again. . . . We just came here but we really wanted to be at our place at Wakulpu.

Those people whose land was not alienated in the land booms of the 1890s or 1920s were able to sustain close ties with their land until very recently. It was the assimilation policy, which informed government actions from the 1940s onwards, that took people away from their land and put in place a quasi-hostage situation for parents who had to remain nearby to see their children. Nungarrayi, now in her late sixties, explains:

I was born at Yanganpali . . . [Wauchope] and grew up there. When I was a little girl, about that high [indicating four feet] my father took me around there, to Wakulpu, Pajipajile, Kuralkinyje, Ngarnapirlapirla, Wurjulungu-langu. . . . My father used to take us around looking for food. If there was no food we would go onto another place. The meat we used to get was mainly possum and we got sugar bag. My sister was living with us . . . at Warnku, the place where all the Warumungu, Warlpiri, Alyawarra people meet up, at Yanganpali, they meet up there for ceremony. We stayed at Warnku, which was like a permanent settlement, a sort of village. Alyawarra, people came there, Kaytej people, Warumungu . . . to that same Warnku place, to that one place, Anmatjirra, Warlpiri come too. They come from all these different countries to Warnku. My father was working at Greenwood Station.

That was where we saw that first white fellow. He had a buggy and a horse. . . . I stayed with my grandmothers [father's mothers and mother's mothers] while my father was showing the missionary the Wakulpu country. . . . After Greenwood we went to Warnku. There were a lot of us living there for a long time at Singleton, Umnurulungku, that's the Aboriginal name for where the old station was . . . and at that old wolfram place too, then he moved to Wauchope to work. My father was still working, then he passed away.

My big children were born while I was still living at Wauchope. . . . We came to live at Alicurang. A white man got us here for school. We were a bit frightened. My two sisters they didn't really want to come, they were frightened, but the white men caught them when it got dark. They wanted us to stay there forever. . . . They brought us in a car.

But we still visit Wakulpu and we want to go there because it is a good place, and plenty fruits, bush tucker. . . . We still go out camping towards that country; we go camping for a number of days in the direction of that country . . . we usually go on weekends. There is water there, a swamp and soakages but we really need a bore to live there. In the olden days we lived at Wilyaninye, where there is a spring and we lived off the spring water. Where all the soakages dried up after that was where we lived, at Wilyaninye, because of the permanent spring water.

A story such as Nungarrayi's is based on intimate and sustained contact with her country. The way the Welfare Department relocated people was traumatic. Different groups were thrown together, resulting in tensions and fights not easily resolved by the customary practices of small hunter-gatherer bands. Important codes were violated. The mixing of peoples was a source of shame, as Napurrula, now in her fifties, a close friend whom I called "aunt," explained in evidence in 1981, to a claim for land some distance from where she has been living.

> This place, Alicurang, is someone else's sacred site and my people are buried in someone else's sacred tree site over there. They want to go back to their own land and sacred site . . . because a lot of old people have passed away, and some of those young people never look back to that country, to their own sacred site, even old people.

Many desert people left their country during the "killing times," the government-sponsored punitive parties of the 1920s. One infamous police action, known as the Coniston Massacre, was sparked by the death of a lone prospector, who had violated Aboriginal codes. The punitive parties ranged through vast amounts of country of Warlpiri, Warumungu, Anmatjira, and Kaytej. Grief and ritualized avoidances have kept people out of the country where these tragedies occurred. Japaljarri was a young boy at the time:

> In the country of witchetty grub Dreaming, which travels north from Yalkaranji on the Hanson River, east of Jarrajarra through the sandhills, one mob went out hunting, another along the creek. We thought we had plenty of time. But about 10 A.M. the white man came and rounded them up and killed them. They killed them everywhere.
>
> At Jalankurlangu, Chicken Jack fought with the white fellow Nugget. He got in more soldiers. The white fellow was making trouble with our women. We poor buggers didn't have two ideas, only one. The white fellow had two ideas. He was cheeky. We were myalls [ignorant bush people]. We left the country then. Some went to Wave Hill [a pastoral property], some to the northeast.

This exodus explains why some people no longer live on their land. Welfare activities, implementation of assimilationist policies, missionary zeal in "settling and civilizing," the growth of the pastoral industry, the establishment of towns, initially on the overland telegraph line put through in the 1870s, and then service centers, mining camps, and later tourist/trade centers, completes the picture of alienation of land and the shattering of the tie of person to place. Despite the tragedy and loss, the responsibility for maintaining land continues and the knowledge is kept alive. Nungarrayi explains how she and her sister continued to do the ceremonies of their country:

> My father was kurdungurlu *[mother's father's line] for that place, for Waake and Wakulpu. . . . He looked after two places, Waake and Wakulpu, and then I lost him; he passed away. Now it is up to me to go on looking after these places, after my own country, Jarrajarra, and also Waake and Wakulpu. My father could not go onto that Waake country, so from when I was a young girl I kept doing the* yawulyu, *looking after the country. . . . My sisters, they are looking after that country too . . . and those daughters of my father and Nakamarra [his second wife].*

The written words seem flat. It is hard to capture the high emotional tone of much of what people say about land. On visiting a site after a long absence, they exercise great care. As they approach, excitement mounts, and when at last the site is reached, there is a ritualized greeting. One that stands out in my mind was recorded in 1979. Charlie Charles Jakamarra was standing on a cliff at Parlkulanji overlooking his country. We had spent months planning the trip, made several unsuccessful attempts to reach it, and at last were within sight. A wind sprang up. He spread his arms and shouted:

> Hey! I'm standing, me! I'm showing it to the children. I'm following the Dreaming. I brought them here. I'm Jakamarra, of Jinpiya. I'm speaking to them as a Parluklanji one, a Jinpiya one, named Kumurlawarru! It was heading westward-eastward. That belonging to the old men, belonging to my father towards the south at Lamangarraji is Jupurrula, for this country still.

This land is now Aboriginal land. It was successfully won back in a land claim. Their desire to live on the land remains strong. The ceremonies have continuity. The colonial rupture of people–land relations has been dramatic, but a new Dreaming is being forged. Not all Aborigines have the possibility of gaining secure title to their land, and even those who may claim land find the legislative provisions and the legal proceedings highly problematic. In order to bring a successful claim as a "traditional owner," one must "prove" ownership according to a standard set by Anglo law.

A New Land Law[6]

At the time of white settlement, Australia was considered by international law to be uninhabited, a desert and uncultivated land, which therefore could be peopled from the "mother" country, Britain. The penal colony, established on the shores of Sydney Cove in 1788 proceeded on the basis that the law of the land was that of eighteenth-century England. In deeming the land *terra nullius*, the land could be settled, rather than conquered. The distinction is critical to the development of the issue of land rights as a legal question for the Australian state. Had the British "conquered" Australia, then they would have had to recognize existing laws of the conquered. But, in a "settled" colony, the colonizing power imposes its own law. At a stroke Aborigines were made subject to British law, but they were subjects who enjoyed neither the protection of law nor the usual rights of Australian citizens.

The fiction that Australia was an empty continent persisted. Until 1992, attempts to bring Aboriginal land rights within the ambit of Australian law failed. In 1971, when a test case was brought by the Yirrkala people of the Gove Peninsula, Mr. Justice Blackburn agreed that the Aboriginal people did have "a doctrine of communal native title" but ruled that this could not be recognized under Australian law. In his view, the matter had been settled in 1788. According to Blackburn's judgment, whether a colony is settled (as distinct from conquered) or ceded is a matter of law, not a matter of fact: the question cannot be reopened by fresh examination of anthropological or historical data.

The Labor Party had promised land rights in the run up to the election in 1972 and, once elected, they wasted no time. Mr. Justice Woodward was commissioned to inquire into the way in which Aborigines might be granted rights in land. He was not asked if they should be granted but, rather, how this might be achieved. His reports of 1973 and 1974 were the basis for legislation that would have given Aborigines secure title to the land already set aside as reserves. It would have allowed them to acquire secure title to unalienated crown land (land that no one else wanted) and to own certain pastoral properties that had been bought by the government. Aborigines were not restricted to land to which they had traditional ties. Woodward envisaged that Aborigines would also be able to claim land on the basis of need. This would have accommodated the peoples living in towns and on pastoral properties. It was a brave and bold conception that could have significantly altered the relationship between Aborigines and settlers in the Northern Territory, but it was not to be. Before the legislation could pass through the parliament there was a change of government, and the incoming conservatives moved to remove the need basis claims from the legislation.

Under the Aboriginal Land Rights (Northern Territory) Act, 1976, Aborigines had to prove they were traditional owners, and the criteria of ownership were set out in the legislation. Aboriginal assertions that the land was theirs were questioned and cross-examined by lawyers. The Aborigines had to show that they were members of a local descent group. This required careful research into their family histories. They had to show they had primary spiritual responsibility for the land. This often meant displaying something of their ceremonial life. The contemporary realities of Aboriginal land relations do not fit neatly into the simple model that would divide land into distinct blocks, each held by a particular clan on the basis of patrilineal descent.

Aborigines also needed to give evidence of traditional attachment to the land by enumerating their visits to the land and showing a desire to live on the land. Aboriginal land claims were thus interwoven with the history of the advance of white settlement on the northern frontier. Where there was water, towns grew up and pastoralists marked out leases. This land could not be claimed under the 1976 Act. In the 1940s assimilation was the official policy. Aborigines were removed by force from their country and brought into large government settlements where they were to be "introduced to the benefits" of white civilization. As a result, many Aborigines are not living on their own land.

In their evidence to land claims hearings brought under the Land Rights Act, Aboriginal people have spoken of their deep attachment to land; of the diverse ways in which they trace relationships to that land; of their continuing responsibility to maintain the land of their ancestors; of their sorrow, frustration, and anger at the way it has been taken away from them. Those whose land is not available for claim are doubly dispossessed. Land rights legislation has created two categories of persons: those with land available for claim, and those whose land is permanently alienated. Ways to achieve a just resolution of this issue are central motifs of Aboriginal campaigns for justice, and many look back to the Woodward vision that accommodated economic and spiritual ties to land as issues shaped by tradition and need.

While seeking legislative solutions may have been a dominant theme of land rights campaigns over the past two decades, politico-legal interrogations of *terra nullius* have continued to provide powerful rallying points for Aboriginal sovereignty and self-determination movements. In their landmark decision of June 1992 in the Mabo Case, the High Court of Australia, in a six-one decision, revisited the Blackburn decision and the doctrine of *terra nullius* and declared "that the Meriam people are entitled as against the whole world to possession, occupation, use and enjoyment of the lands of Murray Island."[7] Although the case entailed the rights of one group of Torres Strait Islanders, and although the decision is written so as to restrict the findings to the specific circumstances of the particular case, many believed the case had wider significance.

It may be that the same circumstances do not pertain in other parts of Australia, but the very fact that the highest court in the land had found that *terra nullius* was flawed in one instance opened up the possibility that its application was similarly flawed elsewhere. For other peoples to run a similar case, they would need similar evidence of continuity of occupation and land tenure system. That was not possible for most Aboriginal people. Also, the court excepted lands that had been lawfully alienated, and thus this could not be a sovereignty case for all Australia. But, the Mabo case had enormous moral and symbolic value, and that translated into political leverage. The case has been cited by other indigenous peoples as evidence that the legal fiction that underwrites the relationship of natives peoples to the modern nation-state has been exposed. In 1993 the Native Title Act passed into law. This act provided the means by which indigenous peoples across Australia might gain native title to their lands. While embodying aspects of the Mabo decision, the Act has come under attack and was significantly amended in 1998.[8]

The restoration of land and the recognition of rights of Original Peoples proceed slowly, and the quest for justice has been marked by trauma and conflict. The media often carry tales of woe from mining companies and pastoralists who see their right to use land being curtailed. Aborigines must constantly defend and justify the little they have. The promise of a "fair go" remains only a promise, and one that is held lightly by many whites who believe in development at all costs. Key questions remain unanswered regarding the economic and spiritual aspects of relations to land, the impact of colonization on current residential patterns, the role of law in dispossessing indigenous peoples, the changing content of customary practice, the shifting value of tradition, and the nature of "affirmative action" legislation that grants rights to minority groups not available to others.

Notes

1. Diane Bell, "Aboriginal Women's Religion: A Shifting Law of the Land," in Arvind Sharma, ed., *Today's Woman in World Religions* (Albany: State University of New York Press, 1994), 39–76.

2. From 1976 to 1978, I undertook intensive participant-observation fieldwork at Warrabri (now Alicurang) in Central Australia on Aboriginal women's religious life. Over the next ten years I undertook applied anthropological work on land claims, sacred site registration, law reform, impact studies, and mining negotiations and gave expert evidence testimony in the Supreme Court (N.T.) and in land claims. The majority of the texts were recorded in the local languages and translated in the field. The style is one Aborigines who speak English find congenial and, since it gives a feeling for the rhythm of speech, I have retained the form and not "tidied up" the translations of the stories. All have been cleared by the speaker as "open," i.e., not containing material that is restricted to men or women.

3. Diane Bell, *Daughters of the Dreaming*, 2d ed. (Minneapolis: University of Minnesota Press, 1993).

4. Further, the notion that knowledge is restricted on the basis of kin, age, gender, skill, and so on does not inform techniques of gaining access to information in western society. Persons in authority in western society (police, doctors, teachers) routinely ask questions to elicit information and test knowledge. This creates an awkward situation when the answer concerns information that is restricted in some way. The person being questioned must deflect, decline, or deny knowledge. Trouble has arisen when answers are given because it has been assumed that if the question was asked, the questioner had the right to ask.

5. Bell, "Aboriginal Women's Religion."

6. In this section, I am addressing the question of land rights as manifest in the Northern Territory, but I am assuming a knowledge of the broad issue of land rights for indigenous peoples, such as Australian Aborigines, Maori, Native Americans, who live and must politic within the bounds of a democratic nation-state. See Diane Bell, "Aborigines and Land" (a background paper prepared for the 1991 "Ancestors and Spirituality" conference at the East-West Center, Honolulu), for a detailed historical account of the legal, moral, political, and cultural issues that have framed and continue to frame the question of land rights in Australia.

7. Eddie Mabo and Others and the State of Queensland, High Court of Australia, 3 June 1992, F.C. 92/014.

8. Michael Bachelard, *The Great Land Grab: What Every Australian Should Know about Wik, Mabo and the Ten Point Plan* (Melbourne: Hyland House, 1997).

Discussion

William Ferea

My hometown is close to Australia and I follow some of the issues there closely. In the earlier part of last year there was quite a controversy about burning the bush and a huge fire that devastated parts of New South Wales.

Diane Bell

I didn't light that one! [laughter]

William Ferea

I'll take your word for it. Anyway, the fire department came to the conclusion that such a disaster could be minimized if the Aboriginal way of burning the bush and cleaning the forest was used.

Diane Bell

Yes, it is sometimes called firestick farming. You burned the country in the cool part of the year so that the trees wouldn't be consumed. You just clean it out and you burn it in kind of a patchwork toward a break like a creek or rocky outcrop. As long as you can do that, which is the Aboriginal method, you prevent large bush fires.

William Ferea

One of the commentators on this controversy also pointed out several incidents where the early western explorers had died in the desert from dehydration and from hunger, even though there were several Aboriginal signs on the rock saying, "This is water." They couldn't find it. They didn't know how to read the land.

Diane Bell

The successful expeditions all had native guides who are recorded in the histories as "Jackey-Jackey." They aren't given real names. It often takes quite a bit of genealogical research to find out who it was, but you can sometimes learn who it was through folk history because it's still close enough to people's memories to know who the actual person was. When you find out who the person was who guided the explorer or the early settler, you find that it was normally the person who spoke for that country, that is, it was the right person to lead them through that land.

John Grim

I want to explore the nature of some of these narratives you presented. I found it especially interesting that when Charlie Jakamarra stood up, there seemed to be a combination of both transmitted knowledge in his narrative and also spontaneity. Could you elaborate on that?

Diane Bell

That particular speech of his is high oratory. There are categories of information that have to be included in it, but the content will depend on who you are, what you're doing, and what it is you want to be transmitted. Since the story was still in the oral domain, he could control how he imprinted himself on the landscape and he could decide how he wanted to negotiate his authority in relation to the other people who were present. One of the ways of being important is to withhold certain things that you know about the land.

Pualani Kanahele

I often meet Aborigines at dance festivals and they talk a lot about Dreaming in relationship to their dances. Could you discuss the connection of Dreaming and dancing?

Diane Bell

So far I've talked about Dreaming mostly in the context of historical narrative, but it's also a ritual process. For example, with Yawulyu I had to dance the travels of that little willie wagtail, which is the one that's like a sister and brother to me. On the ceremonial ground the women cleaned up the women's dancing area, designated one site within that ground as the place that would stand for Pawurrinji, and put in the sacred object, which is a pole painted with the designs of the place in the songs. The designs tell the story of the place but the pole is also decorated as if it's a person. So I would speak to it as sister. I would say, "Good morning, sister. You're looking very fine. Your headband is gleaming white, your body paint looks gorgeous," and things like that. She'd be put in the ground and then we sang in the story. We sang in the travels of the ancestors, which was a way of calling up their presence in the ceremony. In this way the past becomes part of the current ceremony. While you are singing the songs, you paint your body with the designs and then the dancers come in. Their songs are very sacred and cannot be talked about in public. I am not allowed to talk about the content of the songs because it is there you learn the actual mythology. Then comes the public part where you come out of the little shade where you've been sitting, painting, and listening to this information being intoned.

The songs burst into a joyful celebration because at that point the dancers and singers have become the Dreaming. As you dance, you actually dance on the ground the pattern of the landscape that you will find at the site you are singing about. Then at the end, you sing all the power back into the ground, you strip the patterns back down into the little fire that's there. You leave the body paint on, because that's evidence that you've been in the ceremony, and that just wears off. But everything else is returned back down into the ground and the objects are put back in the ritual storehouse. That means that the Dreamings have gone back into the land. That's the process of the dancing.

Esau Tzua

I noticed in your paper, Diane, that you used some relational terms like sister, aunt, and so forth. I come from a tradition where people can be initiated into a tribe when they become related in some way to our people. For instance, a certain missionary came to be considered the biggest chief for our particular tribe. Is it possible that your relationships could be taken into the Dreamtime and put into stories by the Aboriginals with whom you lived?

Diane Bell

I think I'm still too young for that. I'm told that my gray hair helps, though; they say it shows I've spent a lot of time thinking. A student of mine is doing a Ph.D. just a little bit north of where I was and she was with some women who knew me. She said that the women who'd been watching her sighed with relief when she took off her shoes. You see, it's very important for them to be able to see your footprint and relate you to the land. Babies should be born on the ground, you should sleep on the ground, and you should walk on the ground. Anyway, when this student of mine actually took her shoes off, they said, "Thank goodness, just like Nakamarra," which is me. "She always took her shoes off." Then they said, "Come and we'll show you something." They showed her this little winter camp windbreak that I had built a decade before. It was just a little shelter to stop the wind and there was a little series of fires where each of the other families stayed. They showed her where I and my children had camped and told her the story of my travels in that country by reading those physical remains on the land. Now whether that will ever be considered significant enough to be incorporated into a real narrative, I don't know.

Sometimes these relationships were initiated quite by accident. I once discovered that by dancing all night for three successive nights, I was credited with having gone through labor for the rebirth of a young man who was then forever in my debt. I became his relative and at that level I certainly have obligations that enmeshed me. But when I finished doing fieldwork where I was living very closely with people, I went on and did another decade of work in the area of land rights and legal reform. This entailed work with lots of different people right across the north of Australia and those relationships weren't as intimate, nor were they as intense. I think the people with whom I'd worked initially understood that I had other relationships with other Aboriginal people, and because of that I wasn't claimed as their daughter quite as closely as I might have been to start off with. So I think that probably mitigates against me ever becoming a mythic hero.

Honoring the Ancestral Bones
The Grave Protection and Repatriation Act
and the Algonquian Feast of the Dead

John A. Grim

Reverence for ancestors is a widespread phenomenon among human communities. Quite often the bones of the dead figure prominently in the rituals commemorating ancestors. One of the oldest hominid rituals known is that of a Middle Paleolithic burial at Shanidar, Iraq, in which Neanderthals interred flint and animal bones with a buried youth and then covered the site with flowers and pollen from pine boughs.[1] Reverence for ancestors has also resulted in intercultural conflicts and misunderstandings. For example, the "rites controversy" within seventeenth- and eighteenth-century Roman Catholicism involved, in part, the inculturation of Christian doctrine by Jesuit missionaries into the Chinese ritual treatment of ancestors. This early inculturative effort was eventually condemned by papal prohibitions.[2] When one compares the elaborate rituals connected with the Christian "cult of the saints," however, there are distinct parallels regarding spiritual memorials for ancestors.[3]

East Asian ancestor reverence and western "cult of the saints" are paralleled by other comparative practices expressing human regard for ancestors. The African Dogon elder, Ogotemmêli, described the role of drinking beer, believed to have been fermented by the ancestors, as a way of shaming people into performing ceremonies prescribed for dead ancestors by the Dogon cosmology. At one point Ogotemmêli expatiated on the drunken insult "The dead are dying of thirst," which is often shouted out by inebriated participants during the brewing of beer. Ogotemmêli commented:

The words find their ways over walls and through doors till they reach the people responsible for the delay [in holding appropriate rites for dead ances-

tors]. The men staggering in the streets may utter meaninglessly, sing, or shout insults; but their words are heard by all, and some [people] will certainly have an end of mourning ritual to perform or a funeral account to pay. Even if the words of the drunkards are uttered indistinctly, they are clearly understood by all those careless people whose granaries are not full enough to start the rites and by all those poor people whose efforts are in vain.[4]

Here, the chaotic activity of drunkards has been given meaning within the context of death and the chaotic explosion of souls associated in Dogon belief with death. The inebriated state is believed to convey assistance to the ancestors in their afterlife journey as well as to implement fluid ritual relations between the living and their dead ancestors. The capacity to perform these rituals for the ancestors also appears to impart status and designate "wealth" in a spiritual sense. This close relationship of matter and spirit, or "materiality," serves to emphasize a cosmological value.[5] That is, the crops, the beer, the ritual activities, and the cosmological values themselves all hinge on the point of matter-spirit relations, which is also the potion where the living meet the dead ancestors.

Several observations that follow from these opening remarks lead us toward the agenda of this paper. First, reverence for ancestors is a pivotal epistemological act that links community and cosmos, matter and spirit. Second, ritual communication with dead ancestors orients practitioners to an immanent cosmology of forces in the world as much as to transcendental, otherworldly powers. Third, rituals concerning the dead involve basic perceptions of a life-force and the animating character of life, or "soul," as this term is used in discussions of indigenous peoples.[6]

Native American Grave Protection and Repatriation Act of 1990

Having suggested the pervasive and ancient character of ancestor reverence, I want to focus on a contemporary issue, often identified as the "bones controversy." This is a protest initiated by indigenous peoples against the abuse in collection, storage, and display of their ancestors' bones and grave goods.[7] The restoration of ancestral bones to tribal lands for reburial has surfaced as a rallying point for the assertion of indigenous rights in relation to dominant governments and social institutions that often collect skeletal remains, namely, museums and social science agencies. In the United States mounting pressures from Native American religious leaders, especially assisted by the Native American Rights Fund and American Indians against Desecration, has led to an act of

Congress called "The Native American Grave Protection and Repatriation Act of 1990." In the words of two observers, this act may be the most important human rights legislation ever passed for Native Americans by Congress.

> *Repatriation legislation is important for native people because it provides them equal rights regarding their dead. It recognizes that scientific rights of inquiry do not automatically take precedence over religious and cultural beliefs; it provides a mechanism for the return of objects that were not acquired with the consent of rightful owners; and it creates an opportunity for Native Americans and museum people to work in partnership together.[8]*

The Grave Protection and Repatriation Act basically accomplishes four things:

> *1. It increases protection for Native American graves located on federal and tribal lands and provides for disposition of cultural items found there in the future.*
>
> *2. It prohibits traffic in Native American human remains.*
>
> *3. It requires federal agencies and federally funded museums to inventory their collections of Native American human remains and associated funerary objects in five years and repatriate them, if requested, to culturally affiliated tribes or native groups.*
>
> *4. It requires federal agencies and federally funded museums to summarize their collections of Native American sacred objects, objects of cultural patrimony, and unassociated funerary objects in three years and repatriate items to specified native claimants when the agency or museum does not have a right of possession.[9]*

This act marks a transformation in the ways in which institutional America relates to indigenous peoples. Institutional America is legally bound to recognize Native American peoples not as wards of the government living in communities of despair but, rather, as having rights of religious freedom that extend to their communal ancestral bones.

This is a radical shift from the Antiquities Act of 1906. This earlier legislation described all Native American skeletal finds as "cultural resources" that "belonged" to the United States. The act made no provision for any Native American involvement, ownership, or possession of these cultural resources.[10] Recently, however, Bureau of Land Management (BLM) officials in Wyoming forged novel reburial guidelines for all skeletal remains found on BLM land.

These guidelines were innovative, not simply because they quickened the proce-dures for reburial of all bones found on BLM land, but also because they were written and implemented with Native American knowledge, input, and accep-tance.[11] This example of cooperation between dominant and Native American concerns for ancestral bones is a practical example of changing views regarding values and materiality.

The religious issue of materiality also draws our attention to the shift in con-temporary thought regarding the inherent meaning of bones. Cultural studies and scientific analysis prejudiced the question of materiality so that ancestral bones appeared as objects for study by the dominant culture. Social science and cultural study as ritual activity themselves served to enhance the dominant cul-ture and were foundational to colonial identity. Thus, Roy Wagner argued that "The study of culture *is* culture. . . . The study of culture is in fact *our* culture; it operates through our forms, creates in our terms, borrows our words and con-cepts for its meanings, and re-creates us through our efforts. . . . [The dominant culture] is a vast accumulation of material and spiritual achievements and re-sources stemming from the conquest of nature and necessary to the continu-ance of this effort."[12]

Perhaps no other example of the cultural exploitation of indigenous peoples through conquest and subjection is as blatant as that of disinterment of burial remains and collection of skeletal parts for empirical analysis. There is a grow-ing awareness that Native peoples have been systematically denied their basic rights to undisturbed burial grounds. Recently, the world of art investment has added another pressure for continued grave desecration by increased sales and skyrocketing prices for Native American grave goods. In the historical record and in the contemporary marketplace, opaque forces continue to blur subtle forms of racial subjugation and to pit themselves against this basic right of an-cestral burial.

The simultaneous protection and pillage of Native American bones and grave goods has a lengthy history in the United States. Physical anthropologists, such as Samuel Morton in the 1840s and Arles Hrdlicka in the early twentieth century, claimed that Native Americans were racially inferior to white Cauca-sians. These "scientific" theories served to justify the government's policy of di-minishing reservation lands and removing Native peoples from the progressive drive of American society. Working closely with official government agencies, the nineteenth-century scientific community collected Indian crania to build supportive evidence for the racial theory of white supremacy. Thus, many Na-tive Americans killed in battle were decapitated and their heads were sent east for scientific study. One especially vivid description of grave desecration in the name of science is found in a letter of A. P. Hachington from Fort Randall, Dakota Territory, on 18 January 1869. He wrote: "The skull of an old Indian whose father was Yankton and mother Brule [Sioux], died on this post on the 7th day of January, 1869, was buried in his blankets three feet in the ground about half a mile from the fort within a few rods of the teepees occupied by his friends. I secured his head in the night of the day he was buried."[13] This act was not an isolated event; an 1868 order from the U.S. Surgeon General resulted in the heads of Tsistsistas-Cheyenne Indians killed at the infamous Sand Creek massacre being sent east for "Indian Crania Study."

The pain and anguish caused Native communities by such irreverence is only now surfacing in dominant American consciousness. If these realizations are juxtaposed with the sentiments evoked by romantic images of Native Americans, a striking issue surfaces. The 1855 speech by Chief Sea'thl illustrates this paradox. While Chief Sea'thl was a historical figure, his 1855 speech as translated has become controversial regarding its documented accuracy. One section reads:

> Every part of this country is sacred to my people. . . . The soil is rich with the life of our kindred. You wander far from the graves of your ancestors and seemingly without regret. Your dead cease to love you and the land of their nativity as soon as they pass the portals of the tomb and wander away beyond the stars. They are soon forgotten and never return. Our dead never forget the beautiful world that gave them their being.[14]

The irony involved in this narrative is amplified by the transformation inherent in the Grave and Repatriation Act. The words of Chief Sea'thl have been used in innumerable settings to justify the colonial romanticism of the "vanishing Indian." These words have also been used in the neocolonial and postmodern deconstruction of a romantic ideology, showing that the spiritual thought of Sea'thl and of many Native peoples is largely a creation of Euroamerican nostalgia for that which has been conquered.[15] The romantic search for the right Indian ancestor-image is paralleled by a critical attitude that searches out the "absolute fake Indian."[16] The specious imaging by romantic-minded Americans of a noble savage ideal is paralleled by an equally disingenuous dismissal of insightful indigenous leaders like Sea'thl. Thus, the nihilism associated with lost reverence for ancestors, foreseen by indigenous leaders like Sea'thl, plays itself out in the language games of postmodern critical theory.

Native American relations with ancestors continues to find diverse religious expression among the various ethnic groups in North America. Often, the regard among Native American peoples for the body and bones of the dead is expressed in a concern both for initial placement of skeletal remains and for ongoing ritual relations to ancestors. The concern for ancestral bones in the Grave and Repatriation Act of 1990 has both religious and legal dimensions. As Gerald Vizenor has pointed out in his article "Bone Courts: The Natural Rights of Tribal Bones," the reduction of the broader human issues to simplistic religious sentiments further obliterates Native thought. Drawing out the position that bones have narrative rights, Vizenor states:

> Rights, arguments, narratives are discourse, not isolated monologues. The rights of bones to be represented are not semantic, positivist, or religious, but a secular, theoretical, and agonistic interpretation of legal propositions. To overbear tribal narratives, to oppose discourse on bone rights, and to reduce arguments to a religious or radical performance, as the social sciences have done could "demonize science and technology to a point of some great religious convulsion of primitivist simplification."[17]

Vizenor points out, correctly I believe, the error of reducing the issue of the treatment of bones to an exclusively religious issue of the right to ritual reburial. In spiritualizing the "bones controversy," dominant America satisfies another stereotype of the ahistorical Indian who remains trapped in an imagined world of hunting-gathering with primitivist regard for animals and ancestors. This type of media imaging fails to understand the contemporary legal battlefield in which Native Americans continue their fight to recover their sovereignty. It fails as well in its misunderstanding of the spiritual relations with ancestors, or a Native understanding of materiality literally embodied in the bones.

What, then, is the spiritual relationship of Native peoples to ancestral bones? That, of course, is for Native spokespeople to articulate. What I would like to explore as a historian of religions is a particular continuity I observe in the historical records. There is a sequence of concern for ancestral bones among Algonquian peoples from the seventeenth-century Feast of the Dead to the contemporary richness of thought gravitating toward the "bones controversy" among contemporary Native American writers. The ritual complex of the Feast of the Dead, which is still practiced by some Algonquian-speaking peoples in subsequent forms, presents a fascinating picture of the significance of ancestral bones in the community life of these Native peoples. A discussion of this ritual provides insight into both the abiding spiritual reverence with which Native Americans have honored their dead ancestors and the depth of traditional thought that emerges in the Grave and Repatriation Act.

Early Accounts of the Feast of the Dead

The Feast of the Dead is central to any investigation of the Algonquian groups from the mid-seventeenth century to the beginning of the eighteenth century. The ceremonial complex is often thought of as originating among the Iroquoian-speaking Huron peoples formerly located in what is now southern Ontario. The Huron are believed to have transmitted the ritual to their Algonquian-speaking neighbors, who also had seasonal hunting and fishing villages in the Great Lakes area. This major ceremonial seems to have been accommodated to existing funeral rites among these Algonquian peoples as well as into extant modes of political ritualization.

The Feast of the Dead is first documented for these people just before they coalesced as the northern Ojibway and southern Chippewa. The ritual activities underlying the Feast of the Dead provide some insight into the social control needed to effect tribal unity as well as political alliances between village groups preliminary to full tribal formation. Thus, the Feast of the Dead appears in early non-Native journals as a central ritual among interethnic village groups coalescing into larger bands.

The earliest accounts of a Feast of the Dead come from Samuel Champlain, the explorer and trader from 1615; and Gabriel Sagard, a missionary who journeyed to the Huron in 1623–24.[18] Sagard indicated that the Algonquians did not practice a common burial of the dead. A more extensive description of the Huron Feast of the Dead can be found in the records of the Jesuit Jean de Brébeuf for 1636.[19] Brébeuf noted that the Huron used the circumlocution "kettle" in order to talk about the feast indirectly. He also indicated that some villages had formerly celebrated together but, having become alienated from one another, they now competed in drawing villages to their respective feasts.

There are seven accounts of the Feast of the Dead among the Algonquian, varying from passing references about the feast to developed descriptions. One of the joint intendants of French Canada, Antoine Denis Raudot, mentioned the feast in a letter of 1709.[20] Antoine de la Mothe Cadillac, the French commandant of Detroit, mentioned in 1695 the plan of a Miami chief to collect ancestral bones before settling near Detroit the following year.[21] The Jesuit Thierry Beschefer mentioned a Feast of the Dead in 1683 among Nipissing and Achiligouan groups living near the French who were observed by Henry Nouvel.[22] In 1670, the Jesuit Louis André observed a feast at which the Amikwa were host to fifteen hundred to sixteen hundred people of various nations on Quiebichiouan Island in Lake Huron.[23] He described the host's motivation for holding the feast as resuscitation of his father's name. The trader and official Nicolas Perrot gave a generalized account of a feast in his description of Algonquian funeral customs during the period 1665–1700.[24] The trader Pierre Radisson accompanied Saulteur Indians during diplomatic activities among the Dakota and the Cree to the south of Lake Superior in 1660. He described a feast in which the Saulteur were host to Menomini, Cree, Dakota, possibly Ottawa, and other unidentified people.[25]

The most extensive account is the description by the Jesuit Jerome Lalemant who observed a feast in 1641 that was hosted by the Nipissing at Georgian Bay in eastern Lake Huron. Among the two thousand guests were Saulteur and Huron—some of the Saulteur having traveled "a hundred or a hundred and twenty leagues."[26] Moreover, we know from the generalized account of Nicolas Perrot that visitors prepared for their arrival at the host camp by developing a collection of goods for gift-giving to the host village.[27] Lalemant described the ritual arrival, pointing out that the canoes were lined up and that the visitor's chief announced their purpose in traveling. Then the visitors threw some of their gifts into the water. The young men of the host village competed with one another to obtain the articles—beaver skins, hatchets, beads, and other articles. The different groups were divided at the first assembly and the various gifts of the host were exhibited. The visiting chiefs then presented gifts to their hosts, "giving to each present [gift] some name that seems best suited to it."[28]

All of the descriptive accounts mention the variety and vigor of the singing and dancing. Lalemant, however, provided a fuller description of the first dance sequences after the visitors arrived. He indicated three different parts to the opening dances. First, about forty dancers portrayed an encounter with an enemy. Three different types of dress, weapon, and dance step were used to depict the exchange between warriors. The second dance was not described, but Lalemant indicated that it progressively increased in dancers from eight to twelve to sixteen. He described the last dance as a modest dance by the Saulteur women visitors.

The next activity at the 1641 Nipissing Feast of the Dead, according to Lalemant, was a contest of skill that had an unusual turn. At the top of a greased pole the hosts placed a kettle and the skin of a deer as prizes to whomever could climb the pole and take them. All failed until a Huron brave took knife and cord and climbed the tree by cutting notches and securing himself with the cord. He was severely criticized but evidently took the prizes and set out for Quebec. As it turned out, the Algonquian hosts complained to the Huron, who provided "porcelain beads to repair this injustice, which caused the souls of the deceased to weep."[29]

The public acclamation of chiefs followed this contest. Those seeking that position presented themselves in their finest robes. This was followed by a large distribution of gifts by the newly elected chiefs so as to establish their reputation. After this, the names of those who had died since the last feast were formally transferred to relatives. In the feast observed by Louis André, the resuscitation of a prominent chief's name appeared to be the major motivation for holding the celebration. André wrote:

> The Captain of the Beaver [Amikwa] Nation having died three years before his eldest son had invited various tribes to attend the games and spectacles which he wished to hold in his father's honor. He intended, too, to take this opportunity to resuscitate him, as they say, by taking his name; for it is customary to recall the illustrious dead to life at this festival, by conferring the name of the deceased upon one of the most important men, who is considered his successor and takes his place.[30]

On the second day Lalemant mentioned the cabin built for the bones of the dead, "with an arched roof, about a hundred paces long, the width and height of which were in proportion."[31] The bones of the dead were covered with beaver skin robes and porcelain beads. In the longhouse built for the bones, the women sat in two lines facing each other. The host leaders then served food to these women. Then, about a dozen men of good voice entered and sang a mournful chant through the night. Two fires were kept going at either end of the cabin while this most solemn chanting continued. Lalemant wrote:

> The theme of the song consisted in a sort of homage paid to the Demon whom they invoked, and to whom their lamentations were addressed. This chant continued through the night, amid deep silence on the part of the Audience, who seemed to have only respect and admiration for so sacred a ceremony.[32]

Perrot also mentioned the special housing for the guests, but he did not mention the bones of the dead. However, he did describe an opening ritual dance in the cabin. The visitors, from each Indian nation in their own place in the longhouse, removed their outer garments and began a single-file dance around three spruce trees or three cornstalks placed in the cabin. At the end of this dance the hosts took the old clothes and the gifts of the visitors and replaced them with new clothes and trade items. Perrot continued his description, saying that a three-day dance was held during which host families invited twenty or thirty guests for a giveaway. Perrot wrote, "During [these] three days they lavish all that they possess in trade goods or other articles; and they reduce themselves to such an extreme of poverty that they do not even reserve for themselves a single hatchet or knife."[33]

Lalemant concluded his description of the Feast of the Dead by relating the events following the night of sacred chanting. The women distributed craft items or food that had come from their own work. As they chanted the women subtly prepared for a mock attack by the men. The women's chant, "—ever plaintive, and interspersed with sobs—seemed to be addressed to the Souls of the deceased, whom they sped on their way—as it appeared, with deep regret—by continually waving branches that they held in their hands, for fear that these souls might be surprised by the dread of war and the terror of arms, and that their rest might thus be disturbed."[34] At this point an army of men descended from the nearby mountain and feigned an attack on the longhouse, first encircling it and then expanding their formation into an oval. Finally, "after a thousand other figures [of formation] they rushed upon the Cabin." Conquering the women, the warriors of the assembled group danced by turns in the longhouse, performing elaborate dance movements. Then the Algonquian hosts entered, "ten or twelve in line," and prepared a feast serving the separate village groups in places set apart for them. Two meetings followed this feast, one between the hosts and their Algonquian guests and then one with their Huron guests. They gave presents "according to the extent of the Alliance that existed between the Nipissiriniens and them."[35] Lalemant concluded his description of the feast by reporting the contests of skill in which both men and women participated.

Major Themes in the Feast of the Dead

Most noticeable by its absence in the Lalemant account of the Nippissing Feast of the Dead is any description of the burial of the bones, such as is found in Brébeuf's description of the Huron feast.[36] Pierre Radisson does mention such a burial in his account of a feast, along with marriage arrangements made between the allying groups.[37] However, collecting of the bones of the dead, or some clear reference to the dead as being resuscitated, is found in all the sources on the Feast of the Dead. Beschefer, for example, wrote that the feast "is a ceremony in which after bringing the bones of all their kindred who have died within seven or eight years, for the purpose of burying them all together, they engage in dances and feasts."[38]

In an interpretive article, Harold Hickerson suggested, "Perhaps peoples in very close confederacy or in the process of merging interred their dead jointly, but it would seem that among autonomous allies participation in the gift-giving, dancing, and feasting which marked the ceremony was sufficient to affirm friendship and alliance."[39] It may be that, like the circumlocution "kettle" recorded by the Jesuit Brébeuf for the Huron, any direct reference to the ancestral bones, especially to outsiders, was prohibited.

Regardless of how we interpret the presence or lack of a description of the bones of the dead during the feast, this element appears to be the central feature of the Feast of the Dead. Certainly, several types of meaningful behavior during the ritual complex can be isolated, such as gift-giving and complementary gender roles in the feasting, singing, and dancing. So also the contests of skill, the elevation of chiefs, the condolence rites, and the housing of visitors and bones of the dead are all integral religious aspects of political alliance-making. Underlying each of these features, however, are spiritual motivations focused on establishing meaningful and orderly relations with the ancestors. In this section, then, two areas of Algonquian religious concern are discussed, namely, treatment of bones and gift-giving, which served to empower individuals and communities with ancestral presence.

The special treatment of bones by Algonquian peoples is not an isolated phenomenon in the Feast of the Dead. In this particular cultural setting the ritual manipulation of ancestral bones during that ceremonial follows from an ancient Algonquian religious regard for ancestors. Involved in the communication with ancestors is a spiritual language that has been interpreted using Atlantic-Mediterranean concepts of "soul." There are limitations in using such a concept as "soul" to discuss Native American ethnometaphysics, yet some insights can be had using the soul model, which might help mainstream Americans understand the religious character of the contemporary bone controversy for indigenous peoples. It is evident that a relationship between the living person and the spiritual, soul presence of the dead ancestor is established in part by ritual treatment of bones. In fact, the ritual treatment of bones considered in the synthetic context of all the religious acts of the ceremonial became the prototypical act for political alliance-making between disparate village groups during the Feast of the Dead.

Both the Cree of the Canadian shield and the Ojibway of the upper Great Lakes are recorded as holding a dual soul belief. Every human had a stationary soul located in the heart and a free soul that could journey in spiritual realms. At death, the stationary soul went immediately to the afterworld, but the free soul lingered at the grave site for a time until it, too, went to the afterworld.[40] In this context, bones—as the longest lasting part of the body—were seen as related to the free soul. Therefore, ritual treatment of bones was offered as a pleasing act to the dead person.

During the Feast of the Dead the bones of the deceased ancestors were exhumed, dressed in finery, carried to the host village, housed in a special arched longhouse, chanted over, entertained with song and dance, mourned in a solemn night vigil, attacked and captured back from mourners, and eventually buried with the ancestral bones of allied villages. These activities are grouped together as "manipulation of bones" and are seen as part of a synthetic ritual whole, which brought about transformations of the dead in their afterlife journey as well as transformations in the political arena of the living villages. The symbolism inherent in ritual manipulation of bones is called "synthetic" here to indicate its connection to the Ojibway cosmological word of spiritual power of *manitou.* This synthetic symbolism also manifested itself in the treatment of the bones of slain animals by Algonquian peoples,[41] such as divination by "reading" cracks in the heated shoulderbone of select animals,[42] as well as use of the leg bones of particular birds, especially eagles, by the *nanadawi,* or sucking-shaman.[43]

These ritual manipulations of bone are not all identical in function, social context, or religious experience. They are different rituals with unique contents, but they share a similar regard for establishing a synthetic relationship with power (manitou) in the Algonquian worldview. Bone manipulation during hunting is related to the belief in the power-presence associated with the abiding soul-presence of the slain animal. The bones of the animal are treated with respect so that the animal's soul will favorably report to their "Owner," or other-than-human manitou or spirit, who will in turn resuscitate more game for those respectful hunters.

The synthetic character of the bone-manitou relationship is evident when hunters perform divination to locate game by observing cracks in heated bones. These cracks are believed to be caused by the free-soul agency of the hunted animal who, in effect, gives himself to the hunter. The presence of this soul during divination could be harmful to children, so they are prohibited from being present during the ritual. Children can, however, openly carry the cracked bone around to hunters for their inspection after the ritual.

During the Feast of the Dead the ritual treatment of the bones of ancestors established a context for intertribal socialization by drawing on the paradigmatic symbolism of ancestors as that which is orderly, meaningful, and powerful. While communal burial of bones may indicate intervillage cooperation and cohesion on an exoteric level, the esoteric joining with pleased ancestors acknowledged union at a deeper level of materiality. Thus, the intermingling of ancestral bones-as-presences effectively assuaged interclan rivalries and brought political harmony to conflicted totemic groups. The respect and reverence reserved for the souls of ancestors and symbolized by the treatment accorded their bones was now extended to allied villagers. So, formerly autonomous, often isolated villages formed into bands that eventually coalesced during the historical period described above and developed the group spirit and tribal élan displayed by the emigrating Ojibway of the eighteenth and nineteenth centuries.

A second theme in the feast is the reciprocal blessing of gifts. Just as "ritual treatment of bones" during the Feast of the Dead activated the Algonquian synthetic process of empowerment, so also "gift-giving" was related to the central dynamic of the feast, namely, ancestral reverence. For example, the giveaways themselves were connected to the display behavior at the arrival of the guests, at the election of chiefs, at the singing and dancing in the longhouse for the bones of the dead, and, interestingly, with the contests of skill. These related ritual acts were subtly interwoven by a symbol system that knit together the humble giving-as-person with the one who receives and returns blessing-as-person. These interpersonal exchanges, though awkwardly expressed in English, correspond to realities succinctly expressed in an Algonquian language such as Ojibway. That is, verbal forms predominate in Ojibway in which actions determine not simply the form of verb used but also the form of verbal noun used to indicate the subject or object of action.[44] The interpersonal exchanges that occur in the Feast of the Dead derive from the Algonquian view of "person" as a recipient and a result of action. Beings who are acted upon, and who in turn act on others, are "persons." Thus, the quality of "person" is found not solely in humans, but also in features of the environment, and in those other-than-human powers called manitou.[45]

The category of person is consistent with the synthetic worldview of Algonquian peoples and, along with bone manipulation, is an ancient characteristic of these indigenous peoples. "Person" is a covert category in that the Algonquian-Ojibway have not fully articulated their use of this term and the associated ideas. Their belief structure is more comprehensible, however, when the category of person is developed from out of the data.[46] As a basic feature of Algonquian peoples, it is shared by the western and eastern divisions of this extensive language family. The quality of person is found in the older oral narrative cycles of the Ojibway, Pottawatomi, and Ottawa, which confirms the antiquity of the concept at least to the Anishinabe period of these related peoples well before the seventeenth century. As developed in the mythologies and in major ritual performances, the category of "person" connotes human attributes, but not necessarily human form, to beings in the landscape. Persons may be unstable in outer form, but they are constant in inner essence. Thus, they are able to transform themselves, but they are always manitou. Persons are immortal, and persons are capable of speech, understanding, and volition. Persons can enter into social relations, they have values, they are the location of causality, and they possess power in a higher degree than nonpersons in the cosmic realms of existing beings.

Gift-giving during the Feast of the Dead occurs between persons. Visitors collect materials for gifts thrown into the water. Disregard for material wealth is coupled with both the evocation of contact with spiritual forces of ancestors and the youthful skill of the hosts who recover what has been thrown away. The humble hosts welcome their seemingly haughty guests as both groups engage in highly ritualized naming, dancing, and singing. All of these ritualizations augment the stature of those involved in the evocation of ancestral persons. Both groups receive blessings from the ancestral dead, who are believed to be present. The ritual culminates in the solemn vigil of the dead, during which manitou power is evoked. The elaborate display behavior and reciprocal skill exhibitions are ritual exchanges symbolizing the blessings bestowed by the revered ancestors. These blessings parallel the gifts of power given by manitou to vision-fasters. These blessings exchanged at the Feast of the Dead also parallel the game animals given by the "Master" to humans who have earned such reciprocal blessings by their respectful behavior to animal bones after hunting.

The extensive gift-giving during the Feast of the Dead manifested this ancient virtue of ancestral reverence as an expression of cosmological manitou power. The potential of this synthetic force so central to the Algonquian worldview enabled the Feast of the Dead to effect meaningful political alliances between villages. The exchange of named presents, for example, highlighted the personal and the cosmological nature of the reciprocity. The character of the political alliance was not simply conducted on the human level only. Rather, the character of the reciprocal blessing extended the political alliances in the hierarchies of cosmic power in the environment, in the realm of the dead, and in the world of manitou spirits.

Gift-giving also involved entry into the ethical order of power. Thus, when the Huron brave disingenuously climbed the greased tree to claim the prized trade kettle and the deer skin, he was thought to have broken the ethics surrounding the event. Although he was allowed to keep the winnings as a sign of his skill, some recompense had to be made to the manitou offended. Thus, Huron elders responded to the Algonquian complaints that a moral relationship with the dead had been upset. An ethic pervaded the gift-giving and the contests at the Feast of the Dead that moved the political alliance into a transcendent realm. The clever solution of the Huron brave offended this ethic, which crossed ontological levels. It was expected that traditional skills animated by supernatural power were required to win the traditional blessings of the ancestors symbolically tied at the top of the tree. The ethic established in gift-giving was one of reciprocal respect, not simply individual accomplishment. This reciprocity involved human political alliance, as well as the hunting of animals and the healing of sick individuals. This synthetic ethic flowed from the treatment of bones and passed into the giving of game within the Algonquian worldview. Ritual actions established a relationship with manitou-power, which opened the human to visionary experiences and which were maintained by a reciprocal ethics. Similar to humble fasting in an isolated place, the ritual treatment of ancestral bones and the reciprocal giving of gifts marked the exchange of the living with the dead ancestors as spiritual beings.

Conclusion

Drawing on the thought of the Ojibway author Gerald Vizenor, contemporary connections appear between the ancient Feast of the Dead, with its concern for ritual treatment of ancestral bones, and the recent legal battles to implement the Grave and Repatriation Act of 1990. In developing his ideas about the "narrative rights of tribal bones" Vizenor emphasizes the voice that tribal bones bring to legal discussions in America. He writes:

> *Tribal narratives are located in stones, trees, birds, water, bears, and tribal bones. The narrative perspective on tribal remains has been neocolonial; tribal bones held in linguistic servitude, measured and compared in* autistic *social science monologues. Tribal bones are liberated in this proposal, represented in court as narrators and mediators; manumission in postmodern language games. Social and moral contention arises not in tribal remains but in research demands, academic power, material possessions, criminal and accidental exhumation. Archaeologists and anthropologists have assumed an absolute right to burial sites, an improper right to research tribal remains and narratives. Tribal bones must oppose science and narrative simulations; bones have a right to be represented and to have their interests heard and recorded in a federal Bone Court.*[47]

While Vizenor plays the postmodern language game, refusing ideological religious positions as a platform for bones, he does opt for discourse as a context in which ancestral bones can speak. This is similar to the Feast of the Dead in which ritual behavior allowed for the voice of ancestral bones, which spoke efficaciously for village unification during the ceremonial and morally, such as when the clever Huron technician scaled the greased pole. Unlike the typical postmodern language game, however, there is a unique Native American feature to Vizenor's perspective. That is, the narrators in his discourse, namely, bones, stones, trees, and bears, openly challenge the modern Enlightenment view of the world outside of the human as one of a collection of objects. Beginning with the voices of those persons who are no longer among us, the ancestors, the range of potential narrators extends into the whole subjective world whose voices seek "legal standing" as an expression for a larger ethical regard.

Vizenor joins Thomas Berry, author of *The Dream of the Earth*, in describing modern communities as "autistic" because they remain unable to reach outside of the rational analytical bubble to hear the natural world in all its diverse voices.[48] Tribal bones speak, Vizenor claims, and they oppose all modern emphasis on the discontinuity of life. Tribal bones do not oppose scientific investigation, just as they did not oppose more centralized and more complex social arrangements among the coalescing Ojibway. Rather, bones as narratives affirm wonder and inquiry in all its disciplined manifestations. During the ritual of the Feast of the Dead, ancestral bones reminded the Ojibway not only to weep for all of the grief experienced by the people, but also to dance and dress anew in celebration of all that has endured. So also an ancient cosmological reciprocity embedded in these ritual celebrations echoes in the old Ojibway chant:

> It will resound
> Clearly
> The sky
> When I come
> Making a sound.[49]

Notes

1. See Ralph Solecki, *Shanidar, the First Flower People* (New York: Alfred A. Knopf, 1971). Solecki writes: "Emotion is evident too, in the burial of the adolescent. The youth was found in a niche of the cave with provisions of flint and animal bones. Soil samples taken from the grave contained the pollen of pine boughs and mountain flowers. Very possibly, these had been gathered and then placed with the body" (97). This burial is considered 75,000 years B.P.

2. Innocent X forbade the Jesuit policy of inculturation in 1645, a later mitigation was rejected in 1693, and, finally, Benedict XIV issued a final prohibition that effectively ended the China mission for a time. See John C. Dwyer, *Church History: Twenty Centuries of Catholic Christianity* (New York: Paulist Press, 1985), 293–95.

3. See Peter Brown, *The Cult of the Saints* (Chicago: University of Chicago Press, 1981); the chapter by Ewert Cousins, above; and the chapter by Jill Raitt, below.

4. Ogotemmêli's complex discussion of the relation between the impure dead, drinking beer, and the living dead can be found in Marcel Griaule, *Conversations with Ogotemmêli: An Introduction to Dogon Religious Ideas* (Oxford: Oxford University Press, 1965), 183.

5. Charles H. Long, "Matter and Spirit: A Reorientation," in Steven J. Friesen, ed. *Local Knowledge, Ancient Wisdom: Challenges in Contemporary Spirituality* (Honolulu: Institute of Culture and Communication, East-West Center, 1991), 12–16. Long says, "I am placing the locus of matter and materiality precisely at the point of relationships, contacts, and exchanges between and among human beings and between human beings and all other forms of life and meaning" (15).

6. See Åke Hultkrantz, *Conceptions of the Soul among North American Indians: A Study in Religious Ethnology*, Monograph Series, 1 (Stockholm: Ethnographical Museum of Sweden, 1953).

7. See the chapter by Pualani Kanahele, above.

8. Dan Monroe and Walter Echo-Hawk, "Deft Deliberations," *Museum News*, July-August, 1991, 55–58.

9. Ibid., 58.

10. See Walter R. Echo-Hawk, "Sacred Material and the Law," in George P. Horse Capture, ed. *The Concept of Sacred Materials and Their Place in the World* (Cody, Wyo.: The Plains Indian Museum, 1989), 71–72.

11. Raymond C. Leicht, "The Reburial of Skeletal Remains Found on BLM Lands," in *Sacred Materials*, 49–56.

12. Roy Wagner, *The Invention of Culture*, rev. and expanded ed. (Chicago: University of Chicago Press, 1981), 110.

13. Quoted in *Friends Committee on National Legislation Washington Newsletter*, November 1989.

14. From Albert Furtwangler, *Answering Chief Seattle* (Seattle: University of Washington Press, 1997); and *Friends Committee on National Legislation Washington Newsletter*, autumn Indian Report (November/December 1990).

15. Renato Rosaldo, *Culture and Truth: The Remaking of Social Analysis* (Boston: Beacon Press, 1993 [1989]), 68–87.

16. See Umberto Eco, *Travels in Hyperreality: Essays* (San Diego: Harcourt, Brace, Jovanovich, 1986), 3–58; also see Gerald Vizenor, *Crossbloods, Bone Courts, Bingo, and Other Reports* (Minneapolis: University of Minnesota Press, 1990), 77, n. 10.

17. Vizenor, *Crossbloods*, 77. Vizenor quoted from Manfred Stanley, *The Technological Conscience: Survival and Dignity in an Age of Expertise* (Chicago: University of Chicago Press, 1981), 14.

18. Henry P. Biggar, ed., *The Works of Samuel de Champlain* (Toronto: The Champlain Society, 1929), 3:160–63.

19. Ruben Gold Thwaites, *The Jesuit Relations and Allied Documents*, 73 vols. (1896-1901), 10:265–305; hereafter referred to as JRAD.

20. W. Vernon Kinietz, *The Indians of the Western Great Lakes (1615–1760)* (Ann Arbor: Ann Arbor Paperbacks, 1965), 368. Raudot relied extensively on the memoirs of Louis de la Porte de Louvigny for his knowledge of upper Great Lakes Indians.

21. Kinietz, *Indians of the Western Great Lakes*, 210.

22. JRAD 62:201–3.

23. Ibid., 55:137–39.

24. Emma Blair, *The Indian Tribes of the Upper Mississippi Valley and the Region of the Great Lakes* (Cleveland: Arthur H. Clark Co., 1911), 78–92.

25. Gideon D. Scull, ed. *Voyages of Peter Esprit Radisson, being an account of his travels and experiences among North American Indians, from 1652–1684* (New York: P. Smith, 1943), 199–201, 217–19.

26. JRAD 23:209–23.

27. Blair, *Indian Tribes*, 86.

28. JRAD 23:211.

29. Ibid., 23:215–17.

30. Ibid., 55:137–39.

31. Ibid., 23:217.

32. Ibid., 23:219.

33. Blair, *Indian Tribes*, 88.

34. JRAD 23:217–19.

35. Ibid., 10:221.

36. Ibid., 10:265–305.

37. Scull, *Voyages*, 217–19.

38. JRAD 62:201–3.

39. Harold Hickerson, "The Sociohistorical Significance of Two Chippewa Ceremonials," *American Anthropologist* 65 (1963): 89.

40. Hultkrantz, *Conceptions of the Soul*, 241–45; and Diamond Jenness, *The Ojibwa Indians of Parry Island: Their Social and Religious Life*, National Museum of Canada Anthropological Series, 17 (Ottawa: J. O. Patenaude, 1935), 18–20. Compare also the chapter by William Ferea, above.

41. Adrian Tanner, *Bringing Home Animals* (New York: St. Martin's Press, 1979), 122–23; and Alanson Skinner, "Notes on the Eastern Cree and the Northern Saulteaux," *Anthropological Papers of the American Museum of Natural History* 9, no. 1 (1911): 68–76.

42. Tanner, *Bringing Home Animals*, 117–24.

43. John Grim, *The Shaman: Patterns of Siberian and Ojibway Healing* (Norman: University of Oklahoma Press, 1983), 67, 120–29, 140–44; Kinietz, *Indians of the Western Great Lakes*, 305–6; Ruth Landes, *Ojibwa Sociology*, Columbia University Contributions to Anthropology, 29 (New York: Columbia University Press, 1937), 120–21.

44. F. R. A. Baraga, *Theoretical and Practical Grammar of the Otchipwe Language* (Montreal: Beauchemin and Valois, 1978).

45. A. Irving Hallowell, *The Role of Conjuring in Saulteaux Society* (Philadelphia: University of Pennsylvania Press, 1942); "Ojibway Ontology, Behavior and World View," in Stanley Diamond, ed. *Culture in History: Essays in Honor of Paul Radin* (New York: Columbia University Press, 1960), 207–44.

46. Mary B. Black, "Ojibwa Power Belief System," in Raymond Godelson and Richard N. Adams, eds. *The Anthropology of Power: Ethnographic Studies from Asia, Oceania, and the New World* (New York: Academic Press, 1977), 109–17.

47. Vizenor, *Crossbloods*, 66 (emphasis added).

48. Thomas Berry, *The Dream of the Earth* (San Francisco: Sierra Club Books, 1990), esp. pp. 194–215.

49. Gerald Vizenor, trans. and ed., "The Sky Will Resound," *Summer in the Spring: Lyric Poems of the Ojibway* (Minneapolis: Nodin Press, 1965), 59.

Discussion

Laurel Kendall

I'm not going to defend museums. We realize that the time has come to do things very differently. But the argument that collecting was an artifact of nineteenth-century racism needs both elaboration and qualification. Just as Native Americans are finding their own history, we need also to vest the ancestors of modern anthropology with a more complex history. In my museum, the department of anthropology and the subsequent bone-collecting were the products of the work of Franz Boas, the founder of American anthropology. He collected under situations that, looked at today, certainly expressed the hegemony of white, male science. But we must also acknowledge what Boas stood for as an anthropologist. He was trying to fight racism. He devoted his career and trained his students to resist racism on every front. And he felt that the answers to questions of race, the proof of the fundamental equality of all people, were in the bones.

John Grim

Yesterday, Huirangi and I had a chance to speak at a break, and one of the comments that Huirangi made to me was, "The exchange is important." As a person with ancestors speaking with someone who is searching for the meaning of ancestors, he extended his ancestors to me in that exchange. So I agree that collaboration between museums and first peoples could be very beneficial for all sides. Your comments about the history of anthropology and collecting are also important, and I will take them seriously as I continue to work on these issues.

From the audience

How does the knowledge of the ancestors and their bones affect contemporary society? How can that information be transferred to people like myself who don't have the background and understanding of these issues? How can the spread of that knowledge help contemporary society?

John Grim

The question "Why is this important?" is always a crucial one to have before us. My first response is that indigenous people have the knowledge of the treatment of bones, not a person like myself. Indigenous people are the ones who will speak on these issues. But I think the bones are important because Native people are recovering their voices in these bones. The bones are intimately connected with *aloha 'aina*, with the right to determine how land is treated. Native people have a right to stand on the land where their ancestors are buried and to speak from out of that land. For the rest of us, it raises questions about our own bones, about my ancestors and your ancestors, and about the recovery of, in the words of David Kaʻupu, the land as ancestor.

Spiritual Relations, Bodily Realities
Ancestors in the European Catholic Tradition

Jill Raitt

When I was asked to contribute to this conference, two ideas seemed worth pursuing. The first was the relation of Christians to their spiritual ancestors, the Hebrews. My second idea was to consider those ancestors to whom Christians look for examples of the faithful life. These are ancestors in-the-faith rather than in-the-flesh, with the notable exception I shall discuss further on. As I began to work on the subject, the two ways of considering the issues coalesced. Their relation is, of course, temporal and a matter of emphasis, not of exclusion.

As I began working, the realization was again confirmed that these conferences present a unique opportunity. As far as I know, historians of Christianity have not applied their craft in the context of indigenous religions. Nor have I found any historians of Christianity who have addressed the question of *ancestors* in a systematic way. Nor do historians of religion find "ancestors" a meaningful category for understanding Christianity. Nevertheless, a historian of Christianity will find material in studies from both disciplines that make such an enterprise possible. For example, when I turned to the articles on "Ancestors" and on "Genealogies" in the Macmillan *Encyclopedia of Religion*, I found much that was useful even though Christianity was not specifically mentioned under either entry.

The "Ancestors" article is divided into "Ancestor Worship"[1] and "Mythic Ancestors."[2] The first emphasizes practice. Not surprisingly, there is no entry for Christianity among the religious groups who practice ancestor worship. The second article deals with theory. Adam and Eve appear there as "archetypal ancestors of the human community" through sin, which removes them from the fellowship of the Creator and involves them in "sexuality, birth, labor, and death, the universal lot of all human beings." Certainly this is an accurate reading from the Christian point of view since sin and redemption determine Christian scripture, liturgy, theology and practice, whether orthodox or heterodox, formal or popular.[3] One could say that Christianity is the myth of the first Adam who dragged down his progeny and the story of the second Adam who raised up his heirs.[4]

But why is Christianity as such not mentioned in either article? Christianity has ancestors and genealogies: the Hebrews from whom Christianity stems as a religion, and the saints who provide the heroes and legends that relate Christians to their origins and provide continual links between those origins and the present. But before I take up that discussion, I would like to look at some of the reasons why Christianity is not the first example one thinks of in a discussion of ancestors.

Christian theology affirms a doctrine of creation that excludes mediators. The God of Genesis creates directly by a divine word that imposes order on chaos and draws creatures from nothing, *ex nihilo*. The creation of humans follows both the *ex nihilo* pattern (Genesis 1–2:4a) and the molding of humans from earth or mud by a creator who does not mind dirtying the divine hands (Genesis 2:4a–3). In neither case does the Creator call upon helpers. Nor does Christianity want to allow for legend, for a dreamtime, or for a time when there existed beings greater than the present race of humans. This is so in spite of the inclusion of such beings in the stories and genealogies in Genesis up to the time of Abraham.

Yet, both heroic beings and their legends live in Christian art, literature, and practice. Throughout their history, the majority of Christians have welcomed martyrs and saints—including Mary, the human mother of the man-God—as intercessors with Jesus, the second Adam, who is the Mediator between humans and God and who reversed the direction set by Adam and Eve. The Protestant Reformation attempted to clean the slate, so to speak, and has been successful more or less, depending upon how one interprets the various Protestant practices. In this essay, I shall deal with European Roman Catholic Christianity.

In his article on "Genealogy,"[5] Irving Goldman writes, "Genealogical traditions and related rituals evoke, reanimate, and, in some sense, reincarnate ancestors." One might question how well the two genealogies of Christ fit the functions Goldman presents. One of Christ's genealogies opens the Gospel of Matthew and traces his lineage to Abraham. Luke's Gospel (3:23–38) provides a genealogy of Christ that goes back through Abraham to Adam. In his epistles to the Galatians and to the Romans, Paul makes clear both the bond to the Hebrews and the manner in which Gentile Christians relate to them. But Paul's discussion does not evoke Abraham as though he were present. The ancient liturgy of Holy Saturday, however, does so invoke Christian "ancestors," including the Hebrews. Its biblical readings and commentaries claim the major events of the Hebrew Bible as present. An especially poignant and beautiful example is the *Exultet*, the song of the deacon before the blessing of the pascal candle. The *Exultet* repeats *Hoc est nox*, "This is the night," as it evokes the events of creation, the calling of Abraham and the sacrifice of Isaac, and the exodus. Adam, Abraham, and Moses are present to Christians celebrating the passion, death, and resurrection of Jesus Christ.

For the purposes of this paper, however, I will not pursue further the relation of Christians to Jews except to remark upon the difference between the relation of Jews to Abraham, namely, both spiritual and physical, and the relation of Christians to Abraham, which is the spiritual bond of faith. Because of their lack of a genetic tie to Abraham,[6] the ancestors of Gentile Christians are as varied ethnically as the peoples who adopted Christianity or had it thrust upon them. What Christians have in common is the faith of Abraham in the one God and the New Testament interpretation of what that faith meant.

Genealogies, nevertheless, remain potent in some aspects of Christian life. St. Anne, *mater matris*, mother of Mary and therefore grandmother of Jesus, was celebrated in the Middle Ages as the ancestress of French and German royal families and of other notables as well. Thus, St. Anne is represented as the trunk of a tree created in opposition to the standard "tree of Jesse."[7] The first branch is from Anne through Mary to Jesus; the second and third branches provide for Jesus' cousins and their descendants through Anne's two other daughters. All three daughters were named Mary and each had a different father! From Anne's three marriages, the *trinubium*,[8] the story goes, resulted her three daughters, Mary the mother of Jesus and two more Marys from whom Jesus' cousins are derived. Anne was also given a lateral branch, a sister named Esmeria, who was the mother of Elizabeth and grandmother of John the Baptist. Kinship lines could then be drawn from these branches to whomever was considered historically important in the region—a saint, a bishop, or a reigning family.[9]

These aspects of Christian culture are not often considered a legitimate part of Christian history since they are manifestations of popular or folk religion and as such are contaminated by "pagan" influences. Interest in them was therefore restricted to art historians, cultural historians, and, in the instance of the fine study of St. Anne, a concern to recover the contributions of women to Christian history. Now these disciplinary lines are being crossed and historians are studying aspects of folk Christianity and finding that they are not merely popular, but influenced the highest theological discussion; for example, the debate about the trinubium influenced Thomas Aquinas's opposition to the doctrine of the Immaculate Conception of the Virgin Mary.[10] Because the trinubium had been discussed at some length by Peter Lombard,[11] it had become widely known. The "Holy Kinship" was also used politically through its implied sacred legitimation of a ruler's house.

Interesting, too, is the emphasis on the maternal line in the "Holy Kinship" trees, tableaux, and stories. While the New Testament traces Christ's lineage through Joseph who, according to the account, was legally but not genetically related to Jesus, the kinship traditions based on St. Anne establish a matrilinear descent from Jesus' "family" as well as assuring that he was truly human because he had cousins and human relations whose descendants could be traced down through history.

From the earliest days of Christianity, however, lack of a genetic relation was compensated for by the bonds Christians forged to heroic Christians of the past through the recitation of the acts of the martyrs, or of lists of martyrs included in liturgies as martyrologies. Almost as early, that is to say during the second century, relics of the martyrs provided Christians with a bodily relation to their heroic spiritual ancestors. Relics were ideally bones of the martyrs but could also be their clothing or even items that the martyrs had touched. It is important to note that there had to be some sort of immediate physical contact between the relic and the martyr.

Frequently, the discussions of devotion to saints and their relics are gathered up under the term "popular religion" or "popular piety."[12] Where the relation to indigenous religions has been admitted, the reference has frequently been derogatory, especially following the Reformation's rejection of the cult of saints.[13] The proclaimed theological reasons for that rejection were "Scripture alone," and "Christ, the only mediator." But the campaign against devotion to saints, and especially devotion to their relics, was based not only on the charge that it detracted from allegiance to Jesus Christ, but also that such devotion was superstitious, that is, pagan.[14] It was not only sixteenth-century reformers who objected to the "pagan" and "superstitious" elements of aspects of the cult of relics. Bernard of Angers traveled from Chartres to Conques to see at first hand the shrine of St. Foi. He objected to the statue in which the relics of St. Foi were enclosed and which was carried in procession through the town and the fields. He "thought this a superstition and a way of preserving the cult of demons."[15]

Besides the legends, miracle stories, and veneration of their relics, saints are often celebrated through liturgies found either in the Roman Missal or in the special missals of those organizations or areas in which the saint is honored.

Thus, the cult of relics found theological legitimacy as another form of liturgically effective symbolism. The formal sacramental doctrine of Christianity recognizes the power of symbolic action in its use of sacraments and their definition: *res et verba. Res* is taken widely to mean a thing or action that is designated as holy by the accompanying word. Thus, baptism occurs when a person is immersed in water or has water poured over him or her while the minister says, "I baptize you in the name of the Father, the Son, and the Holy Spirit." The application of water without words would not be Christian baptism.[16] In an analogous manner, the presentation of a relic together with the story of the martyr's passion or the saint's life makes of it a sacramental action. In fact, scholars have readily acknowledged that the Eucharist itself was considered to be the relic of relics. Patrick Geary cites a declaration of the Council of Chelsea in 816:

> "*When a church is built, let it be consecrated by the bishop of its diocese. Let the Eucharist which is consecrated by the bishop be placed by him along with other relics . . . in a reliquary and let it be deposited in that same church. And if he is unable to find any other relics, nonetheless this alone is surely sufficient because it is the body and blood of our Lord Jesus Christ. . . .*" Apparently, in the early ninth century, the Eucharist, seen as a relic of Christ, was substituted for other relics because at times none could be found.[17]

It is not far-fetched to conclude that something of the same mentality that understood Christ to be present in the Eucharist understood saints to be present in their relics.[18]

Another aspect of the power of saints is their relation to the continuing life of Jesus as Eucharist, the most exalted "relic" of all. Wonders and miracles are attached to the eucharistic body of Christ, as they are also to the relics of saints whose bodies have not yet risen, but who are nevertheless in the unveiled presence of the risen Christ and can therefore intercede with him on behalf of their protégés on earth.

The body of Christ is also made up of the members of the church. Preeminent among those members are the saints and foremost among the saints are the martyrs whose own blood witnessed to the passion and resurrection of the incarnate God, Jesus Christ. In a profound manner, the elect were members of his mystical body: "Christus . . . totus, cum membris suis." To Augustine and his contemporaries, the martyrs were the *membra Christi* par excellence.[19]

For a better understanding of the subject of saints and relics, I have noted the dominance in saints' stories of one of two sources. Stories of saints in the western Christian tradition until the Reformation, and then continuing in the Roman Catholic Church, stem either from history or from legend. These two primary sources seldom produce a story that is purely one or the other, but rather they are mixed in different proportions from the legend with a tenuous historical base to the biography that is only slightly embellished by legend.

Christianity, like Judaism and Islam, is a religion with its founding events rooted in historical time. As the life and death of Jesus can be dated more or less accurately, so can the lives of Christian saints. The second source is legend, stories of wonderful works by heroes who live in or beyond time and whose relation to history is tenuous. Tales of these saints are told chiefly to exemplify a virtue. These historical-legendary figures and their extraordinary deeds provide edifying examples for the people to weave in and out of their tales and provoke either emulation or simply wonder; in other words, their genre is literary rather than historical.[20]

I have chosen four examples whose *vitae* display different proportions of history and legend: St. Anne, St. Foi, Mary Magdalene, and St. Francis. The first type, the one who is primarily legendary, is St. Anne, the mother of Mary. Mary, the mother of Jesus, is a historical character who therefore had a mother who also lived at a certain time. But that mother is nowhere mentioned in the New Testament and so has no "history." From the eighth through the fifteenth centuries, legends multiplied to provide her with a "vita." As her character was developed in legend and story, she acquired the name and some of the characteristics of Anna, the prophetess who appeared at the presentation of the infant Jesus in the temple (Luke 2:36–38). Beyond that, St. Anne's life is an utter wonder, as are her powers. She represents a figure with a historical foundation but whose life is built entirely of legend.

Another of this type is St. Foi of Conques. Her historical reality is tenuous, the only record being part of the material developed at Conques in the eleventh century. Reputed to have been martyred in 303 at the age of twelve, her relics were moved to Agen in the fifth century and there miracles were attributed to her. In the ninth century, the Conques annals say that a monk stole St. Foi's relics from Agen and brought them to the Cluniac monastery at Conques. She had become a model of faith overcoming torture in martyrdom. Benedicta Ward doubts that she ever existed except in cult stories,[21] but her relics were precious and powerful. As Patrick Geary points out,

Historians, like anthropologists, must accept their subjects' system of viewing reality. Thus, for the purpose of this study, certain phenomena will be

accepted without question: the relics discussed herein are all genuine until proven otherwise by contemporaries; these relics are miraculous, giving off pleasant odors when touched, healing the sick, and otherwise expressing the wills of the saints whose remains they are. Without the acceptance of these postulates, the entire phenomenon becomes incomprehensible and scholarly investigation remains at the level of antiquarian triviality or anachronistc skepticism.[22]

It is not easy to adopt such an attitude and I shall probably slip out of it from time to time, but it seems to me that it is appropriate for our discussions.

Mary Magdalene is a historical person whom the New Testament gives a name and a role, but who has often been interpreted as a composite of the three New Testament Marys. She was claimed by a gnostic sect as one of their leaders. Her legendary travels, which finally brought her to Vezelay, France, her extraordinary asceticism, and her long life were perhaps the least wonderful of her legendary life, which ended, *mirabile dictu,* with the restoration of her virginity.[23]

There is no doubt about the historical reality of St. Francis of Assisi. His life and death are well attested, as are many of his actions, the places to which he traveled, and his *Testament.* But quickly, legends, the *fioretti,* were spun around him that were true to his character if not true otherwise. Unlike St. Foi, Anna, and Mary Magdalene, Francis remains believable and his wonders are based upon his observed character.

Thus, saints, from the holy source of Christian holiness, Jesus Christ, to the most recently canonized saints, share certain characteristics. Stories narrate their lives and deeds. The stories located the saints and those locales then become holy and places of pilgrimage. The bodies of the saints were recovered or things intimately associated with them were gathered as relics and venerated. The relics were enshrined either in the place of the saint's birth or activities or at a place to which the relics had been sent or taken by thieves such as those chronicled in Patrick Geary's fine study, *Furta Sacra: Thefts of Relics in the Central Middle Ages.*[24]

Liturgies, either approved by the church or simply established by custom—or both—organized group veneration. Individual veneration and prayer were encouraged through the attachment of indulgences to a visit to the saint's shrine or to invocation of the saint, and sometimes by the provision of lockets containing miniscule relics that the individual could wear or enshrine at home.

The custom of naming the baptizand after a saint began relatively late.[25] The saints served as models for new Christians who no longer celebrated their own birthdays, but rather their nameday, the day of their patron saint's death, the day the saint was "born" in heaven and on which their liturgy is celebrated.

In this way, the genetic families of Christians yielded to their spiritual families. If parents objected to the choice of their children to become Christians and possibly red martyrs or, later, white martyrs who entered celibate religious life, it was clear which "family" was to be obeyed. To become a member of the body of Christ, the Church, was understood to be far more important than to have been born of a particular pair of parents. "The church was an artificial kin group. Its members were expected to project onto the new community a fair measure of the sense of solidarity, of the loyalties, and of the obligations that had previously been directed to the physical family."[26] Thus the biblical injunction to leave father, mother, et cetera, in order to follow Christ was given the context of joining the greater family of martyrs and saints. Paulinus, bishop of Nola and friend of Augustine, chose the martyr Felix as his heavenly patron. In a way, Paulinus was born with Felix; and by baptism and ascetic withdrawal, he has been "reborn" with Felix. Felix's festival, the day when Felix, by dying, was "born" from earth to heaven, has become Paulinus's true birthday.

> I have always honored this day in such a way that I would treat it as my own birthday rather than that day on which I was born. . . . Ill-starred the day when I came forth, from evil stock to evil deeds; blessed the day when my protector was born for me to Heaven.[27]

While there are likenesses and borrowings from other and often indigenous religions in the initiation ceremony of baptism and in naming for a spiritual ancestor, I must also point out a difference between Christian spiritual ancestry, with its implied and sometimes demanded renunciation of physical ancestry, and the variety of kinship relations among indigenous religions. While young initiates in indigenous communities endure a separation from their families for a given length of time, they eventually return as marriageable adults. Their rebirth is not so much a separation from their birth families as it is a possibility for new ties often based on their kin-groups.

Another difference that underscores the break between the genetic family and the spiritual family of Christians is in the choice that they may make of patrons during their lifetime. Christians may not choose their kin or even, in the case of infants, their baptismal patron saints, but they may turn for help to any saint they wish, drawing upon a well-known pantheon. Peter Brown devotes a chapter to these spiritual relations, entitled, "The Invisible Companion."[28] At its head, Brown cites Theodoret: The philosophers and the orators have fallen into oblivion; the masses do not even know the names of the emperors and their generals; but everyone knows the names of the martyrs, better than those of their most intimate friends.[29] An analogous situation might be the groupies who leave home to follow a rock star. But even this analogy does not do justice to the claim of Theodoret that "everyone knows the names of the martyrs. . . ." One can then choose one's spiritual patron as one chooses one's friends. It is an exercise of freedom.

Another difference between Christianity and indigenous religions can be found in the declaration of Paulinus that he was born "from evil stock to evil deeds." Not only may Christians need to renounce parents who stand in the way of Christian practice, but human flesh is literally heir to sin from which only death and rebirth in Christ can provide a release, while during life heavenly patrons, angels, or saints help Christians to remain faithful to their baptismal vows.

This attitude has two sources. The first is the doctrine of original sin, which won its place over other possible doctrines in Augustine's battle with Pelagius. This doctrine separates western Christianity from indigenous religions, which, so far as I know, make no such absolute break between sinners who inherit sin by being born and saints who become holy through renunciation of bodily relations.

The other source is a more ancient notion of heavenly relations based on a spiritual hierarchy that included one of the components of a human's soul, which was then related to a *daemon, genius,* or guardian angel.[30] The doctrine is important because it develops through Neoplatonism into the influential works of Augustine and later of Pseudo-Dionysius. No two early Christian authors have been more influential on the development of Christian spirituality in the west. This emphasis on a heavenly hierarchy also serves to separate earth from heaven since the heavenly intermediaries are to draw the individual from earthly and bodily attachments to fix their attention on spiritual beings.

It is the doctrines of incarnation and bodily resurrection that insist upon a return to earth. And it is through the martyrs, whose bodily death assured them a heavenly life, that an almost "cozy" relation of *amicitia, patrocinia,* and *familia* with the martyrs (as Peter Brown calls it) replaces the relation between bodied human and angelic spirit and bridges the gulf between heaven and earth.[31]

What better indication of this new bodied relation that replaces the genetic relation of the family than the relic of the new *patronus,* the martyr? Relics are also symbols to which words and narratives give meaning. It is only because one knows that these bones or this bit of cloth belonged to Felix or Perpetua, who died in such and such a way, that the relics represent, re-present, the divine power that gave these martyrs the strength to endure torment and so win heaven. Furthermore, the martyrs have not abandoned their relics, but are in some way present to them so that the faithful can find them at the place of their enshrined relics and invoke them with greater success. Those who desire the help of martyrs make pilgrimages to their shrines. Chief among these is St. Peter's Cathedral, the burial place of the martyred companion of Jesus to whom Jesus gave responsibility for the Christian flock. But the relics of any martyr—and, by the Middle-Ages, of any saint—could establish a shrine and place of pilgrimage, whether local or universal. That place then generated more relics. The most powerful relics were those associated with Jesus and Mary. Constantine's mother, Helen, traveled to Jerusalem and there, miraculously, found the true cross, the crown of thorns, and the nails of the crucifixion.[32] So it came to be that a place, even without relics, could be holy and itself a source of relics. Pilgrims to Jerusalem still bring back earth from the places made holy by Jesus' life and death. They then carry these relics with them and so assure themselves of a constant representation and presence of the holy.

For all the likenesses to some practices of indigenous religions that use various means to maintain the memory of and contact with their ancestors through genealogies and objects like eagle feathers or crystals, which make special power present and effective and so may be called sacraments of communion with their ancestors, there remains a significant difference between indigenous religions and Christianity in this regard. In Christianity, the rhythm of the *ordo sanctorum* has replaced the rhythms of the *ordo naturae*. The feast days of saints were fixed according to the dates of their deaths, their heavenly birthdays. Within that order, there are birthdays and celebrations that were accommodated to the seasons, such as Christmas and All Saints' Day, but their seasonal power is lost when Christianity moves out of the northern hemisphere. Then the significance of light at the time of the winter solstice is lost in the blaze of midsummer. In his discussion of this point, Peter Brown admits that the process of hominization, socialization, and urbanization fostered during sixth-century Christianity deprived natural phenomena of divinity.[33] But he finds comfort in the fact that late-antique Christians ensured that there were places in their world "where men [sic] could stand in the searching and merciful presence of a fellow human being."[34]

It is tempting to conclude, as did Peter Brown, with such a fine flourish. But I must return to the fact that Christianity's later doctrines were built upon the doctrine of universal sinfulness and the probability of each one actually sinning, with the resultant frequent need for forgiveness. "God may pardon sin, but Nature cannot"[35] is a terse summation of the revolution Christianity wrought on the pagan world. In Christianity, the God-man earned the full re-mission of sin, a remission which was applied to individuals through human ministries: the intercession of martyrs and saints and the administration of sac-raments by priests. Thus, the power of forgiving sin determines the structures of Christianity, including the powers of Christian saints and martyrs, the *famuli Christi et patroni Christianorum*.[36]

Notes

1. By Helen Hardacre.

2. By Charles Long.

3. "Through Christianity, the concept of sin was also spread widely in the pagan world." This note deserves a lengthy study in itself. It comes from Robin Lane Fox, *Pagans and Christians* (San Francisco: Harper and Row, 1986), 22.

4. I do not include Eve here because part of the reality of Christianity is its continual patriarchal language. For a medieval instance of the rectification of this perspective, note that the "Holy Kinship" discussed below relates Jesus genetically not only to his Hebrew past but to his Christian "progeny" through the maternal line.

5. *Encyclopedia of Religion*, ed. Mircea Eliade (New York: Macmillan, 1987).

6. With the exception of the "Holy Kinship" discussed below.

7. See, for example the introduction, figs. 2, 9, and especially the chapter by Pamela Sheingorn, "Appropriating the Holy Kinship: Gender and Family History," with all of its illustrations, in Kathleen Ashley and Pamela Sheingorn, eds., *Interpreting Cultural Symbols: Saint Anne in Late Medieval Society* (Athens, Georgia: The University of Georgia Press, 1990), 169–98.

8. Ibid., 13ff.

9. Ibid., 15, cf. 27.

10. Ibid., 16.

11. Ibid., 14.

12. Patrick J. Geary, "The Ninth-Century Relic Trade: A Response to Popular Piety?" in James Obelkevich, ed. *Religion and the People, 800–1700* (Chapel Hill: The University of North Carolina Press, 1979), 1: "If by 'popular piety' is meant a uniquely lay religious tradition separate from that of the clergy. . . ." But see the extended discussion of this problem in Peter Brown, *The Cult of the Saints: Its Rise and Function in Latin Christianity* (Chicago: The University of Chicago Press, 1981).

13. Frederick of Wittenberg, Luther's protector, brought back "the head of St. Anne" from the Holy Land (Ashley and Sheingorn, *Interpreting Cultural Symbols*, 18) and even had himself painted into a Holy Kinship painting by Lucas Cranach the Elder! (189).

14. For example, see John Calvin, *Institutes of the Christian Religion*, III, xx, 22, 27. Cf. Carlos M. N. Eire, *War against the Idols: The Reformation of Worship from Erasmus to Calvin* (Cambridge: Cambridge University Press, 1986), chap. 6, esp. pp. 211ff.

15. Quoted from Benedicta Ward, *Miracles and the Medieval Mind: Theory, Record, and Event, 1000–1215* (Philadelphia: University of Pennsylvania Press, 1982), 41.

16. In those instances (not official sacraments) where no words are spoken, an action or thing becomes a holy thing or action through the ceremony in which it is included, for example, processions, elevations, or showings.

17. Geary, "Relic Trade," 14. This practice raises an interesting question about the preservation and corruption of the eucharist used in such a way; I have not had the leisure to pursue it.

18. This subject needs to be further explored. How early and how closely were these understandings of the "relics" of Christ and his saints related?

19. Brown, *The Cult of the Saints*, 72.

20. Patrick J. Geary, *Furta Sacra: Thefts of Relics in the Central Middle Ages* (Princeton: Princeton University Press, 1978), 9–11.

21. Ward, *Miracles*, 37: "It is very probable that her miracles as recorded at Conques are the earliest written evidence for her cult anywhere, the other material being part of the cult itself." See also Geary, *Furta Sacra*, esp. p. 90; 94–95.

22. Geary, *Furta Sacra*, 4.

23. H. C. Slim, "Mary Magdalene, Musician and Dancer," in *Early Music* 8, no. 4 (1980): 460–73.

24. Geary, *Furta sacra*, 9–11.

25. Lionel Rothkrug, "Popular Religion," in *Religious Practices and Collective Perceptions: Hidden Homologies in the Renaissance and Reformation* (Waterloo, Ontario: University of Waterloo, 1980), 38. Rothkrug says that in Germany, the use of saints' names began only around 1300.

26. Brown, *The Cult of the Saints*, 31.

27. Ibid., 57 with n. 36.

28. Ibid., chap. 3.

29. Ibid., 50, citing *Curatio affectionum graecarum* 8. 67, PG 83.

30. Ibid., 51–53. Citing Plutarch and Plotinus, Brown writes (ibid., 51) that "the soul is not a simple homogeneous substance: it is a composite, consisting of many layers. Above the layers of which the individual is immediately conscious, there lies a further layer, the 'true' soul, that is as immeasurably superior to the soul as we know it, as the soul itself is superior to the body. Thus the self is a hierarchy, and its peak lies directly beneath the divine. At that peak, late-antique men placed an invisible protector. Whether this protector was presented as the personal *daimon*, the *genius*, or the guardian angel, its function was the same: it was an invisible being entrusted with the care of the indiviual, in a manner so intimate that it was not only the constant companion of the individual; it was almost an upward extension of the individual."

31. Ibid., 61.

32. It is not to my purpose to regale you with the multiplication of pieces of the true cross or the discovery of Christ's foreskin, Mary's milk, and even the sound of the bells of Solomon's temple and the sneeze of the Holy Spirit! See John S. Strong, "Relics," in Lawrence E. Sullivan ed., *Death, Afterlife, and the Soul* (New York: Macmillan, 1989), 56.

33. Brown, *The Cult of the Saints*, 124–26.

34. Ibid., 127.

35. James Frazier, *The Golden Bough*, pt. 2 (New York: Macmillan, 1935); cited by Brown, *Cult of the Saints*, 126.

36. There are four ideas that deserve further investigation here. The first comes from a thesis that Lionel Rothkrug suggested to explain the prevalence of saints' shrines in

some areas and the lack of them in other parts of France and the Holy Roman Empire before the sixteenth century; *Religious Practices and Collective Perceptions: Hidden Homologies in the Renaissance and Reformation*; whole issue of *Historical Reflections/ Reflexions historique 7* (1980). His thesis is that among the pre-Christianized Germanic tribes that invaded Europe, some called upon dead chiefs to participate in trials of justice and some did not. In other words, "pagan" peoples who conquered Europe brought with them a continuing relation to their dead and expectation that the dead would participate in important events of the living. Other tribes buried their dead and said a permanent good-bye. Obviously, the former tribes would find veneration of saints and their relics compatible, while the latter would have little patience for such a continuing relation with the dead and buried. The second idea, which I share quite tentatively, is that the martyrs' violent deaths, often involving dismemberment, and followed or accompanied by the vision of Christ, is a shamanic initiation. Some converted tribes may have found the martyr's initiation to be more comprehensive and powerful than the less comprehensible, Roman-derived ordination of priests. A third idea arose in conference discussion, namely, the "portability" of Christianity (see above, the discussion of Cousins's paper). Since "relics" can be sent and carried, they serve a dual purpose. They allow Christianity to "take root" anywhere and, at the same time, tie far-flung churches to Rome, since relics have to be approved by Rome, and, indeed, in the first six centuries relics of the Roman martyrs were sent to Christian churches. Relics, as well as hierarchical structures and ordinations, tethered western Christianity to Rome as the center until the Reformation. The fourth area that should be included is the Roman Catholic doctrine of purgatory and the use of indulgences to maintain a link with ancestors who are not recognized as saints.

Discussion

Sam Kaai

Many of the papers have dealt in one way or another with some kind of rupture in a variety of traditions. In your paper you talked about a rupture that separates people from the order of nature, and I guess one question is, "Was there a rupture?" Hawaiians have experienced their own kinds of ruptures since contact, and we have had to decide whether we want to dwell on the rupture or whether we should go on praising the things we praise. Just because there was an explosion or an ailment or a death or a loss doesn't mean that the original is of no account anymore or that some revisions can't be made. We revise recipes all the time, but we tend to resist changes in our own spiritual life.

Ewert Cousins

Yes, I would agree with you about the rupture. For many generations, modernity has looked upon itself as having been caught up in, and the main cause of, a radical rupture. But things seem to be changing and at least some people who have been influenced by modernity are now very interested in the wisdom of the distant past as being extremely relevant to the present and the future. I don't believe that's characteristic of the rupture of modernity, in the sense of a rupture that shattered the connection with the past. It's almost as if there is a recovery of the past, not in a unilinear way but in a collective global way, as if the human community has to go back even farther into its past in order to be fully in the present.

Lawrence Sullivan

I've been working on the notion that critical thinking grows out of particularly generative images of crisis, and it seems to me that there are different ways in which to imagine a fundamental crisis that propels you toward the critical thought that's characteristic of culture. In traditions that have a lively acknowledgment of ancestors, many of these fundamental crises are located in the lifetime or in the actions of those ancestors who made fundamental breakthroughs for their culture. Those become paradigmatic models for ritual life or for thinking one's way through other new episodes. Modernity, on the other hand, more often locates the break that allows for critical thought in the choices of the individual. The crisis is there but it's relocated. Instead of invoking paradigmatic ancestral crises as the source for critical thinking, people act as though they now have the choice to think rationally about themselves in new ways. When I say this, I want to avoid some kind of cheap universalism that glosses over our differences. I'm looking for continuities of thought that define us as human and that do not deny the distinctive orientations of various cultures. So in regard to ancestors, it seems to me that critical thinking grows out of images of crises, but they can be variously located.

There is something ironic about the general western impression that traditional religions are carried on by people who blindly follow tradition without an awareness of why they're doing what they're doing. Yet, it seems that all people operate off of the precedents and momentum of the past. The irony is that traditions that have kept the lively ancestral imagery and vocabulary often prove themselves to be much more self-conscious than communities of modernity. Traditional communities at least prove to speak about these things more directly than those that are indifferent to the ancestors who are actually constitutive of their reality. In so doing, they do not equip themselves either with the vocabulary or with the regular occasions to examine their ancestry. So it may be that in certain regards, modernity, which prides itself on being a transcendental breakthrough and being rationally self-aware, is quite limited and not as self-conscious as traditions that have kept the lively veneration of ancestors.

Jill Raitt

I'm wary of talk about going back, even after what Charles Long said about going home the hard way. Western traditions have so far to go back, I'm not sure we would ever work our way there. "Reaching out" may be a more fruitful strategy than "going back." A lot of people are tired of a consumption-based society that pushes us to acquire more and more things that mean less and less. People are beginning to see that there is no future in such a system, but they don't feel they have a past to go back to. I think that part of the interest of people in the United States in Native American traditions is that we can't go back to our own ancestors in their simplicity, if there ever was such a time. Where would I like to stop in time and find solutions? In my own ancestry I don't think I can find a place where I would want to look for guidance and values. But I do think that given the situation in the world we must reach out, not back, to indigenous peoples. It won't do to borrow someone else's ancestors, but maybe we can reach out on the basis of being human, as Larry said. Maybe we can reach out as human beings to human beings who have successfully negotiated with the environment for a long, long, time without destroying it. Maybe there are things there we can learn.

Laurel Kendall

I have a great deal of sympathy for what Jill has said, and yet it raises a lot of questions. What is the form and what are the means whereby reaching out takes place? As you were talking about consumerism, the images of "native commodities" were flashing in my mind: the magazines on shamanism, the paperbacks, the books, the marketing, the crystals. That is all part of that same juggernaut. We have to acknowledge that and think about where that begins, where that takes off, what it means. It's this cheap universalism that Larry was alluding to, and I find it very disturbing.

Pualani Kanahele

Here's an example of what you're talking about. I teach at the community colleges, and a few years ago when I was at Maui Community College, I was coming out of my class when a woman approached me. I never saw her before in my life, but she knew who I was and what I did. She said she just came from the mainland. Twenty years ago she had a dream about me and so she came to find me. I invited her into my office and she told me I have to share the knowledge that I have with her and with the rest of the world. She said that I have some of the knowledge of the earth that has to be shared with the world. I was taken aback. I was thinking, "Who is this crazy *haole* lady coming into my office, telling me I have to share my knowledge with her?" But when you talk about reaching out, people like that are going to be coming and insisting the rest of the world has a right to our "primal wisdom" in a way that makes it little more than a religious commodity. And there are people who will start spiritual workshops, invite people to share a cave with them for the weekend and feel the vibrations of the earth, and that kind of thing. People set themselves up as authorities on primal religion and lead a lot of people astray. Sometimes we don't have a choice; it is a part of our culture to share, but then it eventually gets out of control.

Laurel Kendall

Welcome to the marketplace.

Sam Kaai

I've had people come to me and tell me that in their channeling they've learned that they were Hawaiian in a previous life and that I'm the anointed one to reveal this. It's really painful.

Puanani Burgess

I'm a beneficiary of Charles Dickens. Charles Dickens had a choice to write for the elite or to write in a way that shared his stories with the common people. The elite said he was cheapening his craft, but he felt that the only way he could reach the common people was to put it in a form that they could afford and understand. Common people need to have access to the kinds of information and issues that we are talking about as well. Maybe those "religious commodities" say the wrong thing, but what often happens—and I've seen it—is that people will read something superficial that starts them on their own journey to deeper levels. And perhaps for that reason, the popular writing is useful sharing. Without that kind of dissemination, a lot of people wouldn't know that these issues are alive and well and throbbing in university circles.

Lawrence Sullivan

I want to go back to a question that has come out in several different ways, and that is the relationship of ancestors and death. As I've been thinking about it over the last couple of days, it seems to me that one reason why death and ancestors are linked is that death is something that renders significance. Ancestors are of course significant, but death seems to have the power to add meaning to an event or person. Maybe this is one reason why accounts of ancestors in mythology seem to be so filled with deaths and disappearances and mayhem and disasters. There are all kinds of things dying and disappearing or transmuting themselves and undergoing radical disappearance and change. Perhaps these deaths rendered the various groups or the various places significant in ways that they might not have been had something ultimate not occurred there. It brings something to an end, but thereby also renders it significant.

The other thing that occurred to me about ancestry and death is that death in the cases that have been presented seems to have a kind of "fusive" quality that joins things of significance to one another or draws things into significant relationships, things that would not have been significant without death somehow being attached to them. For example, our personal histories may not seem to have any significant intersection except for being in this meeting together. But if some disaster would strike or the building would collapse on us, our personal histories and their conjunction might be rendered significant in ways that would not have been realized if we had just passed like ships in the night. When death occurs, and these conjunctions or fusions are made, it mobilizes divinatory teams, whether these teams be insurance investigators or police detectives or others, who sift through the enigma and the rubble for signs of what happened. I think that death in the stories and images of ancestors function in this way, that the enigmas and absences of ancestors give rise to this labor that is distinctively human—the labor of the imagination—that knits together what has happened to figure out why this is significant.

Charles Long

On the point about whether all who die are sacred, I think that generally it is the case that the place of repose is sacred. You have a community, and those people who have died and rest in that sacred place are part of that community. The other thing is that you don't have efficacious ancestors unless there is an afterlife. Unless you have a community that knows there is a life after this life, you cannot have efficacious ancestors because they have nowhere to go. That means that the reason death functions in the way you were describing is precisely because death is an exchange between this world and that world. It's an ultimate exchange between this world and that world, as well as an initiation into the other world. So the issue of having ancestors and having an afterlife is a crucial one for modernity. If there is no afterlife, if the dead are just dead and that's the end of it, then there's no reason for anyone to be worried about the recovery of ancestors. It's just the undertaker's job. One of our problems with ancestors in modernity is where to locate a meaning for life that extends beyond the life of the flesh in relationship to the integrity and meaning of the human community.

I wonder whether or not it's even possible for various sorts of modern people in modern communities to learn anything from so-called primal people. It's not a matter of getting a little piece of knowledge about learning to live with nature, because what we call "the way they live with nature" means that they don't consider it "nature." One reason that modern people don't have a meaning of the afterlife is precisely because they've created something called "nature," over which they are in control, where nature becomes an object, a commodity, a thing. Now, along with that goes a whole spectrum of other structures in the modern world. It will require a rethinking of the very nature and constitution of the human community and of the human self, rather than a little patching up.

The problem has to be addressed at a deeper level than has been attempted by the environmentalists or the ecologists or the theologians. Basically, they are still talking about human beings in control of nature. Now that we have messed up this thing called nature, we think we can fix it, as if it were an automobile and primal people have the tool we need. That is why I am a little reluctant about all this "reaching out" and "sharing." We need to probe deeper into what it means to be human in our time. Instead of learning from primal traditions, I think we need to stand and be interrogated by those traditions. That interrogation itself might afford the possibilities for some new constitution of the self, but it hasn't happened yet. We know a great deal about all kinds of people in the world. But the one thing we have not done is to allow those of us who claim to be the knowers of these traditions to be interrogated by those traditions.

Disconnection and Reconnection

Puanani Burgess

I would like to begin with a poem that introduces me. It is called

"Choosing My Name"

When I was born my mother gave me three names,
Christabelle, Yoshie, and Puanani.

Christabelle was my "english" name,
my social security card name,
my school name,
the name I gave when teachers asked me
for my "real" name,
it was a safe name.

Yoshie was my home name,
my every day name,
the name that reminded my father's family
that I was Japanese, even though
my nose, hips and feet were wide,
the name that made me acceptable to them
who called my Hawaiian mother *kuroi* (black),
it was a saving name.

Puanani is my chosen name,
my *piko* name connecting me to the *ʻāina* and the *kai* and

to the *poʻe kahiko*;
it is my blessing; my burden,
my amulet; my spear.

Charles Long gave me a phrase that articulated something that has bothered
me for a long time. He talked about the hard way home; not the long way home,
but the hard way home.[1] That is what my presentation is about. I had not
thought enough about that. What would the hard way home be for someone
like me? For me, that means I have to be American, Japanese, Christian; to be
modern, to live in this time; to be an intellectual, to be educated; to be Hawaiian; to be animal, spirit, *ʻāina*. That would be the path for me in order to take the
hard way home.

I have a poem that talks about the hard way home. The poem is called "The
Liturgy." It was written by a group of us from Waiʻanae. We were asked to develop a liturgy that would be distributed throughout the world by a national,
ecumenical organization of Christian women. We were asked to speak to issues
that we as women in Hawaiʻi face—land, loss of identity, and so on. But when
we sat down as a group to talk about the liturgy, we were led back to the source
of where and how we worship. And there we found tensions between us that we
needed to discuss before we could even talk about the politics of our spirituality.

"The Liturgy"

In the Hawaiian tradition, language is believed to be a gift of the gods. As
we speak each word, the spirit of the Gods lives within the word. Words,
then, if spoken with the knowledge of their spiritual content, can become prayers. And as we speak, even to each other, Sisters and Brothers,
we are praying and the god or gods whom we thank for Life are with us.

To you, Sisters and Brothers, we send these words, our prayers. We hope
they will evoke in you the reality of the pain and the conflicts we as Native Hawaiian women have felt in having to disown our gods, our spirituality, our culture, our symbols, our language and our dignity and have as
their replacement the Christian god.

That our experience speaks to and acknowledges the experience of other
native peoples is significant. The Hawaiian Experience is not an isolated
experience.

It is not our purpose to produce guilt, but understanding; not merely repentance, but lasting change and an end to the use of the Cross as a symbol of conquest and a partner of the Flag.

E 'ŌLELO KAKOU, SISTERS AND BROTHERS
(Let us speak together, Sisters and Brothers)

E PULE KAKOU, SISTERS AND BROTHERS
(Let us pray together, Sisters and Brothers)

Sisters and Brothers,
Hear our prayer to you.

In the Spirit of Aloha which our gods
bequeathed to us and to you,
we ask you to hear our words and feel our pain.

Long before your Christian forefathers and mothers
came upon our sacred 'Āina (Land)
We were nine hundred thousand strong.
Strong in body, mind and spirit.
Our gods, our ways, our 'Āina, our sea and sky
provided for and nourished us.

But your forefathers and mothers came to our shores
and brought with them the Cross and
   the Flag, and
   Disease, and
   Alcohol, and
   Despair, and
   Greed, and
   Shame for what we were—"lowly heathens," I think they said.

They offered, no, demanded,
that we accept the Cross and the Flag
   (those Siamese twins of Power)
And said, "Here. With these you will prosper."

We tried to put into their hands, our symbols:
    The Kalo (Taro), from whose body we take sacred nourishment.
    The 'Āina (Land), from whose body we take sacred nourishment.
    The Wai and the Kai (the inland and the sea Water), from whose body
        we take sacred nourishment.

But they scorned our symbols. They scorned us.
They said, "Here. With these, you will prosper."

But look at us now, Sisters and Brothers.
    We are the poorest.
    We live in cars, tents, on benches and sidewalks.
    We occupy more jail cells, more hospital beds, more morgue slabs and
        coffins than any other race in Hawaii.
    Our children are labelled "DISADVANTAGED" and
                              can't read
                              can't write
                              can't get a job
                              can't get an education.
We are beggars in our own homeland.

But no more.
As we lay down the Cross,
As we lay down the Flag,
We search and have found those symbols which spring from
                              this place
                              this time
                              this People.

In our hands we offer you
a scoop of earth, the 'Āina
a scoop of water from the land and the sea, Life
a rainbow, Hope
and Aloha, Love.

But let us be clear.
Whether you accept our symbols
    or not,

We will continue to speak the truth of our history
the truth of our pain
the truth of our oppression
the truth of our colonization.
And through these Truths we will be free.

This is our prayer to you, Sisters and Brothers.
Listen to it with your soul, Sisters and Brothers.

Amene.

In writing this poem, I was the redactor, the one who brought the ideas and the themes of the women together. There was more pain among the women who wrote this than I can sometimes bear to remember. You see, there was a way to acknowledge historical facts, but not a great deal of knowledge or desire to heal. There was no way to do it; a hug was not enough. It seemed to us that something more systematic, more institutional was needed, something other than a mere handshake or embrace. But how do you do that when you are a group of people who are only beginning to become conscious of your history, just grappling with the information and the power of that history? How do you work with that and not be consumed by the hatred? How does Hatred become transformed into Love that can be seen, like the beautiful woman that it is? That hatred has the power within its miraculous body to transform into soul, into Aloha, into love, that can feed and nourish all of us. That was a challenge for us. Could we escape the stereotyping? In a painful process like that, it is sometimes easier to deal with stereotypes than to break through the masks.

I listen to the tremendous amount of hope and joy of the Hawaiians here who know the names of their ancestors, who know their 'aumakua. Once I asked Ulunui if I could come visit her, and she knew what I was asking. I wanted to find a way to reconnect with my ancestors. When I asked, I waited for the answer with greater anticipation than when I was admitted into law school. The anticipation was greater because I was hungry, because I didn't know, and yet was unwilling to ask for something that was not mine. It belonged to someone else and had to be given in a way that was appropriate. I was not quite sure how to proceed; I had no footsteps to follow, no protocol.

My case is similar to the situations of many, many people in Hawai'i. I was born to a Hawaiian mother and a Japanese father, but they lived at a time when it was not popular to be Hawaiian. My mother tried to hide the fact that she was Hawaiian, which was very odd because there was absolutely no way to hide the fact. She looked Hawaiian and her only given name was Hawaiian. All her brothers and sisters had English names behind which she felt they could hide, but she never could. Everyone who ever saw her name knew instantly who she was and there could never be any peace for her in the world into which she was born. When she introduced me to her friends that we met on the road, she would say, "This is my daughter, Yoshie. She is so fair. Isn't she beautiful?" She systematically tried to remove from me every vestige of Hawaiian-ness that I had picked up along the way.

My mother's mother, however, was a *kahuna* who had chosen me to be a repository of the family's knowledge, and there was an ongoing fight between them. My mother sent me to Japanese classical dancing for five years. In the evenings my grandmother, who was blind, would steal me away. We would hide in the darkness and she would pound the *ipu* (gourd used as a drum). She tried to teach me the songs and the dances and the rituals. My mother would ferret us out, she would find us wherever we were, and she would drag me away from there as I kicked and screamed. One time I remember her pulling me this way, sticking my arm in the kimono and dragging me out into the street. It is that kind of tearing that many of us face who are of mixed blood and mixed culture, and it is very difficult to find some form of spirituality in between the worlds.

My father's parents were Shinto as well as Buddhist. There were altars in their house and early on I was taught the details of the rituals that went along with respect for the ancestors. My maternal grandmother offered not just the Hawaiian way, but also the Christian way. She was both, she had her existence in both systems. My mother, however, forced me toward Japanese and so, for eighteen years of my life, I was Japanese. Then I did what my mother probably thought was the most unforgivable thing I could do. I married a Hawaiian man. I rejected the Hawaiian and Japanese cultures and took comfort in "local culture," which was a mixture of all sorts of things. I don't know if you can find comfort and solace in something so mixed, having no single identity, but I tried very hard to do just that.

In those first eighteen years of my life I invested myself heavily in books. I decided I would get a college education and try to go the intellectual route. I was very successful and made it to law school. I even made it to my last semester of law school, but at that point I called the dean and told him I could no longer continue. You see, people kept telling me, "Pua, you've got to stop crying all the time!" I would be reading the cases in a class on Hawaiian rights and I would start to weep. The stories that were in those pages leaped out at me. I couldn't ignore them. I couldn't ignore the pain of people who had to reject their hearts in favor of their minds. But it wasn't just the case stories. Many of my classmates wanted to experience the world with their hearts and their minds, but law school relentlessly separated the two. The heart and the mind had to be pursued in different contexts. It was only when we had beer parties after hours that the professors would unwind and start to weep in their own way. Or they would bemoan the fact that there was no emotional or spiritual content within the law. My question to them was, "Why not? Who says there can't be? It must be you." When I told them I no longer found that acceptable, I became both a hero and a demon at the same time to that group of people.

For those of us who do not have the knowledge of our genealogy, where do we go? David Ka'upu talked about the 'āina as ancestor, and when you think about it, you realize that the 'āina made us Hawaiian. It is the 'āina that made you Papua New Guinean, or Japanese, or Irish. The 'āina made you what you are. When I brought questions to my *kupuna*, I once asked her how I could possibly reconnect without the rituals, without the protocol. She answered, "You have a Hawaiian heart, don't you? You have a Hawaiian mind, don't you? That is all your ancestors had." If this is the case, then you must construct your world with the clues and the bits that you have left.

There is a wonderful book by Germaine Greer in which she talks about the gaps that she had in her life, in her mythology, in her ability to relate to her ancestors. It talks about how she became a detective and pieced it together, how she bravely made up places where she knew she must have a bridge but could not find anyone to ask. That is my case, and the case of many of the people I work with in my community.

The name of my community is Wai'anae, "the water where the mullet runs." It is a very famous community, but unfortunately it is famous for negative things. The image comes from outsiders, but it is becoming the perception of insiders as well. That is where the danger lies. Wai'anae is made up of about forty thousand people. Most people think of us as ocean people. We have that character, but we also have the character of beautiful uplands and green lush places where the *kalo* (taro) grow. My husband comes from Wai'anae; he's an insider there. When he took me back there, it was not easy to go into that community. About half of the people are ethnically Hawaiian and Hawaiian culture affects the whole character of the place. So we call ourselves a Hawaiian community. It is like any small community—there are many invisible, visible lines that connect us in mysterious and wonderful spiritual ways. I was not part of any line, any song, so I had to find a line or a song that would make me an insider. I'm still looking.

One way that I have tried to make the connections between myself and the spirituality that I know is my right is through the Hawaiian concept that "work is medicine." Hawaiians believe that work in itself is healing and in that work we are connected to the land, the 'āina. That is why we initiated a project to grow kalo, and specifically to grow kalo in a context where we are able to share what kalo means as a symbolic and spiritual source for the people who live in Hawai'i. After all, kalo is my ancestor. If I cannot name the people who are my ancestors, I know that I can go back to kalo. It is my first ancestor and there is comfort and strength in that knowledge. This project is located in Ka'ala, the oldest and highest mountain range on O'ahu; it is the birth mother of this island. Ka'ala means "path" or "way," and for many people, including myself, it is just that. It is not the only path or the only way, but it is one way. When people come to Ka'ala, we never ask them to leave their modern self on the outside by the stream that runs along the edge of the project. We ask them to bring their modern self across the stream onto the path, to see, to feel, to touch, to know that the 'āina lives today. It is our contemporary and our peer. It has an ancient genealogy, but like us, it carries that genealogy in itself right now. The 'āina is alive. It may not be well everywhere, but it is alive. So we try to share with the children and people who visit the culture at Ka'ala as we have come to understand it. Our effort is an attempt to give people a source of values and experience in which they do not have to choose between the modern or traditional, they do not have to choose between being Christian or traditional.

One of the things we do at Ka'ala is to provide a place where adults and children can work in the lo'i, the kalo patch. The children always ask, "Are we really going into the lo'i? Are we really going into the mud? Are there frogs and crayfish? What will it be like?" We also have meetings where the children can learn from the kupuna, the elders. Many of the children no longer have the experience of learning from kupuna. So we have kupuna show the children how to pound the kalo into pa'i 'ai, how to fish. And most important, we try to show them the respect that comes from working with kalo or from working with fish.

For instance, one of our kupuna is a master fisherman, and he helped us relearn that the fish has a spirit. He reminded us that in the Hawaiian way, you feed the fish so that when it is your turn the fish will feed you. It is not a random approach to fishing. They go out consistently to feed the fish at the same place. When Uncle Walter gets there in his canoe, he hits the side of the canoe and the fish come. These are the same fish he's always been feeding, so when it's time for him to harvest, he puts out the nets, he throws in the palu (bait), and the fish will come. Then he thanks the spirit of the fish and the ocean for this contribution and returns some of the fish back to the sea. What is interesting is he recognizes some of the "elders." He takes these fish and puts them back so that they will call the new fish to come to this place at the appropriate time. That is the kind of wisdom, the kind of spiritual attachment to everything that is alive, that many of our elders have. But they do not have the younger people to help manage the process so that they can do the work that they need to do and want to do.

When people come to Kaʻala, some think of the work as cultural, some think of it as spiritual, and some think of it as just a place for recreation or as a place to be entertained. We tell them that Kaʻala has the ability to be that, but it is something else as well. Their response is usually confusion and many of them approach such a place only intellectually. Only when they go into the loʻi do they begin to experience what that primal mud is. They begin to understand what it means to grow kalo and the kind of science that was required to grow more than two hundred varieties of this plant.

Music and dance have been a significant influence in Hawaiʻi for those of us who are searching for our ancestors. There are so many people in my community who have no sense of what it means to be Hawaiian, but if you play Hawaiian music, there is something that reaches out to them and touches them. For the moment that they are singing that song, they know very deeply what it means to be Hawaiian. When they see Pualani's *halau* dance, they have a sense of what it means to come from a tradition that spoke to the gods in this form. For many of them, the form itself is no longer accessible except as an observer. So, many people involved in education ask how we can reach these people, how we can reach these children who have no alignment, who have no access to these ways of knowing and expression.

We have another project that demonstrates the use of modern technology wrapped around by our tradition. We grow fish called *tilapia* in small backyard tanks about twelve feet in diameter that are managed by families. Tilapia are red and beautiful; they look like puffed-up gold fish. Nine Hawaiian families are growing these fish, not for their own consumption, but for the sake of the community. A reason for doing this project was something like Gandhi's idea when he urged the women to continue to use the spinning wheel, to regain their own sweat, to have their own production nourish their own people and their own community. The technology that we use comes from a place in Pennsylvania. We took this technology and modified it for our own use. In the tanks we have a rotating bio-filter that allows the water to be cleansed by the bacteria and algae so that we can use the water many times. The water then goes into the loʻi where it nourishes the kalo. Soon we will be expanding to hydroponics so that the water will go from the fish to the hydroponically grown vegetables and then on to the terrestrial crops. This is the Hawaiian Way, to use over and over and over to complete the cycles of life.

There is a young man who works for us as the manager of this project, and one day I saw him standing at the tank. He reached in and netted three fish, about a pound each. He walked to the kitchen, gutted them, cleaned them, and fried them. In about ten minutes, it was on the table. That really is the essence of why we do this. We want people to see that they have control over their own spirituality, which is expressed in the production and sharing of food.

In the quest for finding ourselves and the roots of our spirituality, we try to write books ourselves. They are imperfect. They are based on some of the information that we have gotten from our elders. For us, it is a way of memorializing, but also of passing on this form of knowledge to our young people and to the institutions that teach them. One of the books is a manual called *From Then to Now: A Manual for Doing Things Hawaiian-Style*. We tried to include not just techniques, but also the motivation. When we do our work, people say to us, "Why do you use a bulldozer? That's not a Hawaiian tool. Why don't you stick to the adze?" Our response is that we try to use the bulldozer in the way the Hawaiians used the adze, in a way that would conserve and benefit the land. Our ancestors did not ignore mechanical advances. They embraced them and made them their own.

The dress that I'm wearing today symbolizes what I mean. Hawai'i has a way of Hawaiianizing things: the musics, the languages, the clothes. This dress is not Hawaiian, although we all call it a Hawaiian mu'umu'u. American and European women wore dresses like this, and we Hawaiianized the style. This particular dress has Chinese and Japanese characters on it. I wore it to show how life is lived with many layers here in Hawai'i. The dress acknowledges the many languages here, the many cultures, the many ways of knowing and being. How does someone like me, a Japanese-Hawaiian-Chinese-German-French woman, separate them all? Sometimes I think, or at least hope, that my mother did not give me three names to remind me of the separateness. Maybe deep inside she wanted to help me claim that richness.

The genius of a community lies in its ability to dream itself back into existence and health. It is not through government intervention that this dreaming is taking place, not through a fear of the future or a dread of the past that this dreaming is taking place. Our community is dreaming of being well again. It is a very natural desire, for which we hope against all odds. So I would like to conclude with a poem I call

"The Mouse Is Dreaming"

In a dark hole behind the washing machine
　　the house-mouse is dreaming.
Whiskers, body, tail—twitching and trembling,
　　paws scratching the air.

That house-mouse he's a dreamin'
    of chunks of cheese, and whole loaves of bread,
of a nest made of the finest pieces of cloth and paper—dry,
    warm and snug,
of living out in the open once again, to feel sun-warmed and
    star-shined;
of walking. Of walking slowly through the territory patrolled
    by the Cat.
            Of cat traps and cat cages;
            and cats without claws and teeth;
            of a world without Cats.

And this mouse she's a-dreamin'
    of acres of loʻi kalo, of nets filled with ʻōpelu,
    of rocks choke with opihi and limu,
    of forests of koa and iliahi and wiliwili,
of buildings empty and crumbling which no longer scrape the
    sky;
of living in the open once again, to feel sun-warmed and star-
    shined;
of walking. Of walking slowly through the territory controlled
    by the Cat.
            Of cat traps and cat cages;
            and cats without claws and teeth;
            of a world without Cats.

And the mice dream dreams
that would terrify the cats.

Note

1. See the discussion following Charles Long's chapter, above.

Discussion

Pualani Kanahele

I have a story to add and it's not even a Hawaiian story. It's an Indian story and maybe some of you have heard it before. It has to do with the beginning of the Indian Buffalo Dances. In our festivals we've come across a lot of different Indians who do the Buffalo Dance and bring the buffalo along with them. The story as it was related to me is that the Indians used to try to catch the buffalo by stampeding them over the cliff. And they would be able to get whatever buffalo went over the cliff for food and clothing and other uses. Well, this one year they tried to stampede the buffalo over the cliff but the buffalo would come right to the edge and turn off to the side. They tried it over and over for many days but the buffalo just wouldn't go over the cliff. The people were starving because they needed the buffalo meat, so finally in the evening this one Indian maiden went down to the waterhole. As she looked up on the cliff, she saw the buffalo milling around up there. So she says, "Why don't one of you just come here and fall down. If any of you fall down, I'll marry you." To her surprise, the buffalo who seemed to be the leader, the shaman of all the buffalo, says, "Okay." So they all ran over the cliff and here was all of this dead buffalo. Then one of the buffalo got up and he says, "Okay, girlie, you got to marry me now!" She answered, "First, I have to go home and tell my father!" "No, no, no! You said if we jump over the cliff you're going to marry me. And so you have to stay here and marry me." So she had to stay and marry the buffalo because that was what came out of her mouth.

Pretty soon the girl's father started to miss her, so he asked where she'd gone. The other people in the tribe said, "We don't know. She went down to get water." The father looked around and he saw the tracks and realized that his daughter had gone off with the buffalo. He went to look for her but he didn't find her. Then he saw a magpie flying by, and he called out, "Did you see my daughter anywhere around here? She's a pretty girl." He describes her and the magpie replies, "Oh, yeah. I saw a girl. She's just right over there with the buffalo."

Meanwhile, the head buffalo told his new wife, "I want you to take this jug and go and get water for us." So the girl took the jug and headed for the waterhole. But on the way, she met her father and she was so happy! Her father said, "Come on home with me now." But she says, "No, I cannot. I made a promise to the buffalo and I have to stay there. I have to get back before they miss me or it will be very dangerous for me." But as soon as she started to go back, the buffalo came over and they saw the father and trampled him. They stampeded until there was nothing left of the father. He was dead and there wasn't a scrap of him left. So she started to cry and cry and cry, "Oh, my father! My father! He's gone!" And her husband says, "Why are you crying?" She says, "I'm crying because you killed my father and I can't find anything left of him. He's all gone." Her buffalo husband answered, "When my ancestors fall down and die, you don't cry." And she says, "But he's my father and I'm very sad for him."

Now, after all the buffalo went away, the magpie came back to her and she asked, "Can you find a little piece of my father? Maybe there's a chance of bringing him back." So the magpie sifted through the dust and everything and found one little bone left. He gave it to the girl, and she put it under a large skin. Then she started her chanting and her wailing and her praying. She carried on for hours and pretty soon the blanket started to lift up; it started to look like the shape of a man under the blanket. But the full form wasn't there so she continued her prayers and she continued her chanting until the full form was there. And when she lifted up the blanket, there was her father, alive and well.

Then her buffalo husband came back and says, "Why don't you do that for us? When we fall off the cliff and die, nobody does that for us! They just let us lie there dead and then they eat us. Why don't you go and make us come back to life after you've eaten us and our bones are all scattered?" Then the husband says, "I've got it! I know a way that you can make us come back. This is how you'll do it." And he taught her the Buffalo Dance. He started stamping his buffalo dance and he says, "This is how you'll bring us back. This is how you'll allow our ancestors to live."

Now, I can relate to the part of the story about the dancing and bringing back the ancestors, but the part that I like best is where there was only a little piece of the father and from that little piece the girl was able to bring him back whole. To me, the moral of that story is that even if you think that everything is gone and there's nothing left, and even if people tell you, "It's dead! Everything that you believed in before is gone!" even if all that seems to be true, as long as there is a piece of it left, just a little string of it left, it can grow and it can exist for you.

Does anyone have another story?

Works Cited

Aarni, Teddy. *The Kalunga Concept in Ovambo Religion from 1870 Onwards.* Stockholm Studies in Comparative Religion, 22. Stockholm: Almquist and Wiksell International, 1982.

Adams, William Howard. *Jefferson's Monticello.* New York: Abbeville Press, 1983.

Ahern, Emily M. *The Cult of the Dead in a Chinese Village.* Stanford: Stanford University Press, 1973.

Ariès, Philippe. *The Hour of Our Death.* New York: Alfred A. Knopf, 1981.

Attwater, Donald. *The Penguin Dictionary of Saints.* New York: Penguin, 1983.

Baraga, F. R. A. *Theoretical and Practical Grammar of the Otchipwe Language.* Montreal: Beauchemin and Valois, 1978.

Beattie, J. *Other Cultures.* New York: Free Press, 1964.

Bell, Diane. "Aboriginal Women's Religion: A Shifting Law of the Land." In *Today's Woman in World Religions,* edited by Arvind Sharma, 39–76. Albany: State University of New York Press, 1994.

———. "Aborigines and Land." Background paper prepared for the "Ancestors and Spirituality" conference at the East-West Center, Honolulu, 1991.

———. *Daughters of the Dreaming.* 2d ed. Minneapolis: University of Minnesota Press, 1993.

Berglund, Axel-Ivar. *Zulu Thought-Patterns and Symbolism.* London: C. Hurst, 1976.

Berry, Thomas. *The Dream of the Earth.* San Francisco: Sierra Club Books, 1988.

Biernatzki, William E. "Varieties of Korean Lineage Structure." Ph.D. diss., St. Louis University, 1967.

Biggar, Henry P., ed. *The Works of Samuel de Champlain.* Toronto: The Champlain Society, 1922–36.

Black, Mary B. "Ojibwa Power Belief System." In *The Anthropology of Power: Ethnographic Studies from Asia, Oceania, and the New World,* edited by Raymond Godelson and Richard N. Adams, 109–17. New York: Academic Press, 1977.

Blackman, Margaret B. *During My Time: Florence Edenshaw Davidson, a Haida Woman*. Seattle: University of Wshington Press, 1982.

Blair, Emma. *The Indian Tribes of the Upper Mississippi Valley and the Region of the Great Lakes*. Cleveland: Arthur H. Clark Co., 1911.

Brennan, Paul W. *Let Sleeping Snakes Lie: Central Enga Traditional Religious Belief and Ritual*. Adelaide, South Australia: Australian Association for the Study of Religion, 1977.

Brian, James. "Ancestors as Elders in Africa." *Africa*, 43, no. 2 (1973): 122–33.

Brown, Peter. *The Cult of the Saints: Its Rise and Function in Latin Christianity*. Chicago: University of Chicago Press, 1981.

Burstein, Andrew. *The Inner Jefferson: Portrait of a Grieving Optimist*. Charlottesville: University of Virginia Press, 1995.

Ch'oe, Kil-song. *Han'guk ui chosang sungbae* (Korean Ancestor Worship). Seoul: Seoul National University Press, 1986.

Choi, Chungmoo. "The Artistry and Ritual Aesthetics of Urban Korean Shamans." *Journal of Ritual Studies* 3 (1989): 235–49.

Chun, Kyung-soo. *Reciprocity in Korean Society: An Ethnography of Hasami*. Seoul: Seoul National University Press, 1984.

Clifford, James. *Person and Myth: Maurice Leenhardt in the Melanesian World*. Berkeley and Los Angeles: University of California Press, 1982.

Cousins, Ewert, ed. *World Spirituality: An Encyclopedic History of the Religious Quest*. New York: Crossroad, 1985– .

Crapanzano, Vincent. *Tuhami, Portrait of a Moroccan*. Chicago: University of Chicago Press, 1980.

de Heusch, Luc. *Sacrifice in Africa: A Structuralist Approach*. Manchester: Manchester University Press, 1985.

Deuchler, Martina. "Neo-Confucianism in Action: Agnation and Ancestor Worship in Early Yi Korea." In Kendall and Dix, eds., *Religion and Ritual*, 26–55.

Driberg, J. H. "The Secular Aspect of Ancestor Worship in Africa." *Journal of the Royal African Society* 36 (1936), supplement.

Dwyer, John C. *Church History: Twenty Centuries of Catholic Christianity*. New York: Paulist Press, 1985.

Echo-Hawk, Walter R. "Sacred Material and the Law." In Horse Capture, ed., *The Concept of Sacred Materials*.

Eco, Umberto. *Travels in Hyperreality: Essays*. San Diego: Harcourt, Brace, Jovanovich, 1986.

Eire, Carlos M. N. *War against the Idols: The Reformation of Worship from Erasmus to Calvin*. Cambridge: Cambridge University Press, 1986.

Eliade, Mircea, ed. *The Encyclopedia of Religion*. 16 vols. New York: Macmillan, 1987.

Flannery, Wendy. "Appreciating Melanesian Myths." In *Powers, Plumes, and Piglets: Phenomena of Melanesian Religions*, edited by N. C. Habel, 161–72. Bedford Park, South Australia: Australian Association for the Study of Religions, 1979.

Fortes, Meyer. *Oedipus and Job in West African Religion.* Cambridge: Cambridge University Press, 1959.

———. "Pietas in Ancestor Worship." *Man* 91, no. 2 (1961): 166–91.

Fox, Robin Lane. *Pagans and Christians.* San Francisco: Harper and Row, 1986.

Frankel, Stephen. *The Huli Response to Illness.* Cambridge: Cambridge University Press, 1989.

Frazier, James. *The Golden Bough.* New York: Macmillan, 1935.

Freud, Sigmund. *Totem and Taboo.* London: Routledge and Kegan Paul, 1950.

Fry, Peter. *Spirits of Protest: Spirit-Mediums and the Articulation of Consensus among the Zezuru of Southern Rhodesia (Zimbabwe).* Cambridge: University of Cambridge Press, 1976.

Furtwangler, Albert. *Answering Chief Seattle.* Seattle: University of Washington Press, 1997.

Geary, Patrick J. *Furta Sacra: Thefts of Relics in the Central Middle Ages.* Princeton: Princeton University Press, 1978.

———. "The Ninth-Century Relic Trade: A Response to Popular Piety?" In *Religion and the People, 800–1700,* edited by James Obelkevich, 8–19. Chapel Hill: University of North Carolina Press, 1979.

Glasse, Robert M. "The Huli of the Southern Highlands." In Lawrence and Meggitt, eds., *Gods, Ghosts and Men,* 27–49.

Gluckman, Max. "Some Processes of Social Change Illustrated from Zululand," *African Studies* (Johannesburg) 1 (1942): 258ff.

Goldman, Irving. "Genealogy." In Eliade, ed., *Encyclopedia of Religion,* 5:502–6.

Goody, Jack. *Death, Property, and the Ancestors: A Study of the Mortuary Customs of the LoDagaa of West Africa.* Stanford: Stanford University Press, 1962.

Griaule, Marcel. *Conversations with Ogotemmêli: An Introduction to Dogon Religious Ideas.* Oxford: Oxford University Press, 1965.

Grim, John. *The Shaman: Patterns of Siberian and Ojibway Healing.* Norman: University of Oklahoma Press, 1983.

Guillemoz, Alexandre. "La dernière rencontre: Un rituel chamanique coréen pour une jeune morte" (The Last Encounter: A Korean Shaman Ritual for a Dead Young Woman)." In *Transe, chamanisme, possession: Actes des deuxièmes Rencontres internationales sur la fête et la communication,* 69–80. Nice: Editions Serre, 1986.

Hachington, A. P. Quoted in *Friends Committee on National Legislation Washington Newsletter,* November, 1989.

Hallowell, A. Irving. "Ojibway Ontology, Behavior and World View." In *Culture in History: Essays in Honor of Paul Radin,* edited by Stanley Diamond, 19–52. New York: Columbia University Press, 1960.

———. *The Role of Conjuring in Saulteaux Society.* Philadelphia: University of Pennsylvania Press, 1942.

Hardacre, Helen. "Ancestor Worship." In Eliade, ed., *Encyclopedia of Religion,* 1:263–68.

Harvey, Youngsook Kim. "The Korean Shaman and the Deaconess: Sisters in Different Guises." In Kendall and Dix, eds., *Religion and Ritual,* 149–70.

Hereniko, Vilsoni. *Woven Gods: Female Clowns and Power in Rotuma*. Pacific Island Monograph Series, 12. Honolulu: University of Hawaii Press, 1995.

Hesse, K. *Baining Life and Lore*. Port Moresby: Institute of Papua New Guinea Studies, 1982.

Hickerson, Harold. "The Sociohistorical Significance of Two Chippewa Ceremonials." *American Anthropologist* 65 (1963): 67–85.

Hood, Robert E. *Must God Remain Greek? Afro Cultures and God-Talk*. Minneapolis: Fortress Press, 1990.

Horse Capture, George P., ed. *The Concept of Sacred Materials and Their Place in the World*. Cody, Wyo.: The Plains Indian Museum, 1989.

Hultkrantz, Åke. *Conceptions of the Soul among North American Indians: A Study in Religious Ethnology*. Monograph Series, 1. Stockholm: Ethnographical Museum of Sweden, 1953.

Im, Ton-hui [Dawnhee Yim Janelli]. "Han'guk chosang sungbae ui pyonch'on sa" (A History of the Transformation of Korean Ancestor Worship). *Chont'ong Munhwa* 8 (1986): 47–53.

Isichei, Elizabeth. "Introduction." In *Studies in the History of Plateau State, Nigeria*, edited by Elizabeth Isichei, 1–57. London: Macmillan, 1982.

Jacobson-Widding, Anita. "The Fertility of Incest." In *The Creative Communion: African Folk Models of Fertility and the Regeneration of Life*, edited by Anita Jacobson-Widding and Walter van Beek. Uppsala Studies in Cultural Anthropology, 15. Uppsala: Academiae Ubsaliensis; Stockholm: Almquist and Wiksell International, 1990.

Jacobson-Widding, Anita, and Walter van Beek. "Introduction." In *The Creative Communion: African Folk Models of Fertility and the Regeneration of Life*, edited by Anita Jacobson-Widding and Walter van Beek. Uppsala Studies in Cultural Anthropology, 15. Uppsala: Academiae Ubsaliensis; Stockholm: Almquist and Wiksell International, 1990.

Janelli, Roger, and Dawnhee Yim Janelli. *Ancestor Worship and Korean Society*. Stanford: Stanford University Press, 1982.

———. "The Functional Value of Ignorance at a Korean Seance." *Asian Folklore Studies* (Nagoya) 38 (1979): 81–90.

———. "Lineage Organization and Social Differentiation in Korea." *Man*, n.s., 13 (1978): 272–89.

Jenness, Diamond. *The Ojibwa Indians of Parry Island: Their Social and Religious Life*. National Museum of Canada Anthropological Series, 17. Ottawa: J. O. Patenaude, 1935.

Johansen, J. Prytz. *The Maori and His Religion in Its Non-ritualistic Aspects*. Copenhagen: Munksgaard, 1954.

———. *Studies in Maori Rites and Myths*. Copenhagen: Munksgaard, 1958.

Jordan, David K. *Gods, Ghosts, and Ancestors: The Folk Religion of a Taiwanese Village*. Berkeley and Los Angeles: University of California Press, 1972.

Jules-Rosette, Benetta. "Symbols of Cultural Transformation in Urban Africa: Indigenous Religions and Popular Art as New Expressive Forms." In *Transformation and Resiliency in Africa as Seen by Afro-American Scholars*, edited by Pearl T. Robinson and Elliott P. Skinner, 231–50. Washington, D.C.: Howard University Press, 1983.

Junod, Henri A. *The Life of a South African Tribe.* 2 vols. Neuchâtel: Attinger Frères, 1912–1913.

Kendall, Laurel. "Caught between Ancestors and Spirits: A Korean *Mansin's* Healing *Kut.*" *Korea Journal* 17, no. 8 (1977): 8–23.

————. "Initiating Performance: The Story of Chini, A Korean Shaman." In *The Performance of Healing*, edited by C. Laderman and M. Roseman, 17–58. New York: Routledge, 1996.

————. *The Life and Hard Times of a Korean Shaman: Of Tales and the Telling of Tales.* Honolulu: University of Hawaii Press, 1988.

————. *Shamans, Housewives, and Other Restless Spirits: Women in Korean Ritual Life.* Honolulu: University of Hawaii Press, 1985.

————. "Wives, Lesser Wives, and Ghosts: Supernatural Conflict in a Korean Village." *Asian Folklore Studies* (Nagoya) 43 (1984): 215–25.

Kendall, Laurel, and Griffin Dix, eds. *Religion and Ritual in Korean Society.* Berkeley: Institute for East Asian Studies, University of California, 1987.

Kim, Kwang-Ok. "Rituals of Resistance: The Manipulation of Shamanism in Contemporary Korea." In *Asian Visions of Authority: Religion and the Modern States of East and Southeast Asia*, edited by Charles F. Keyes et al., 195–219. Honolulu: University of Hawaii Press, 1994.

Kim, T'aek-kyu. *Tongjok purakui saenghwal kujo yon'gu* (A Study of the Structure of Social Life in a Lineage Village). Seoul: Ch'onggu, 1964.

King, Noel Q. *African Cosmos: An Introduction to Religion in Africa.* Belmont, Calif.: Wadsworth, 1986.

Kinietz, W. Vernon. *The Indians of the Western Great Lakes (1615–1760).* Ann Arbor: Ann Arbor Paperbacks, 1965.

Kopuka, N., and R. Tawhiwhi, "He panui kawanga whare nui. . . ." *Te Pipiwharauroa* 58 (1902) 8.

Kopytoff, Igor. "Ancestors as Elders in Africa." *Africa* 41 (1971): 124–42.

Laleye, Isiaka Prosper. *La conception de la personne dans la pensée traditionnelle Yoruba.* Berne: Herbert Lang, 1970.

Lan, David. *Guns and Rain: Guerrillas and Spirit Mediums in Zimbabwe.* Berkeley: University of California Press, 1985.

Landes, Ruth. *Ojibwa Sociology.* Columbia University Contributions to Anthropology, 29. New York: Columbia University Press, 1937.

Lawrence, Peter, and Mervyn J. Meggitt, eds. *Gods, Ghosts and Men in Melanesia: Some Religions of Australian New Guinea and the New Hebrides.* Melbourne: Oxford University Press, 1965.

Lee, Diana, and Laurel Kendall. *An Initiation Kut for a Korean Shaman.* Video distributed by University of Hawaii Press.

Lee, Kwang-Kyu [Yi Kwang-gyu]. "Ancestor Worship and Kinship Structure in Korea." In Kendall and Dix, eds., *Religion and Ritual*, 56–70.

Leenhardt, Maurice. *Do Kamo: Person and Myth in the Melanesian World.* Chicago: University of Chicago Press, 1979.

Leicht, Raymond C. "The Reburial of Skeletal Remains Found on BLM Lands." In Horse Capture, ed., *The Concept of Sacred Materials*, 49–56.

Lincoln, Bruce. "Two Notes on Modern Rituals." *Journal of the American Academy of Religion* 45 (1978): 147–60.

Little, Kenneth L. *The Mende of Sierra Leone: A West African People in Transition.* Rev. ed. London: Routledge and K. Paul, 1967.

Long, Charles H. "Matter and Spirit: A Reorientation." In *Local Knowledge, Ancient Wisdom: Challenges in Contemporary Spirituality*, edited by Steven J. Friesen, 12–16. Honolulu: Institute of Culture and Communication, East-West Center, 1991.

———. "Mythic Ancestors." In Eliade, ed., *Encyclopedia of Religion*, 1:268–70.

MacDonald, Mary N. *Mararoko: A Study in Melanesian Religion.* New York: Peter Lang, 1991.

———. "Pajapaja and Jesus: Indigenous Religion and Christianity Among the Huli." Paper read at the Third East-West Center Workshop on Primal Spirituality, Honolulu, January 1993.

———. "The Power of Intentions: Thinking about Kewa Ethics." *Journal of Religious Ethics* 20 (1992): 331–51.

Meggitt, Mervyn J. "The Mae Enga of the Western Highlands." In Lawrence and Meggitt, eds., *Gods, Ghosts and Men*, 105–31.

Merriam, Alan P. *An African World: The Basongye Villiage of Lupupa Ngye.* Bloomington: Indiana University Press, 1974.

Metcalf, Peter. *A Borneo Journey into Death: Berawan Eschatology from Its Rituals.* Philadelphia: University of Pennsylvania, 1982.

Monroe, Dan, and Walter R. Echo-Hawk. "Deft Deliberations." *Museum News*, July-August, 1991, 55–58.

Naipaul, V. S. *A Way in the World.* New York: Alfred A. Knopf, 1994.

Orbell, Margaret. *Hawaiki: A New Approach to Maori Tradition.* Christchurch, New Zealand: Canterbury University Press, 1985.

———. *The Natural World of the Maori.* Auckland: Bateman, 1985.

Panzer, K. *Garagab Egerenon Anutu Imuam en Anzob Egereneran.* Logaweng-Neuguinea: Neuendettelsauer Missionsdruckerei, 1917.

Parsons, Robert T. *Religion in an African Society: A Study of the Religion of the Kono People of Sierra Leone.* Leiden E. J. Brill, 1964.

Peden, William. "The Jefferson Monument at the University of Missouri." Ellis Library, University of Missouri-Columbia.

Phillipps, W. J. "Carved Maori Houses of the Eastern Districts of the North Island." *Records of the Dominion Museum* 1 (1944): 107–8.

Potter, Jack M. "Cantonese Shamanism." In *Religion and Ritual in Chinese Society*, edited by Arthur P. Wolf, 207–31. Stanford: Stanford University Press, 1974.

Rappaport, Roy. *Pigs for the Ancestors: Ritual in the Ecology of a New Guinea People.* Rev. ed. New Haven, Conn.: Yale University Press, 1984.

Ray, Benjamin C. *Myth, Ritual, and Kingship in Buganda.* New York: Oxford University Press, 1991.

Reedy, Anaru, trans. *Ngā Kōrero a Mohi Ruatapu: The Writings of Mohi Ruatapu.* Christchurch, New Zealand: Canterbury University Press, 1993.

Reedy, Anaru, trans. *Ngā Kōrero a Pita Kapiti: The Teachings of Pita Kapiti.* Christchurch, New Zealand: Canterbury University Press, 1997.

Rosaldo, Renato. *Culture and Truth: The Remaking of Social Analysis.* Boston: Beacon Press, 1993 [1989].

Rothkrug, Lionel. *Religious Practices and Collective Perceptions: Hidden Homologies in the Renaissance and Reformation.* Special issue of *Historical Reflections/ Réflexions historiques* 7 (1980).

Schnepel, Burkhard. "Continuity despite and through Death: Regicide and Royal Shrines among the Shilluck of Southern Sudan." *Africa* 61 (1991): 40–70.

Scull, Gideon D., ed. *Voyages of Peter Esprit Radisson, being an account of his travels and experiences among North American Indians, from 1652–1684.* New York: P. Smith, 1943.

Senghor, Léopold S. "Totem." In *The Collected Poetry,* translated by Melvin Dixon. Charlottesville: University Press of Virginia, 1991.

Sharp, Andrew. "New Zealand, naming of." In *An Encyclopedia of New Zealand,* edited by A. H. McLintock. Wellington: R. E. Owen, 1966.

Sheingorn, Pamela. "Appropriating the Holy Kinship: Gender and Family History." In *Interpreting Cultural Symbols: Saint Anne in Late Medieval Society,* edited by Kathleen Ashley and Pamela Sheingorn, 169-98. Athens, Georgia: University of Georgia Press, 1990.

Schiefenhoevel, Wulf. "Of Body and Soul among the Eipo of Irian Jaya," *Bikmaus* 4 (1983).

Shigematsu, Mayumi. "Saishin ni mirareru josei no shakai kankei" (The Women's Social Sphere in Korean *mansin's kut*). *Minzokugaku Kenkyu* (1980): 93–110.

Shima, Matsuhiko. "Kinship and Economic Organization in a Korean Village." Ph.D. diss., University of Toronto, 1979.

Shostak, Marjorie. *Nisa: The Life and Words of a !Kung Woman.* Cambridge, Mass.: Harvard University Press, 1981.

Sinclair, Charles, trans. *The Divine Comedy of Dante Alighieri: II Purgatorio; III Paradiso.* New York: Oxford University Press, 1961.

Skinner, Alanson. "Notes on the Eastern Cree and the Northern Saulteaux." *Anthropological Papers of the American Museum of Natural History* 9, no. 1 (1911) 68–76.

Slim, H. C. "Mary Magdalene, Musician and Dancer." *Early Music* 8 (1980): 460–73.

Smith, Huston. *The World's Religions.* San Francisco: Harper, 1991. Rev. and updated version of *The Religions of Man* (1958).

Smith, Wilfred Cantwell. "Objectivity and the Humane Sciences: A New Proposal." In *Religious Diversity,* edited by Willard G. Oxtoby, 158–80. New York: Crossroad, 1982.

Solecki, Ralph. *Shanidar, the First Flower People.* New York: Alfred A. Knopf, 1971.

Song, Sunhee. "Kinship and Lineage in Korean Village Society." Ph.D. diss., Indiana University, 1982.

Stanley, Manfred. *The Technological Conscience: Survival and Dignity in an Age of Expertise.* Chicago: University of Chicago Press, 1981.

Steinbauer, F. *Melanesian Cargo Cults: New Salvation Movements in the South Pacific.* St. Lucia: University of Queensland Press, 1979.

Stephens, Frank F. *A History of the University of Missouri.* Columbia: University of Missouri Press, 1962.

Strong, John S. "Relics." In Eliade ed., *Encyclopedia of Religion,* 11:275–82.

Sun, Soon-Hwa. "The Work and Power of Korean Shamans." Unpublished ms.

Tanner, Adrian. *Bringing Home Animals: Religious Ideology and Mode of Production of the Mistassini Cree Hunters.* New York: St. Martin's Press, 1979.

Taylor, Pat Ellis. *Border Healing Woman: The Story of Jewel Babb.* Austin: University of Texas Press, 1981.

Thwaites, Ruben Gold. *The Jesuit Relations and Allied Documents.* 73 vols. Cleveland: Burrows Bros. Co., 1896–1901.

Trompf, G. W. *Melanesian Religion.* New York: Cambridge University Press, 1991.

Turei, Mohi. "Te hui ki Mataahu." *Te waka Maori o Niu Tirani* 8/17 (1872): 109–18.

Tuza, E. "A Melanesian Cosmological Process." In *Total Cosmic Vision of Life: An Introduction to Melanesian Philosophy,* edited by H. Olela, 52–65. Port Moresby: University of Papua New Guinea, 1981.

Uchendu, Victor C. "Ancestorcide: Are African Ancestors Dead?" In *Ancestors,* edited by William H. Newell, 282–96. The Hague: Mouton, 1976.

Underhill, Ruth M. *Papago Woman.* 1936. Reprint, New York: Holt, Rinehart, and Winston, 1979.

Vizenor, Gerald. *Crossbloods, Bone Courts, Bingo, and Other Reports.* Minneapolis: University of Minnesota Press, 1990.

———, trans. and ed. "The Sky Will Resound." In *Summer in the Spring: Lyric Poems of the Ojibway.* Minneapolis: Nodin Press, 1965.

Wagner, Roy. *Habu: The Innovation of Meaning in Daribi Religion.* Chicago: University of Chicago Press, 1972.

———. *The Invention of Culture.* Rev. and expanded ed. Chicago: University of Chicago Press, 1981.

Ward, Benedicta. *Miracles and the Medieval Mind: Theory, Record and Event, 1000–1215.* Philadelphia: University of Pennsylvania Press, 1982.

Wendt, Albert. "Novelists and Historians and the Art of Remembering." In *Class and Culture in the South Pacific,* edited by Anthony Hooper et al., 78–91. Auckland: Centre for Pacific Studies, University of Auckland; and Suva: Institute of Pacific Studies, University of the South Pacific, 1987.

Wurm, Stephen A. *Papuan Languages of Oceania.* Tübingen: Narr, 1982.

Young, T. Cullen. "The Idea of God in Northern Nyasaland." In *African Ideas of God: A Symposium*, edited by Edwin W. Smith, 36–60. London: Edinburgh House Press, 1950.

Zahan, Dominique. *The Bambara*. Iconography of Religions. Leiden: E. J. Brill, 1974.

Zuesse, Evan. *Ritual Cosmos: The Sanctification of Life in African Religions*. Athens: Ohio University Press, 1979.

List of Conference Participants
"Ancestors and Spirituality"
7–11 January 1992
East-West Center, Honolulu

Dr. Diane Bell, George Washington University, Washington, D.C.

Ms. Puanani Burgess, Wai'anae Coast Alternative Development Corp., Wai'anae, Hawai'i.

Dr. Ewert Cousins, Theology Department, Fordham University, Bronx, New York (retired).

Dr. William Ferea, Philosophy Department, University of Papua New Guinea, Port Moresby, PNG.

Dr. Steven Friesen, Department of Religious Studies, University of Missouri-Columbia.

Ms. Ulunui Garmon, Edith Kanaka'ole Foundation, Hilo, Hawai'i.

Dr. John Grim, Bucknell University, Department of Religion, Lewisburg, Pennsylvania.

Dr. Futa Helu, 'Atenisi Institute, Nuku'alofa, Kingdom of Tonga.

Dr. Rubellite Johnson, Department of Indo-Pacific Languages, University of Hawaii, Honolulu (retired).

Mr. Sam Kaai, Pukalani, Hawai'i.

Ms. Pualani Kanahele, Edith Kanaka'ole Foundation, Hilo, Hawai'i.

Rev. David Ka'upu, Kamehameha Schools, Kapalama Heights, Honolulu, Hawai'i.

Dr. Laurel Kendall, American Museum of Natural History, New York.

Dr. Charles Long, Religious Studies and Research Center for Black Studies, University of California-Santa Barbara (retired).

Dr. Mary MacDonald, LeMoyne College, Syracuse, New York.

The Reverend Toyotaka Ogaki, Institute for Shinto, Isei, Japan.

Dr. Jacob Olupona, African and African-American Studies, University of California-Davis.

Dr. Margaret Orbell, Department of Māori, University of Canterbury, Christchurch, New Zealand (retired).

Dr. Jill Raitt, Department of Religious Studies, University of Missouri-Columbia (retired).

Dr. Lawrence Sullivan, Center for the Study of World Religions, Harvard Divinity School, Cambridge, Massachusetts.

Dr. Esau Tuza, University of the South Pacific Center, Honiara, Solomon Islands.

Mr. Huirangi Waikerepuru, Pukaka, New Plymouth, New Zealand.

Index

Religions of the World

Johannes Wilbert, *Mystic Endowment: Religious Ethnography of the Warao Indians.* 1993.

Winnifred Fallers Sullivan, *Paying the Words Extra: Religious Discourse in the Supreme Court of the United States.* 1994.

Gerardo Reichel-Dolmatoff, *Yuruparí: Studies of an Amazonian Foundation Myth.* 1996.

Johannes Wilbert, *Mindful of Famine: Religious Climatology of the Warao Indians.* 1996.

Enchanting Powers: Music in the World's Religions, edited by Lawrence E. Sullivan. 1997.

The Apocryphal Acts of the Apostles: Harvard Divinity School Studies, edited by François Bovon, Ann Graham Brock, and Christopher R. Matthews. 1999.

Lindsay Jones, *The Hermeneutics of Sacred Architecture: Experience, Interpretation, Comparison.* Volume 1: *Monumental Occasions: Reflections on the Eventfulness of Religious Architecture.* 2000.

Lindsay Jones, *The Hermeneutics of Sacred Architecture: Experience, Interpretation, Comparison.* Volume 2: *Hermeneutical Calisthenics: A Morphology of Ritual-Architectural Priorities.* 2000.

Ancestors in Post-Contact Religion: Roots, Ruptures, and Modernity's Memory, edited by Steven J. Friesen. 2001.

Religions of the World and Ecology

Buddhism and Ecology: The Interconnection of Dharma and Deeds, edited by Mary Evelyn Tucker and Duncan Ryuken Williams. 1997.

Confucianism and Ecology: The Interrelation of Heaven, Earth, and Humans, edited by Mary Evelyn Tucker and John Berthrong. 1998.

Christianity and Ecology: Seeking the Well-Being of Earth and Humans, edited by Dieter T. Hessel and Rosemary Radford Ruether. 2000.

Hinduism and Ecology: The Intersection of Earth, Sky, and Water, edited by Christopher Key Chapple and Mary Evelyn Tucker. 2000.

Indigenous Traditions and Ecology: The Interbeing of Cosmology and Community, edited by John A. Grim. 2001.

Daoism and Ecology: Ways within a Cosmic Landscape, edited by N. J. Girardot, James Miller, and Liu Xiaogan. 2001.